# Teaching Materials and the Roles of EFL/ESL Teachers

**Also Available from Bloomsbury Academic**

*Changing Pedagogy*, Xin-Min Zheng and Chris Davison
*Developing Materials for Language Teaching*, Brian Tomlinson
*English Language Learning Materials*, Edited by Brian Tomlinson
*Research for Materials Development in Language Learning*, Edited by Brian Tomlinson and Hitomi Masuhara

# Teaching Materials and the Roles of EFL/ESL Teachers

## Practice and Theory

IAN McGRATH

BLOOMSBURY
LONDON · NEW DELHI · NEW YORK · SYDNEY

**Bloomsbury Academic**
An imprint of Bloomsbury Publishing Plc

50 Bedford Square  175 Fifth Avenue
London  New York
WC1B 3DP  NY 10010
UK  USA

www.bloomsbury.com

First published 2013

© Ian McGrath, 2013

All rights reserved. No part of this publication may be reproduced or transmitted in any form or by any means, electronic or mechanical, including photocopying, recording, or any information storage or retrieval system, without prior permission in writing from the publishers.

Ian McGrath has asserted his right under the Copyright, Designs and Patents Act, 1988, to be identified as Author of this work.

No responsibility for loss caused to any individual or organization acting on or refraining from action as a result of the material in this publication can be accepted by Bloomsbury Academic or the author.

**British Library Cataloguing-in-Publication Data**
A catalogue record for this book is available from the British Library.

ISBN: HB: 9781441190604
PB: 9781441143693
PDF: 9781441162717
ePub: 9781441194923

**Library of Congress Cataloging-in-Publication Data**
A catalogue record for this book is available from the Library of Congress

Typeset by Newgen Imaging Systems Pvt Ltd, Chennai, India
Printed and bound in India

*To Natasha, as always, and the new generation.*

# CONTENTS

*Acknowledgements* viii
*Preface* ix

1 Introduction: Materials, the roles of teachers and learners, teacher education  1

**PART ONE** External perspectives: 'Theory'  27

2 Publisher and coursebook writer perspectives  29
3 The professional literature  49
4 Teacher educator perspectives  81

**PART TWO** Teacher and learner perspectives: 'Practice'  103

5 How teachers evaluate coursebooks  105
6 How teachers adapt and supplement coursebooks  127
7 Learner perspectives  149
8 Contextual influences and individual factors  167

**PART THREE** Implications  185

9 Implications for teachers, managers, ministries, publishers and coursebook writers, and research  187
10 Implications for teacher educators: A practice-based proposal  203

*References*  220
*Author Index*  235
*Subject Index*  238

# ACKNOWLEDGEMENTS

My thanks are due to a number of people who responded to requests for help during the writing of this book or provided other kinds of support. They are: Lubna Alsagoff, Rod Bolitho, Cheng Xiaotang and Chen Zehang, Tamas Kiss, Bo Lundahl, Nick Sampson, Phil Quirke, Margaret Sands, and Saad Shawer.

I am also grateful to those of my former students who agreed to be interviewed or gave their consent for their work to be quoted; some are named in the text, while others preferred to be anonymous. My thanks to Afidah Bte Ali, Ramasamy Anusuya, Dhilshaadh Balajee, Jack Hsiao, Sandra Kanj, Tomo Matsumara, Rayhan M. Rashad, Rong Rong, Asmoraniye Shaffie, Kitty Yuen and Zheng Yiying – and to the many others who have helped to shape this book through the insights they provided into their working contexts and needs.

# PREFACE

## 1. Teachers, learners, contexts

The teachers referred to in the title of this book have one thing in common: all teach English to learners who are not speakers of English as a first language. These learners may be children, teenagers or adults, in countries where English is spoken as a first, second or foreign language, and studying English for a specific purpose or for no particular reason. The teachers, who may or may not be native speakers of English, have different levels of education, training and experience, and vary in their personal characteristics. The contexts in which they teach will also be very different, not only as regards the resources available or class size but also in terms of institutional expectations and the status accorded to teachers (reflected in, for example, workload, pay, and autonomy). So, apart from the fact that they are all teaching English, do these teachers have anything else in common? Well, yes: they all use materials.

## 2. The value of materials

The importance of materials in language teaching and learning is widely recognized. As Richards (2001a) notes:

> Teaching materials are a key component in most language programs. Whether the teacher uses a textbook, institutionally-prepared materials, or his or her own materials, instructional materials generally serve as the basis for much of the language input learners receive and the language practice that occurs in the classroom. In the case of inexperienced teachers, materials may also serve as a form of teacher training – they provide ideas on how to plan and teach lessons. (Richards, 2001a: 251)

Other writers have pointed to particular functions fulfilled by textbooks. For instance, where learning objectives have already been specified in the form of a syllabus, a textbook can 'put flesh on the bones' of that syllabus (Nunan, 1991: 208), and 'suggest the intensity of coverage for syllabus items, allocating the amount of time, attention and detail particular syllabus items or tasks require' (Richards & Rodgers, 1986: 25); more generally, textbooks support learning, stimulate interest, and are a source of information about the language (Cunningsworth, 1995; Dudley-Evans & St John, 1998). In short, they support the teacher, complement the teacher and support the learner. It is therefore hardly surprising that 'the most commonly found elements in second and foreign language classrooms around the world are teachers, learners and textbooks' (Richards, 1998a: 125). Yet, as Richards points out in the same paper, 'while the roles of teachers, teaching and learners have been the focus of a vast body of discussion and research over the years, much less attention has been given to textbooks' (ibid.). The implication is clear: since textbooks, and materials more generally, are such a key component of language classrooms, their appropriateness and usefulness require our critical attention.

## 3. Materials as an object of study and research

Richards was right in his contention that, relatively speaking and at the time he was writing, research had focused more on teachers, teaching and learners than on textbooks. However, we cannot infer from this that materials had received very little attention in the professional literature. In one area of English language teaching in particular (English for Specific Purposes – ESP), there had been concerted activity around course and materials design since the 1960s, particularly relating to English for science and technology (EST). This activity was to be reflected in such major publications in the 1970s as Allen and Widdowson's *English in Focus* series, Bates and Dudley-Evans' *Nucleus* series and the 4-volume *Reading and Thinking in English* coordinated by Moore, and in collections of academic papers such as Perren (1969, 1971, 1974); British Council (1975, 1978); Richards (1976); Holden (1977); Mackay and Mountford (1978); and Todd Trimble, Trimble and Drobnic (1978). In the United Kingdom, in 1972, lecturers responsible for pre-sessional courses for overseas students set up an organization initially known as Special English Language Materials for Overseas University Students (SELMOUS) specifically to share materials (see, for example, Cowie & Heaton, 1977; Johnson, 1977), and material development has remained a focus for ESP and its various sub-branches such as English for Academic Purposes (EAP) – see, for example, Alexander (2007). Robinson (1980) contains a very helpful review and detailed bibliography of early publications.

Interest in materials was not confined to ESP. By 1998, when Richards's paper was published, several more general book-length publications dealing with materials had appeared (Madsen & Bowen, 1978; British Council, 1980; Cunningsworth, 1984; Grant, 1987; Sheldon, 1987; McDonough & Shaw, 1993; Byrd, 1995a; Cunningsworth, 1995; Hidalgo, Hall & Jacobs, 1995);

and this steady stream has continued (see, for example, Tomlinson, 1998a; Fenner & Newby, 2000; McGrath, 2002; Renandya, 2003; Tomlinson, 2003a; Mishan, 2005; Tomlinson, 2008a; Harwood, 2010a; Mishan & Chambers, 2010; Tomlinson & Masuhara, 2010a). A second edition of Tomlinson (1998) was published in 2011; a third edition of McDonough and Shaw, with Masuhara as third author, was scheduled to appear in 2012, and a second edition of McGrath in 2013. On a broader front, this recognition of the importance of materials has also been reflected in conferences devoted to this topic, and the setting up of the British-based Materials Development Association (MATSDA) and the Materials Writers Special Interest Section within TESOL, the American-based international association of teachers of English to speakers of other languages. Outside the world of English language teaching, the International Association for Research on Textbooks and Educational Media (IARTEM) was founded in 1991; it holds biannual conferences and publishes conference reports (see www.iartem.no/) and an e-journal (see http://biriwa.com/iartem/ejournal7/).

## 4. The focus of this book

It appears to be the case, then, that materials have for some time been receiving the kind of serious attention that Richards called for. However, it has been argued that materials development is still seen in applied linguistics circles as 'an essentially atheoretical activity, and thus unrewarding as an area of research' (Samuda, 2005: 232), and that such research as has been carried out has been too narrowly focused (Tomlinson & Masuhara, 2010b). A focus on the textbook, for example, to the exclusion of the teacher and learners fails to take account of their interconnected dynamic relationship. The better materials are, the more helpful they will potentially be; but since they are merely designed to be aids to teaching and learning their effectiveness will depend on how appropriate they are for a particular context (which depends partly on selection processes) and how they are perceived and used by teachers and learners. Graves (2000) compares a textbook to a piano:

> The piano ... cannot produce music on its own. The music is produced only when you play it. Playing well requires practice and familiarity with the piece. The more skilled you are, the more beautiful the music. ... Clearly the quality of the instrument also affects the quality of the music. However, if it is in tune, even the most humble piano can produce beautiful music in the hands of a skilled musician. The musical analogy falls short because it involves only one performer, while success in teaching with a textbook depends also on the students who use it. (Graves, 2000: 175–6)

Efforts to improve materials are important, but an increased emphasis on research into the selection, use and, indeed, the effects of materials is also necessary (Hutchinson & Torres, 1994; McGrath, 2002; Tomlinson & Masuhara, 2010c). As Littlejohn (2011: 181) points out: 'Analysing materials . . . is quite a different matter from analysing "materials-in-action" '. This book reviews the most widely available studies on teachers' evaluation and use of materials, but more are needed.

There are, of course, others outside the classroom who potentially have some influence on the nature of the materials that are used and how they are used by an individual teacher. Among them are those in positions of authority within an institution (institutional managers), who may select materials and coordinate teaching and testing based on them; fellow teachers, who may offer advice and ideas or alternatively discourage experimentation; and beyond them, a Ministry of Education, which develops curricula, syllabuses and national examinations, and perhaps publishes or approves textbooks. Where a textbook is the main teaching-learning aid, publishers and textbook writers play an obvious role, since 'the textbook . . . influences what teachers teach and what and to some extent how learners learn' (McGrath, 2002: 12). One might expect that teacher educators will also give guidance in materials selection and use.

Ultimately, the book is about this web of relationships. It draws on the published literature to describe the influences at work in the production of commercial materials such as textbooks, and synthesises what is known about English language teachers' relationships with materials and learners, and the effects of both institutional context and the wider educational context. It also presents what I hope is a compelling argument for the role of teacher education in helping teachers to develop the knowledge, skills and confidence to select, adapt, and design materials that will make learning more effective and more enjoyable.

## 5. Aims and target audience

Some years ago, the well-known author and teacher educator, Alan Maley, was asked in an interview what changes he would like to see in the ELT field. He replied:

> I'd like to see a re-equilibration of the power relationship between the academic research/theorizing community (which has most of the power and prestige) and the classroom teaching community (where most of the work gets done). What academics do is fine and perfectly valid in their community. But most of it is mistakenly taken to be relevant for a completely different community, with different needs, goals and aspirations. (Maley, 2001)

Maley puts forward a number of propositions here, not all of which would be accepted by those involved:

- The research/theorizing community (i.e. university academics) has both more power and more prestige than the classroom teaching community (presumably school teachers, though there are many classroom language teachers in universities who would agree with this).
- The classroom teaching community does most of the work.
- This community deserves a higher status.
- Differences in what academics and school teachers are expected to do and the contexts in which they work mean that the ideas that emerge from universities are often not relevant for those working in schools.
- These ideas are, however, assumed to be relevant.

This is not exactly an attack on academics in ivory towers. Maley has himself occupied academic positions in universities and is careful to state that what academics do is 'fine and perfectly valid in their community'. Rather, it is a warning that theories developed in one context may not be applicable in another, and an implied assertion that the practices of school teachers have their own validity and deserve credit.

One of the purposes of this book is to present the work of these communities side by side so that the nature of the gap can be seen, and the work needed to bridge that gap appreciated. However, because its focus is on teaching-learning materials, two other communities also feature: those who produce commercial materials (publishers and textbook writers) and those who might be expected to train teachers in the evaluation, use and development of materials (teacher educators). The intention is that each of these groups – and other groups with a vested interest, such as syllabus writers, institutional managers and educational administrators – should also benefit from a better understanding of the work of the others.

The principal aims of the book are as follows:

- To raise awareness among Ministries of Education and other language teacher education providers of the necessity – and, I would argue, centrality – of a materials evaluation and design component in language teacher education programmes, both pre-service and in-service (including postgraduate programmes in TESOL/TESL/ELT/Applied Linguistics).
- To raise awareness of classroom realities and teacher needs among teacher educators responsible for the planning and teaching of

- To raise awareness among publishers and coursebook writers of what teachers need and expect.

- To raise awareness among institutional managers of the kinds of support that teachers need if they are to fulfil their responsibilities and continue to develop as professionals.

- To stimulate reflection and informed action in teachers themselves.

- To stimulate further research to strengthen the knowledge base of teacher education by identifying examples of effective practice among both classroom teachers and teacher educators.

## 6. Structure of the book

Following an introductory chapter (Chapter One) which introduces the major themes (materials, roles of teacher and learners, teacher education), the book consists of three parts. Part One contains three chapters which present views on materials and their use by teachers from perspectives which are external to the classroom. These chapters deal with the perspectives of, in turn, publishers and textbook writers (Chapter Two); the professional community, defined as those who write about materials and their use, and therefore a more inclusive term than Maley's 'academic community' (Chapter Three); and teacher educators, specifically those who have written about teacher education in materials evaluation and design (Chapter Four). Taken together, these chapters represent the theory of the title of this book – that is, the expectations that groups external to the classroom have of teachers and the roles they will play in their interactions with materials and learners. Part Two then considers how far these expected roles appear to be reflected in the practices of teachers in relation to materials evaluation (Chapter Five) and materials adaptation (Chapter Six), and the value that teachers, in turn, attach to learner involvement in evaluating or supplying materials (Chapter Seven). What emerges from these chapters is that there are some gaps between teacher practice and the theory discussed in earlier chapters. The final chapter in Part Two, Chapter Eight, offers explanations for these gaps. Part Three consists of just two chapters, both concerned with implications. Chapter Nine presents implications for teachers themselves; for the other groups that have an impact on teacher practice – publishers and textbook writers, institutional managers and Ministries of Education; and for research. Chapter Ten outlines a practical proposal for teacher education in materials evaluation and design.

## 7. A personal note

At the time of writing, I am based at the National Institute of Education in Singapore, where I teach courses on materials as part of in-service BEd and MEd programmes. Previously, I have run workshops and courses on materials evaluation and design for English language teachers in Europe, the Middle East, the Indian subcontinent, South East Asia, South America and for many years in the United Kingdom, at the universities of Edinburgh and Nottingham. Contexts may vary, but participants tend to have three things in common: they think materials are important (and are often critical of those they are expected to use); they are interested in developing their ability to select materials and/or develop their own; and they have had little or no *practical* training in materials evaluation or design.

As a teacher educator, I could not be more delighted. Motivation to learn and a similar starting point – what more could I ask? Seen from a wider, more objective standpoint, however, teachers' lack of training is a source of great concern. If the majority of teachers have never received any systematic training relating to materials, I asked myself, what are the effects on the ways in which they select and use materials? And what can be done to improve the situation? These were the initial questions which stimulated me to write this book. However, in the course of my research, as often happens, other intriguing questions emerged, among them: why do teachers not do what they are expected to? None of these questions lends itself to a simple answer, and because the literature which links teachers, materials and teacher education is so limited and materials, contexts and individual teachers so varied, the answers that I have provided are inevitably partial and, to some extent, personal. I hope that the answers that I have provided are nevertheless useful and, perhaps more important, that the questions will spur on others to formulate questions and publish answers that are meaningful for their own contexts.

Singapore<br>
1 December 2011

# CHAPTER ONE

# Introduction:

# Materials, the roles of teachers and learners, and teacher education

> ... far too many institutions seem to view materials and equipment as being more important than students and/or teachers. ... We are, after all, teaching students – not materials.
>
> (Edwards, 2010: 73)
>
> As teacher preparation increases, the importance of the textbook diminishes.
>
> (McElroy, 1934: 5)

## 1. Introduction

The Preface highlighted the importance of materials in language teaching and the need to gain a better understanding of how teachers select and use materials. It also hinted at a key role for teacher education. The three sections of this chapter reintroduce each of these themes. **Section 2** takes a closer look at what we mean by 'materials', the arguments for textbooks and criticisms of textbooks; **Section 3** examines teachers' roles in relation to materials and learners; and **Section 4** deals with teacher education.

## 2. Materials

### 2.1 What do we mean by 'materials'?

If you ask 100 English language teachers who are teaching learners of different ages, with different needs and in different contexts what materials they use in their teaching their individual answers will vary considerably. Some lists may contain only one item; others will be much more extensive. Certain items will appear in most lists; others may be much less frequent. The master list, containing all the items from the individual lists, will almost certainly include:

- **A textbook,** produced by a commercial publisher (i.e. for profit), a Ministry of Education or a large institution (e.g. university language centre, private language school chain); this will normally be accompanied by some combination of the following: teachers' notes, a student workbook, tests, visual aids (e.g. wallcharts, flashcards), a reader, audio and video material / computer-based (CALL) exercise material / Smartboard software / web-based materials.

- **Commercial materials that are not provided as part of the textbook package:** for example, reference material (dictionaries, grammar books, irregular verb charts) and practice material (supplementary skills books, readers).

- **Teacher-prepared materials,** selected by or devised by the teacher or a group of teachers working together:
    - authentic print materials (e.g. newspaper and magazine articles, literary extracts, advertisements, menus, diagrams and other print materials downloaded from the internet which were not designed for language teaching)
    - authentic recordings (e.g. songs, off-air recordings, recordings of academic lectures; Internet sources such as YouTube)
    - worksheets, quizzes and tests downloaded from the internet or photocopied from other sources
    - teacher-developed materials (e.g. oral or written activities developed to accompany authentic or textbook materials,

     self-standing tasks and exercises, tests, overhead projector transparencies, PowerPoint presentations, CALL materials)
- games (board games, Bingo, etc.)
- realia (real objects, including classroom items) and representations (photos, drawings, including drawing on the board).

Some teachers will also enlist the aid of learners to supply or create materials. Indeed, we might broaden the notion of materials to include all use of the target language by learners and the teacher in that this is a potential input to learning, especially when it is captured by a recording or takes a written form. If we stretch the notion of materials still further, we might also add any other visual or auditory means (e.g. facial expression, gesture, mime, demonstration, sounds) used by the teacher or learners to convey meaning or stimulate language use. Tomlinson (2001) takes this kind of broad view of materials, defining them as 'anything which can be used to facilitate the learning of a language. They can be linguistic, visual, auditory or kinaesthetic, and they can be presented in print, through live performance or display, or on cassette, CD-ROM, DVD or the internet' (p.66).

## 2.2 *Some distinctions*

The list above has been organized in such a way that certain distinctions are immediately apparent: between, for example, textbook packages, other (supplementary) commercial materials and materials prepared by teachers themselves; between reference material and practice material; and between various types of teacher-prepared materials. McGrath (2002: 7), writing specifically about text materials, differentiates between four categories of material:

> those that have been specifically designed for language learning and teaching (e.g. textbooks, worksheets, computer software); authentic materials (e.g. off-air recordings, newspaper articles) that have been specially selected and exploited for teaching purposes by the classroom teacher; teacher-written materials; and learner-generated materials.

We might also wish to distinguish on the basis of where materials were produced ('global' vs 'local' textbooks), their intended audience (General English – sometimes dubbed Teaching English for No Obvious Reason (TENOR) – or English for Specific Purposes (ESP)) or their linguistic focus (on a language system such as grammar or phonology, or a language skill such as listening or speaking).

However, there are other distinctions which are perhaps more important because they concern the roles that materials play: that between non-verbal and verbal materials, for instance, that between materials-as-content and materials-as-language, and the four-way distinction made by Tomlinson (2001) between materials which are *'instructional* in that they inform learners about the language, ... *experiential* in that they provide exposure to the language in use, ... *elicitative* in that they stimulate language use, or ... *exploratory* in that they facilitate discoveries about language use' (p.66, emphases added).

Non-verbal materials such as representations can help to establish direct associations between words and objects and clarify meanings; they can also be used to stimulate learners to produce language, spoken and written. However, for language learning purposes they are much more limited than verbal (or text) materials: spoken language in the form of classroom talk or recordings, materials containing written language and multimedia materials (literally, anything combining more than one medium). The form in which ideas are expressed in these materials may serve as examples of language use – and, indeed, of discourse structure; this language also carries content, ideas to which learners may react and from which they may learn.

The importance of materials-as-content should not be underestimated. One of the beliefs which links the communicative approach to methods of a century and more earlier, such as the Direct Method, is that learning to speak a language is a natural capacity which is stimulated by three conditions: 'someone to talk to, *something to talk about*, and a desire to understand and make yourself understood' (Howatt, 2004: 210, emphasis added). In language classrooms, that 'something to talk about' may be a subject selected by the teacher or initiated by a learner, including some aspect of the language itself, or it may be a topic, text or task in the materials. In language learning terms, what matters is that it should trigger in learners the 'desire' to understand and make themselves understood. The implication is clear: the more engaging the content, the more likely it is to stimulate communicative interaction. Learning thus takes place through exposure and use – or in Tomlinson's (2001) terms – through experiencing the language or responding to elicitation. Content selected for its relevance to learners' academic or occupational needs can, of course, also fulfil broader learning purposes, and content and language integrated learning (CLIL) has aroused much interest in recent years.

In reference materials such as dictionaries and grammar books, language *is* the content; and explicit information about the language, plus exercises, also forms the bulk of student workbooks and some textbooks. Tomlinson refers to this as the 'instructional' role of materials. Helpful though this approach to the language may be for analytically inclined learners, it needs to be complemented by text-level examples of language in use. These texts, spoken and written, together with all instructions and examples, must illustrate language which is accurate, up-to-date and natural. They can then serve both as language samples in which rules of use can be 'discovered' by learners – Tomlinson's 'exploratory' role for materials – and as a model for learners' own production. We might describe this way of looking at materials as a materials-as-language (rather than materials-as-content) perspective.

## 2.3 Coursebooks and their advantages

As far as language learning is concerned, then, the importance of materials-as-content lies primarily in their value as a stimulus for communicative interaction, and of materials-as-language as the provision of information about the target language and carefully selected examples of use. The modern textbook, now normally referred to as a 'coursebook' because it tends to be used as the foundation for a course, is designed to combine these functions.

It is easy to understand why coursebooks are so popular. Their advantages include the following:

1. **They reduce the time needed for lesson preparation.** Teachers who are teaching full-time find coursebooks invaluable because they do not have enough time to create original lessons for every class.
2. **They provide a visible, coherent programme of work.** Teachers may lack the time and expertise to design a coherent programme of work. The coursebook writer not only selects and organizes language content but also provides the means by which this can be taught and learned: 'the most fundamental task for the professional writer is bringing together coherently the theory, practice, activities, explanations, text, visuals, content, formats, and all other elements that contribute to the finished product' (Byrd, 1995b: 8). Coursebooks are also reassuring for the parents of younger learners who are keen to know what their children are doing and to offer their help if it is needed.
3. **They provide support.** For teachers who are untrained or inexperienced, textbooks (and the Teacher's Books that normally accompany them) provide methodological support. Those who lack confidence in their own language proficiency can draw on linguistically accurate input and examples of language use (Richards, 2001b). At times of curriculum change, coursebooks offer concrete support for the inexperienced and experienced alike (Hutchinson & Torres, 1994).
4. **They are a convenient resource for learners.** The visible coherence – or sense of purpose and direction – referred to above is also helpful for learners. Because coursebooks enable a learner to preview or

review what is done in class, they can promote 'feelings of both progress and security' (Harmer, 2001: 7). In short, they provide a framework for learning as well as for teaching – 'A learner without a coursebook is more teacher-dependent' (Ur, 1996: 184). Compared to handouts, coursebooks are also more convenient.

5  **They make standardized instruction possible.** If learners do the same things, at more or less the same rate, and are tested on the same material (Richards, 2001b), it is easy to keep track of what is done and compare performance across classes. From this perspective, coursebooks are thus a convenient administrative tool.

6  **They are visually appealing, cultural artefacts.** The attraction for learners of the modern global coursebook lies in no small part in its visual appeal – the use of colour, photographs, cartoons, magazine-style formats. Cultural information is conveyed by these means as well as through the words on the page (Harmer, 2001).

7  **Coursebook packages contain 'a wealth of extra material'** (Harmer, 2001: 7). Beyond the student book, the modern coursebook package makes available a range of additional resources for both classroom use and self-access purposes.

This last point is graphically illustrated in McGrath's (2007) analysis of eight global coursebook packages (see Table 1.1). The materials surveyed were as follows:

| Cambridge | *face2face* (1) | *Interchange (3rd edn)* (2) |
| --- | --- | --- |
| Longman | *Cutting Edge* (3) | *Total English* (4) |
| Macmillan | *Straightforward* (5) | *Inside Out* (6) |
| Oxford | *New English File* (7) | *New Headway* (8) |

As McGrath (2007: 347–8) notes, one feature of such packages is that they provide *integrated* resources for teachers. For example, Teacher's Books (or resource packs) may now contain photocopiable activities, supplementary materials offering 'extra support/challenge' for mixed groups and warm-up activities (*New English File*), and further resources for teachers include:

- Teacher's Video Guide (*Inside Out* contains guidance and worksheets)
- customizable texts (*face2face*)

**Table 1.1** Content of coursebook packages

|  | C | | L | | M | | O | |
|---|---|---|---|---|---|---|---|---|
|  | 1 | 2 | 3 | 4 | 5 | 6 | 7 | 8 |
| **Student's book** | √ | √ | √ | √ | √ | √ | √ | √ |
| **Teacher's book** | √ | √ | √ | √ | √ | √ | √ | √ |
| **Teacher's resource pack** |  | √ |  |  | √ | √ |  | √ |
| **Workbook (various versions)** | √ | √ | √ | √ | √ | √ | √ | √ |
| **Audiocassettes** | √ | √ | √ | √ | √ | √ | √ | √ |
| **Audio CDs** | √ | √ | √ |  | √ | √ |  | √ |
| **Lab audio CDs** |  | √ |  |  |  |  |  |  |
| **Videocassettes** |  | √ |  | √ |  | √ | √ | √ |
| **DVD** |  | √ |  |  |  | √ |  |  |
| **Teacher's Guide to video** |  |  |  |  | √ |  |  |  |
| **Tests** |  | √ |  |  | √ | √ |  | √ |
| **CD-ROM** | √ | √ |  |  |  |  | √ | √ |
| **Linked website** | √ | √ | √ | √ |  | √ | √ | √ |
| Other website resources (T) | √ | √ |  |  | √ | √ | √ | √ |
| Other website resources (S) |  |  |  |  |  |  | √ | √ |

(McGrath, 2007: 347–8)

- customizable tests on CD (*Inside Out*)
- publishers' websites linked to specific courses (Oxford sites include articles, downloadable worksheets and activities, and discussion groups)
- publishers' websites available to any teachers (e.g. Macmillan's *onestopenglish.com*).

Additional materials for learners are also provided – for example:

- a CD-ROM to accompany the student's book (*face2face*) or workbook (that for *New English File* includes video extracts and activities, interactive grammar quizzes, vocabulary banks, pronunciation charts and listen and practise audio material; the

workbook for *Inside Out* comes with either an audio cassette or an audio CD)
- publishers' websites for students linked to specific courses (e.g. *New English File*)
- publishers' websites available to any learner.

Linked resources which can be used in combination with specific courses are also available. These include specially designed supplementary materials and stand-alone resources. Examples include:

- business Resource Books (*New English File*)
- pronunciation course; interactive practice material on CD-ROM (*Headway*)
- bilingual (Dutch/French/German) 'Companions' containing listing of words/phrases with pronunciation, translation and contextualization (*Inside Out*).

Such developments are impressive: '25 years ago, who would have dreamed of website resources linked to courses or freely available general website resources for teachers and learners? And more is being offered almost daily. For instance, whiteboard software is available to accompany the two Cambridge titles, and learners can register for free e-lessons with Macmillan' (McGrath, 2007: 348). At the time of writing, e-books and e-readers have begun to have an impact on ELT publishing. Macmillan's Dynamic-Books software will reportedly allow teachers to edit e-book editions of Macmillan coursebooks in order to tailor them to the needs of their students (Salusbury, 2010). In a few years' time, other innovations will no doubt have been introduced.

## 2.4 Doubting voices

Given these potential benefits, it is hardly surprising that, despite occasional warnings of the demise of printed coursebooks in the face of technological development, coursebooks continue to be published and, particularly in contexts where English is taught as a foreign language by non-native English speaking teachers (NNESTs), 'whether we like it or not, represent for both students and teachers the visible heart of any ELT programme' (Sheldon, 1988: 237). Yet Sheldon's interpolated 'whether we like it or not' is telling. Despite their obvious appeal, coursebooks have attracted a number of criticisms, most of which are aptly captured by Rinvolucri's (2001) phrase 'a human, cultural and linguistic disaster' (cited in Harmer 2001: 5).

**Coursebooks do not cater for the whole person; nor do they do take adequate account of differences in learning preferences.** Underlying the humanistic approaches of the 1960s was the belief that, to be effective, teaching must engage the learner on an affective level as well as a cognitive level, and the same belief underpins one line of criticism of coursebooks. Tomlinson (2003b: 162) notes that many of the coursebooks he has used 'concentrated on the linguistic and analytical aspects of learning and . . . made insufficient use of the learners' ability to learn through doing things physically, to learn through feeling emotion, to learn through experiencing things in the mind', and the same criticism is implicit in the title of Rinvolucri's (2002) resource book *Humanising the Coursebook*. Tomlinson (2011b: 18) also claims that although 'most current coursebooks . . . favour learners with a preference for studial learning [i.e. focussed on linguistic form and correctness] and an apparent assumption that all learners are capable of benefiting from this style of learning' such learners are actually in a minority, and that other learning styles (or preferences), such as the auditory and experiential, also need to be catered for. A similar point in relation to the need to cater for multiple intelligences is made by Botelho (2003).

Global coursebooks (i.e. those produced for an international market) derive from an anglocentric view of the world and cultural realities that have little relevance for the majority of learners studying English outside English-speaking countries; native speaker norms predominate. The transmission of 'western' values is a form of cultural imperialism. The charge of anglocentrism is typically voiced by teachers working outside Britain, Australasia and North America (abbreviated to BANA by Holliday, 1994) or those representing their views (see, for example, Canagarajah, 1993; Altan, 1995; Gray, 2000). It draws attention to the fact that when marketing materials UK and US publishers tend to blur very real differences between the learning environments and learning purposes of those studying English within BANA – who comprise both immigrants and long-term/short-term student visitors – and those outside BANA (Masuhara & Tomlinson, 2008). While it is perfectly logical for materials intended for use within BANA to be oriented towards interaction with native speakers and familiarization with the culture of a specific BANA region (and this is appreciated by students – see, for example, Crawford, 2002), it is difficult to justify such an emphasis in materials intended for use in contexts where most English use is between non-native speakers of English. Specifically on the level of language, the debate on the role of English (as a lingua franca/international language) may rage over the question of appropriate models and exposure to relevant varieties, but the issues are complex (see, for example, Gilmore, 2007) and how this might translate into textbooks is as yet uncertain. Two recent studies of the accents used in recordings accompanying Finnish textbooks for English language learners (Kopperoinen, 2011; Kivistö, 2005) suggest that in the meantime native speaker norms continue to dominate.

The issue is not simply one of relevance. Global textbooks originating in 'the west' inevitably embody western values, which are reflected in both their content and their underlying pedagogical approach. Seen from the perspective of societies where such values are not simply alien but potentially malign in their influence, they have been characterized as a vehicle for cultural imperialism (see, for example, Alptekin & Alptekin, 1984; Dendrinos, 1992; Phillipson, 1992; Canagarajah, 1999). Pennycook (1994) has argued forcefully that global textbooks, through both their content and their recommended teaching practices and implied classroom role relationships, represent a belief in and 'advocacy for a particular way of life, a particular understanding of the world' (p.178). He concludes, nevertheless, that 'there are . . . possibilities . . . for resistance, appropriation and change' (p.179). This may take the form of teachers encouraging learners to engage critically with textbooks and other sources of materials (see, for example, Paran, 2003; Haig, 2006) or an instinctive learner response. Altan (1995) observes: 'When both the materials we use and the way we use them are culturally adverse, then inevitably learners switch off and retreat into their inner world to defend their own integrity' (p.59). Retreat may not be the only strategy. In some contexts, learners may resist more overtly. For instance, the Sri Lankan students described by Canagarajah (1993) not only demonstrated a reluctance to participate in the role plays and conversation activities that featured in the global textbook they were using but also showed what they expected of the teacher by moving the chairs he had placed in a circle before the lesson back into the more traditional rows.

Though the global textbook may have been the focus for such criticisms, it is important to note that ideology may also be explicit in 'national' textbooks, which deliberately promote national values and culture to further the aim of social cohesion (see, for example, Lund & Zoughby, 2007) – and one could, of course, envisage more sinister aims. Moreover, national textbooks are no different from other materials in embodying, in their rubrics and activities, implicit messages about the nature of language learning and the relationship and roles of teacher and learners. Graves (2000: 202) suggests a number of questions to be asked when analysing the hidden curriculum of a textbook. See also Jazadi (2003) and Littlejohn (2007, 2011) on what task analysis can reveal.

**Coursebooks do not reflect the findings of research into language, language use or language acquisition; and their representation of cultural realities is limited, biased or inaccurate.** Critics of the language content in coursebooks have argued that coursebooks do not represent authentic language use, illustrating this view with reference to reported speech (Barbieri & Eckhardt, 2007), the language of modality (Holmes, 1998), suggestions (Jiang, 2006), complaints (Boxer & Pickering, 1995), conversation strategies (McCarten & McCarthy, 2010), closing conversations (Bardovi-Harlig, Hartford, Mahon-Taylor, Morgan & Reynolds, 1991), telephone conversations (Wong, 2001) and differences between spoken and written grammar (Cullen & Kuo, 2007); Harwood (2010b) provides a useful overview of such content analyses. Other writers have looked at whether the treatment in coursebooks of a specific skill appears to take account of applied linguistic research. McDonough and Shaw (2003: Chapters 6–10), for example, summarize research on each of the main skill areas and integrated skills and examine how far this research is reflected in teaching materials. Studies of ESP textbooks have revealed a similar divide between the findings of linguistic research and teaching materials. Ewer and Boys (1981) drew attention to the fact that textbooks, particularly in ESP, were based on shaky linguistic foundations. Twenty years on, Candlin, Bhatia and Jensen (2002: 300), searching for suitable materials to teach legal English writing, concluded that of the 56 books they studied 'few, if any, are premised on any type of research-based linguistic analysis of legal texts and language' (cited in Harwood, 2010b: 10). Harwood's (2005) review of EAP textbooks found only one book (Swales & Feak, 2004) based on corpus research (see also Hyland, 1994 and Paltridge, 2002 on writing in EAP). Angouri (2010: 373) found 'a discrepancy' between the language used in Business English materials concerned with meetings and that used in real contexts (see also Williams, 1988 and Chan, 2009). Gilmore (2007), who provides a usefully wide-ranging review of studies comparing authentic and textbook discourse, distances himself a little by arguing that authenticity should not be seen as inherently 'good' and contrived examples/discourse as 'bad'; instead, the basis for judgement should be 'fitness for purpose' (Hutchinson & Waters, 1987: 159).

The language syllabuses in coursebooks and such aspects of their pedagogy as task design have also been a focus of critical attention. Auerbach and Rogers (1987, cited in Graves, 2000) drew attention to the fact that the language functions in US 'survival' textbooks for adult learners emphasized an acquiescent role as regards the status quo rather than one which involved questioning, analysis and problem-solving, and therefore represented a 'hidden curriculum'. More recently, a major impetus has been research in the field of second language acquisition (SLA), which has called into question the validity of the traditional grammatical syllabus and the presentation-practice-production (or 3 Ps) approach on which the coursebooks of the late 1960s and many of their 'communicative' successors were based. Thornbury and Meddings (2001: 12), for example, comment: 'Unfortunately, there is not a lot of research evidence to suggest that grammar mcnuggets are internalized in the order and at the pace that they are delivered', and Tomlinson and Masuhara (2010b), surveying the results of 23 research projects, conclude that 'none of the researchers seems to provide any evidence supporting either the typical textbook approach of Practice/Presentation/Production or the typical textbook procedures of listening and repeating, dialogue reproduction, filling in blanks or answering comprehension questions' (p.399). This may have been because their focus was not so much on evaluating the effectiveness or otherwise of such procedures but rather on researching, for example, the effect on motivation of using authentic texts, of exposure to extended language use through reading and listening or of discovery learning. While all the research described appears to have achieved positive results, these fall short of a clear cause and effect relationship between procedure and evidence of acquisition. A recent review of the effects of SLA theorizing and research on grammar teaching (Ellis, 2010) is similarly inconclusive. While arguing that the design of communicative tasks and techniques for grammatical consciousness-raising have been influenced by work in SLA, Ellis concedes that little else of this research can be applied directly to language teaching. The 'typical' textbook approach and procedures may now seem questionable, but as yet no clear research-based alternative has emerged.

A further very common criticism is that coursebooks perpetuate gender and other stereotypes and misrepresent reality – for instance, by excluding minorities and by depicting a world that is free of problems and sanitized (see, for example, Littlejohn & Windeatt, 1989; Thornbury, 1999, 2010; Gray, 2002; McGrath, 2004; Arikan, 2005; Lund & Zoughby, 2007). Global textbook publishers try to counter stereotypes in their guidance notes for authors, but their whitewashing approach to textbook content, reflected – as Gray (2002) notes – in what has been called PARSNIP (avoiding reference to politics, alcohol, religion, sex, narcotics, -isms – such as communism, and pork), is clearly pragmatic rather than principled. This is not only an issue for global textbooks, of course.

Underlying many of these criticisms is the feeling that in the world of textbooks little changes. As Sheldon (1988) observed, in the course of a wide-ranging critique, 'textbooks merely grow from and imitate other textbooks and do not admit the winds of change from research, methodological experimentation, or classroom feedback' (p.239). The development of large language corpora means that as far as *language* research is concerned this is perhaps less true now than at the time Sheldon was writing (see, for example, Stranks, 2003; Richards, 2006; and papers in Harwood, 2010a). However, complaints of bland content in textbooks persist (Masuhara, Haan, Yi & Tomlinson, 2008) and researchers are still finding evidence of stereotyping (e.g. Mukundan & Nimehchisalem, 2008).

**Coursebooks marginalize teachers. Coursebooks should be replaced by resource books. All external materials are an obstacle to real communication.** On the face of it, the variety of resources offered by a modern global coursebook package is one of its major strengths. However, concerns about this ever-increasing provision have also been expressed. Writing more than 20 years ago, Rossner (1988) commented: 'Current materials tend to overburden the user with an embarrassment of riches . . . [and] create more work for the teacher, who is forced to spend more time coming to grips with these materials' (p.214). One result of this increased complexity is that 'the structure of the textbook is becoming much tighter and more explicit – more like a prepared script. Less and less appears to be left to the teacher to decide and work out' (Hutchinson & Torres, 1994: 316), a point echoed by Littlejohn (2011): 'The extent to which materials may now effectively structure classroom time from a distance has . . . increased considerably' (p.180). According to this view, teachers risk being marginalized.

The argument, then, is not simply about the expansion in the resources available. More fundamentally, it is about the roles of textbook and teacher. Brumfit (1979: 30) expresses the view that 'even the best textbooks take away initiative from teachers by implying that there is somewhere an "expert" who can solve problems' for teachers and learners. The consequence of taking away (or lost) initiative is 'de-skilling' (Shannon (1987), cited in Richards 1993, 1998a). If teachers hand over responsibility for decision-making to textbooks, the argument goes, this reduces their role to that of mere technicians. When the selection of a textbook is the starting-point for course planning, rather than a stage which follows consideration of aims, learners' needs and teachers' capacities and preferences, the teacher (or whoever else takes decisions for course-planning) has abdicated from a key responsibility: there is now a real danger that it is the coursebook which determines course aims, language content and what will be assessed. In effect, the book becomes the course and the teacher teaches the book. Swan (1992) warns against the resulting false sense of security:

> ... textbooks ... can seem to absolve teachers of responsibility. Instead of the day-to-day decisions that have to be made about what to teach and how to teach, it is easy just to sit back and operate the system, secure in the belief that the wise and virtuous people who produced the textbook knew what was good for us. Unfortunately this is rarely the case. (Swan, 1992: 33, cited in Hutchinson & Torres, 1994: 315)

Allwright (1981) presents two contrasting perspectives on the role of materials and the teacher-textbook relationship. If teachers are seen as *deficient*, the textbook becomes a form of insurance against their deficiencies (limitations). Materials therefore need to be teacher-proof. From the *difference* perspective, the teacher is seen as having expertise which is different from but complementary to that of the materials writer. Materials are therefore seen as a resource. Siding with this latter perspective, he concludes that 'the management of learning is far too complex to be satisfactorily catered for by a pre-packaged set of decisions embodied in teaching materials' (p.9).

As alternatives to the textbook, Brumfit and Allwright make rather similar proposals. Brumfit (1979: 30) envisages 'resource packs, sets of materials with advice to teachers on how to adapt and modify the contents', while Allwright (1981: 9) conceives of a 'guide to language learning' for learners and 'ideas books' and 'rationale books' for teachers, supported by learner training and an appropriate focus within teacher training, all within a framework of the cooperative management of learning by learners and teachers – effectively a process syllabus.

In essence, these are arguments for replacing a textbook by other types of materials. A more extreme view dispenses altogether with what might normally be thought of as materials. In a short and undated paper in which he traces the shifts in his own use of and attitudes to coursebooks, Underhill writes: 'I have

... found that materials, especially coursebooks, can come between me and my students ... If I'm not careful I reduce myself to a "materials operator", separated from my students by a screen of "things to do"'. Acknowledging this paper as an influence, Thornbury published in 2000 the first of several papers on 'dogme' in ELT (the term 'dogme' comes from the manifesto Dogme 95 published by a Danish film collective, which called for a return to basics in film-making). Pointing to the vast array of published resources now available, Thornbury (2000) asks, 'Where is the inner life of the student in all this? Where is real communication?' Questions such as these led him to call on ELT colleagues to join him in 'a vow of EFL chastity' enshrined in the dictum that 'Teaching should be done using only the resources that teachers and students bring to the classrooms – that is, themselves – and whatever happens to be in the classroom' (Thornbury, 2000). Although the burning of textbooks, following the example of Sylvia Warner, seemed to be advocated at one point (Thornbury & Meddings, 2001), a later paper accepts that textbooks might be among the resources that teachers or learners bring to the classroom and, indeed, offers a number of interesting ideas for exploiting coursebooks:

> A 'Dogme' approach doesn't necessarily exclude the use of a coursebook ... The idea is to use the coursebook, but sparingly ... It does *not* mean, however, propping up the book's weaknesses by bringing in yet more materials in the forms of photocopied exercises, for example ... The idea is to include activities that provide optimal exposure, attention, output and feedback, thereby maximising the chance of language emergence. (Thornbury & Meddings, 2002: 36–7, original emphasis)

The occasional use of coursebooks might be tolerated, but technology is a definite taboo, and this 'pedagogy of bare essentials', to use the strapline from the group's archived website, now tends to be promoted as 'Teaching Unplugged'. The website, at http://www.thornburyscott.com/tu/sources.htm, offers convenient access to a variety of the early papers, including that by Underhill, and a number of resources; a discussion group can be accessed at http://groups.yahoo.com/group/dogme; and the book 'Teaching Unplugged' (Meddings & Thornbury, 2009) has developed the argument. Edwards (2010) concludes her review of this book with the comment that it is unlikely to lead to the disappearance of the coursebook or to affect the growth of technology, but points out in support of the underlying Dogme concerns: 'As a teacher, one of my major worries is the fact that far too many institutions seem to view materials and equipment as being more important than students and/or teachers ... We are, after all, teaching students – not materials' (p.73).

Given all these criticisms, it is perhaps surprising that, as Hutchinson and Torres (1994) put it, 'the textbook not only survives, it thrives' (p.316). Undoubtedly, one of the reasons for this is, as noted earlier, its convenience. As Hutchinson and Torres point out, textbooks provide 'the structure that the teaching–learning system – particularly the system in change – requires' (p.317). We also need to distinguish, of course, between the first three of these criticisms, which relate to the coursebook as a product, and the final criticism, which relates to the way in which the coursebook is perceived and used. Harmer argues that fears of teachers being led by the nose have been somewhat overstated:

> Coursebook critics, it seems to me, focus on *unthinking* coursebook use to make their case – as if all teachers used them in this way all the time. Yet that is to suggest that all teachers see coursebooks in the wrong light – as monolithic manuals which have to be followed to the letter, like playscripts. But coursebooks are not like that and never have been. Like any lesson plan or succession of plans, they are *proposals* for action, not instructions for use. Teachers look at these proposals and decide if they agree with them, if they want to do things in the way the book suggests, or if, on the contrary, they are going to make changes, replacing things, modifying activities, approaching texts differently, or tackling a piece of grammar in a way which they, through experience, know to be more effective than the exercise on page 26. You can use a textbook without slavishly following every word; you can love a friend without agreeing with everything they say or doing everything in the same way they do. In the hands of engaged teachers, coursebooks, far from being straitjackets, are spurs to creativity, somewhere to start, something for teachers to work with and react with or against. (Harmer, 2001: 8, original emphases)

Many teachers do, as Harmer claims, make changes to coursebook materials based on their beliefs or experience, and engaged teachers may simply use the materials as a springboard. As we shall see in later chapters, however, there are also teachers who, for one reason or another, treat a coursebook as a manual or playscript to be followed.

Rather than simply condemning this as inappropriate, we might ask why this is, and who is responsible if teachers do treat coursebooks as playscripts. Where elements of a coursebook package, including technology, are closely integrated this may be a factor (McGrath, 2007), but there are also implications for institutional management and teacher education.

## 2.5 *Teaching without a coursebook*

Not all teachers use a coursebook. Confident, experienced teachers working in environments which give them freedom to use whatever materials they like may prefer to draw on materials from a wide variety of commercial and authentic sources, and create their own. Teachers involved in specific-purpose teaching, and especially 1:1 courses, who feel that no suitable textbook exists may find themselves in the same situation through necessity rather than choice. Other teachers, who are working towards a specific examination, may base their teaching largely on previous examination papers. Yet other teachers may be using an approach or method which is not based on a textbook. In Singapore, for example, the Ministry of Education has been phasing out the use of English language textbooks in primary schools in favour of an approach based on the shared reading of Big Books. The books provide a context for target language items and a stimulus to discussion and writing; and additional resources are supplied by the Ministry. In effect, this is a rejection not only of textbooks but also of teaching based on a textbook. Further examples would be three of the innovative 'humanistic' methods that emerged during the 1960s. For instance, Community Language Learning (CLL – also known as Counseling Learning) is based on the language produced by learners, recorded by the teacher, and then written up for analysis. The early stages of both Total Physical Response (TPR) and Silent Way are purely oral: in TPR learners follow oral instructions; and Silent Way makes use of Cuisenaire rods (the small coloured wooden sticks originally designed for mathematics) and other materials specifically designed for this method, such as sound/colour charts, which contain blocks of colour representing phonemes. (For further discussion of these methods, see, for example, Stevick, 1980; Richards & Rodgers, 2001.) Richards (1985) makes the interesting point that the lack of a textbook has limited the spread of these methods.

In some contexts, traditional resources of all kinds may be non-existent. Gebhard (1996) cites a personal communication from Ed Black: 'I was teaching English to Chinese immigrants in Jamaica. There was no chalk, no paper, no books. Me, no Chinese. They, no English' (p.107). Gebhard comments:

> I am very familiar with such settings . . . it is often difficult to obtain materials and media through which to teach. But . . . I enjoy the challenge of creating materials out of everyday things. For example, we can teach students to write in the air and on the earth, make use of clouds (what do you see? I see a horse) and of folded leaves and sticks (e.g. to form a town to practice giving directions), and use our fingers to practice counting. (Gebhard, 1996:107–8)

He adds:

> I believe that those who are fortunate enough to teach in difficult settings have an advantage. They are challenged to reach deep within their creative selves and observe everyday things as possible teaching materials. This is an education within itself, one that provides an awareness that teaching first of all concerns what goes on between people, as well as an awareness that at our fingertips there is an infinite number of materials that are possible resources for teaching. (Gebhard, 1996:108)

Gebhard's enthusiasm is infectious. He is right, of course, that teaching is essentially an interaction between people and teachers need to exploit fully whatever means are available to make that encounter as useful and memorable as possible. He is no doubt also right that difficult circumstances, which include large classes as well as limited or non-existent resources, bring out the best in responsible and creative teachers, and in this way contribute to their professional development. Whether teachers working in such circumstances or their less resourceful colleagues feel themselves to be 'fortunate' is much less certain. Faced with a choice between a book and no book, most teachers would probably choose the book, on the grounds that it is another resource, at least. Sadly, this section was omitted from the second edition (2006) of Gebhard's book, thus giving the impression at least that such difficult settings no longer exist. Two short papers by J. Hadfield and C. Hadfield (2003a, 2003b) offer not only a corrective but also a range of practical suggestions for teachers working with 'almost nothing' (defined as paper, pens and blackboard) or nothing at all in the way of provided resources. The papers also raise interesting questions about teachers' wants and needs as far as technology is concerned – questions that will be taken up in Chapter Four.

There are, then, situations in which for one reason or another teachers are not using a textbook as the basis for a course. Ultimately, of course, what is important is not what kinds of material are used but whether they help to accomplish the desired learning outcomes; and this will depend in part at least on how they are viewed and used.

## 3. Teachers and learners

### 3.1 *Teachers' relationships with materials and learners*

Drawing on his discussions with teachers, Bolitho (1990) outlines four ways of representing symbolically the relationship between teachers, learners and materials. Slightly reorganized, these are illustrated below:

(i) The most common representation, Bolitho notes, is of a line from materials through teacher to learner (Figure 1.1):

This suggests, he adds, not only that the teacher has a mediating role between materials and learners but also that learners cannot access the materials directly – they can do so only through the mediation of the teacher. What

Materials ⟶ Teacher ⟶ Learner

**FIGURE 1.1**
(Bolitho, R. 1990. 'An eternal triangle? Roles for teacher, learners and teaching materials in a communicative approach'. In Anivan, S. (ed.) *Language Teaching Methodology for the Nineties* (pp.22–30). Singapore: SEAMEO Regional Language Centre. © SEAMO RELC, reprinted with permission.)

the diagram also implies, of course, is that materials are a form of external provision, given to the teacher rather than selected by the teacher.

**(ii)** In Figure 1.2, the relationship between teacher and materials has changed. The teacher now has equal status with materials:

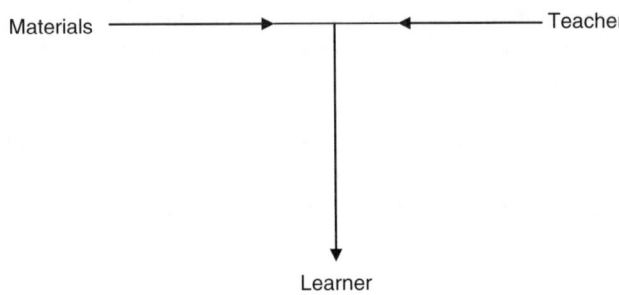

**FIGURE 1.2**
(Bolitho, R. 1990. 'An eternal triangle? Roles for teacher, learners and teaching materials in a communicative approach'. In Anivan, S. (ed.) *Language Teaching Methodology for the Nineties* (pp.22–30). Singapore: SEAMEO Regional Language Centre. © SEAMO RELC, reprinted with permission.)

Bolitho comments: 'the teacher and the materials are seen as superordinate, conspiring (as one teacher put it only half-jokingly) to make the learner's life difficult' (p.23). Notice that there is no arrow between learner and materials.

**(iii)** The third representation (Figure 1.3), with arrows going in both directions between the three points on the circle, differs from the first two most obviously, as Bolitho observes, in that it recognizes

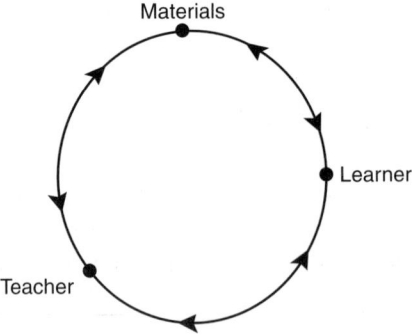

**FIGURE 1.3**
(Bolitho, R. 1990. 'An eternal triangle? Roles for teacher, learners and teaching materials in a communicative approach'. In Anivan, S. (ed.) *Language Teaching Methodology for the Nineties* (pp.22–30). Singapore: SEAMEO Regional Language Centre. © SEAMO RELC, reprinted with permission.)

the importance of learners being able to access materials directly as well as through the teacher's mediation.

We might also comment on four further aspects of this particular representation. First, the materials are not shown as deriving from an external source; they might therefore include not only commercial materials but also materials created by teachers or supplied by learners. Second, materials are represented as a source for both teacher and learners on one side of the diagram, but on the other, teacher and learners are free of any influence of external materials – implying that such materials do not determine all classroom interaction. Third, if we take a broad view of materials as anything which contributes to learning, we might wish to see that unfettered interaction between teacher and learners (or between learners) as resulting in *co-constructed* materials, and assign these materials their own place on the empty side of the diagram. Finally, this circular representation also takes account of the fact that materials do not have to be treated in a serial fashion ("We've done Unit 3. Let's go on to Unit 4."). Both learners and teachers may wish to review what has already been 'done'; learners may also wish to preview what will be done in future lessons.

**(iv)** On the face of it, the triangle depicted below (Figure 1.4) says exactly the same as the circle in (iii).

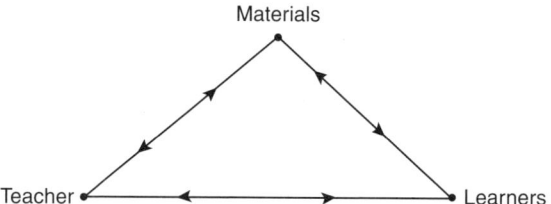

**FIGURE 1.4**
(Bolitho, R. 1990. 'An eternal triangle? Roles for teacher, learners and teaching materials in a communicative approach'. In Anivan, S. (ed.) *Language Teaching Methodology for the Nineties* (pp.22–30). Singapore: SEAMEO Regional Language Centre. © SEAMO RELC, reprinted with permission.)

However, not all triangles are equilateral. If the base were shorter than the two sides, this might imply that both teacher and learner were distant from the materials, either because they are too difficult or, perhaps, not used very much. If the side linking materials and teacher were short, on the other hand, that might imply that the teacher identifies closely with the materials. The teachers surveyed by Bolitho also pointed out that triangles like the one depicted have an apex and a base, which suggests a hierarchy, with materials dominating; one teacher felt that the diagram illustrated 'the tendency that teachers have to blame materials (or learners) when things go wrong, and the similar tendency displayed by learners to blame teachers (or materials)' (p.23).

At the heart of this discussion, of course, are the attitudes of teacher and learners to materials. Richards (1998a: 131) has commented on the danger of 'reification' ('the unjustifiable attribution of qualities of excellence, authority and validity') of textbooks by teachers, adding that in some parts of the world this tendency may be reinforced by cultural conditioning: 'Teachers . . . tend to assume that any item included in a textbook must be an important learning item for students, and that explanations (e.g. of grammar rules or idioms) and cultural information provided by the author are true and should not be questioned' (ibid.). Moreover, 'they assume that they do not have the authority or knowledge to adapt the textbook' (ibid.). Learners, similarly, may perceive published materials as more authoritative than those produced by their own teachers and therefore attach more value to them.

## 3.2 New roles for learners

Bolitho (1990) makes a number of important points about the relationships between materials, teachers and learners.

> Let us start with *materials*, which means textbooks first and foremost. Here the weight of tradition is heavy. Ever since the advent of the printed word in the Middle Ages, textbooks in education have represented knowledge. The handing over of a set of textbooks by a teacher to a class is an act with symbolic significance: 'Here is your textbook. If you learn what is in it you will succeed' is the implication. This tradition still holds good in the overwhelming majority of educational contexts, worldwide. (Bolitho, 1990: 23)

The book, in this tradition, constitutes the course. The teacher's role is to teach – and finish! – the book. Learners know that they will be tested on what is in the book (in some cases, not only on the language but also the content of texts). The book defines what is to be taught and learned.

> Learners . . . have been able to take the book home, to revise from it perhaps with the help of parents educated in the same tradition, and to go into end-of-year examinations confident of having covered all the materials necessary for success. Vocabulary lists and grammar rules could be learned by heart and applied in tests of linguistic competence. Set texts could be memorised and liberally quoted in literature examinations. Learning a language had more to do with acquiring knowledge than with developing skills. (Bolitho, 1990: 24)

With the advent of the communicative approach, materials changed and expectations of teachers and learners changed. As Bolitho notes:

> ... publishers, methodologists and textbook authors have been encouraging teachers to see a communicative textbook as a resource to draw on in teaching a course, even as a point of departure for classroom activities, rather than as a convergently conceived framework for study. But has anyone bothered to tell learners this? ... Learners are entitled to know *why* they are asked to behave in certain ways ... and *how* they can learn most effectively. Yet how many teachers go into classrooms and simply expect learners to do as they are asked without a word of explanation? (Bolitho, 1990: 24–5)

Bolitho is right, of course. These days, many textbooks do include sections on 'learning to learn', but especially when what is expected of learners represents a break with cultural tradition, an explanation needs to be offered, and the teacher is in the best position to give this. This point applies even more strongly to attempts to give learners more responsibility. For instance, it has been proposed that learners should:

- be involved in textbook evaluation and selection or decisions about which parts of a textbook should be studied
- be shown how to make independent use of both classroom materials and out-of-class resources
- be encouraged to interact critically with the content of textbooks and other materials
- provide supplementary materials to be used in class
- generate materials that can be used by other learners.

(See, for example, Wright, 1987; Clarke, 1989; Tudor, 1993; Deller, 1990; Campbell & Kryszewska, 1992 – and McGrath, 2002 for reviews of these and other sources.)

What lies behind all these suggestions is the belief that motivation is enhanced when learners have some control over and investment in their own learning, when decisions about what is done and how it is done are not imposed but taken with teachers or by learners themselves. For these ideas to take root, however, teachers have to be prepared to share responsibility with learners; learners have to be willing to accept these new roles; and both teachers and learners have to look at materials with fresh eyes. We return to the topic of learners and materials in Chapter Seven.

## 3.3 Teacher roles

### 3.3.1 Choice

In situations where more than one textbook is available, or a course is based on materials other than a textbook, there is a need to choose. Choice is generally held to be a good thing, but it is not always simple. Even when there was much less choice than there is now, the selection of a textbook might be influenced by a variety of factors, as the following quotation from an American educator makes clear:

> The color of a salesman's necktie and the crease in his trousers, the beauty of binding and illustrations, and the opinions of officious administrative officers have all been potent factors in choosing books. More consequential have been the prestige of author and publisher, and the influence of wide current use.
>
> (McElroy, 1934: 5)

Almost half a century later, British commentators were still warning about teachers being taken in by skilful marketing (Brumfit, 1979) and jazzy covers (Grant, 1987: 119); and popularity, as evidenced by sales figures (Sheldon, 1988), and the reputations of the major publishers and writers of best-selling textbooks continue to be seen as guarantors of textbook quality. McElroy himself is in no doubt, however, that 'whether the author be great or small, the publisher powerful or unknown, the final determinant should be the book itself: what it contains and how the material is presented' (ibid.).

Much rests on the choice of book, and care therefore needs to be taken over the selection process. As McElroy points out:

> To experiment haphazardly with new books is expensive. In former times the Board of Education took sole responsibility for selecting books. In larger school systems today, the Superintendent, the High School principal, or a supervisor exercise practically final authority. Preferred practice delegates this authority to a small textbook committee representing not only those who are responsible to legal authorities but classroom teachers as well. (McElroy, 1934: 5–6)

The financial implications of a bad decision referred to in the first part of this quotation are certainly one consideration. Where institutions or parents are buying textbooks in the expectation that they will be reused, they are seen as a kind of investment. However, the choice of an inappropriate textbook will also affect teachers. Whenever a new book is adopted, teachers spend time familiarizing themselves with it; and the less appropriate it proves to be the more time will be needed to compensate for its inadequacies. For learners, moreover, an inappropriate textbook has limited value as a learning resource. The consequences are less serious when courses are not based on a single textbook, but time has still been wasted and learning opportunities lost, and the search for suitable materials has to begin again.

Bad decisions can, in theory at least, be avoided if proper processes are in place. As can be seen from the quotation above, 'preferred practice' in

America in the 1930s delegated textbook selection to a small committee on which classroom teachers were represented. These days, materials may be selected by an institutional manager, a group of teachers, or the teacher teaching a particular class. In the latter case, the impact of a bad decision may affect fewer people, but it will be just as great on those it does affect. Teachers therefore need to be able to make or contribute to informed selection decisions. We return to textbook selection processes and materials evaluation more generally in Chapter Three.

## 3.3.2 Control

Commercial coursebooks are written to appeal to as wide a population as possible and even national coursebooks have to cater for some degree of variation in learners, teachers and learning environments. If we therefore accept that the perfect coursebook for a particular teacher and group of learners not only does not but cannot exist, and that a coursebook should be seen primarily as a *resource* book, then it follows that the responsibility for deciding what to use from the coursebook and how to use it lies with the teacher:

> The coursebook should never be allowed to assume an authority it does not merit and consequently be blamed for failing to 'work', but rather seen as a friendly guide, suggesting areas of study and approaches, but always open to manipulation by the teacher who ultimately will have the best opportunity to 'know' his/her students and their particular needs. (Acklam, 1994: 13)

In short, it is the teacher and not the coursebook who should control or manage what happens, and one of the ways in which that control can manifest itself is through creative use (or 'manipulation', in Acklam's terms) of the coursebook.

## 3.3.3 Creativity

Dudley-Evans & St John (1998), writing about ESP, state that 'practitioners have to be . . . good providers of materials' (pp.172–3). A good provider, for them, needs to have the ability to:

1. select appropriately from what is available
2. be creative with what is available
3. modify activities to suit learners' needs and
4. supplement by providing extra activities (and extra input) (Dudley-Evans & St John, 1998: 173).

This list of abilities is applicable not just to ESP but to all forms of English language teaching, of course, and corresponds very closely to the teacher roles identified in earlier sections: (1) may be understood as both selecting from material that has been provided (e.g. a textbook) and the process of selecting a suitable textbook, where this is possible; (2) refers to exploitation – that is, getting something extra out of the material; (3) to adaptation; and (4) to supplementation which is designed to provide more exposure to the language or more opportunities for practice, which, at its least adventurous, may involve no more than borrowing from other published materials. However, point 4 could extend to selecting authentic texts and designing suitable exploitation activities or creating wholly original practice materials such as worksheets or tasks. A curriculum document for Hong Kong secondary school teachers cited in Samuda (2005: 236) states that: 'All English teachers must take on the responsibility for selecting and adapting suitable tasks from different materials or designing tasks for their own learners' (Curriculum Development Council, Hong Kong, 1999: 48). Samuda (ibid.) notes: 'The clear expectation is that both redesign and original design work will be incorporated into a second language teacher's "normal" professional repertoire'. There is no explicit reference in Dudley-Evans and St John's list of roles to creating original materials; indeed, they state explicitly that 'one of the myths of ESP has been that you have to write your own materials'. Nevertheless, aspects of creative design run through the set of roles they specify; even the decision not to use certain elements of a textbook can be seen as an act of reshaping or redesign. As Madsen & Bowen acknowledge:

> Every teacher is in a very real sense an adapter of the textbook or materials he uses. . . . He adapts when he adds an example not found in the book or when he telescopes an assignment by having students prepare 'only the even-numbered items'. He adapts even when he refers to an exercise covered earlier, or when he introduces a supplementary picture, song, realia or report. (Madsen & Bowen, 1978: vii)

With experience, all teachers will instinctively adapt materials in many or all of the ways described by Madsen and Bowen. However, if we wish them to go beyond such low-level adaptation and supplementation to forms of provision which are more demanding in terms of creativity, expertise and potentially time, we may need to persuade them of the need and help them to develop the necessary confidence and skills. We may also want to encourage them to accept learners as active partners rather than as recipients of materials and teaching. The implications for teacher education are clear.

## 4. Teacher education in materials evaluation and design

### 4.1 The need

The need for teacher education in materials evaluation and design and the focus of this may have been implicit in the discussion of teacher roles in the last section, but this need has also been explicitly recognized. In an international survey of perceptions of teacher needs (Henrichsen, 1983), a questionnaire was sent to 500 teachers and employers in the United States of America and more than 30 other countries. Recipients were asked to rate the importance of 60 content areas (e.g. educational psychology, American literature, intercultural understanding, transformational grammar, Total Physical Response) divided into eight uneven groups (e.g. Education, Linguistics, Literature, TESL/TEFL Methods, TESL/TEFL Materials). TESL/TEFL Materials consisted of just two items: Materials Selection and Evaluation and Materials Development and Production. One hundred and fifty three responses (a return rate of 31%) were received from a total of 30 countries. These were analysed along a number of dimensions. Overall, training in materials selection and evaluation ranked top for respondents from outside the United States of America and second when all respondents were considered; when respondents were broken down by institution type or geographical area, materials selection and evaluation generally came out 'considerably' higher than materials development and production.

That very strong message from both teachers and employers about the importance of teacher education relating to materials endorses Cunningsworth's (1979) view that 'trainees on EFL teacher training courses need to be shown what to look for when evaluating course materials, and should be helped to develop criteria against which they can make a professional judgement when confronted with new or unfamiliar material' (p.31). Hutchinson and Torres (1994) suggest that the scope of such programmes should be broader, arguing that 'a central feature of all teacher training and development' should be to help teachers 'to be able to evaluate textbooks properly, exploit them in the class, and adapt and supplement them when necessary' (p.327); Richards (2001b) goes still further: 'teachers need training and experience in adapting and modifying textbooks *as well as in using authentic materials and in creating their own materials*' (p.16, emphasis added). This combined set of stated needs corresponds perfectly to that articulated by Dudley-Evans and St John (1998) cited in the previous section. Many years ago, McElroy (1934), who was thinking of both formal teacher education and the value of experience, observed: 'As teacher preparation increases, the importance of the textbook diminishes' (p.5). As an argument for teacher education in materials evaluation and design, this is just as true now as it was then.

## 4.2 Provision

Such calls notwithstanding, the study of materials does not as yet constitute a universally accepted core component of even pre-service teacher education programmes. None of Fredriksson and Olsson's (2006) small-scale sample of four experienced Swedish teachers of English and other languages 'had ever heard of any guides or literature on this topic' (p.7) and the authors conclude that in Sweden 'materials evaluation . . . is not a well known concept' (ibid). González Moncada (2006), who surveyed 12 undergraduate teacher education courses in Colombia, found that only one other than her own provided training in materials. Writing about the Arab Gulf, Bahumaid (2008) notes that though there is a materials production component in the MA TESOL programme at the American University of Sharjah, there is no comparable component in undergraduate or postgraduate programmes in TEFL at Sultan Qaboos University in Oman, The United Arab Emirates University or Kuwait University, and concludes that training in both materials evaluation and development is needed for teachers and inspectors in the region. Writing more generally, Canniveng and Martinez (2003) claim that 'teacher training courses give little importance (or even sometimes ignore this area) in their programmes' (p.479).

One explanation for this apparent invisibility may lie in the fact that materials are treated as one element of the larger picture (e.g. within courses dealing with 'curriculum development' or 'syllabus planning') or, as Tomlinson (2001) has suggested, seen as a subsection of methodology. Block (1991) was thinking of lacunae in the professional literature when he commented: 'The assumption seems to be that materials selection, adaptation and development will take care of themselves' (p.211), but he might have been referring to language teacher education. The argument that will be advanced in this book is that even if teachers are expected to carry out no more than three of the roles identified by Dudley-Evans and St John (1998) – selecting appropriately from what they are given, being creative with what is available (i.e. exploiting it) and modifying activities to suit learners' needs – they need guidance and hands-on practice in the form of a dedicated course. If, in addition, they are expected to supplement the core materials by providing extra activities (a minimal interpretation of Dudley-Evans and St John's fourth role) or develop their own materials, as advocated by some writers (e.g. Block, 1991; Richards, 1998a; Tomlinson, 2003c; Jolly & Bolitho, 2011) and required in Hong Kong, then that argument is even stronger. We return to the theme of teacher education in Chapters Four and Ten.

# PART ONE

# External perspectives: 'Theory'

# CHAPTER TWO

# Publisher and coursebook writer perspectives

> We, like the publishing houses, were interested in innovation and principled pedagogy; however, our perspectives were different.
>
> (Mares, 2003: 136)
>
> In using textbooks . . . teachers have to put back some of the creativity that may have been lost in the process of textbook publication.
>
> (Richards, 2001b: 14)

## 1. Introduction

Commercial publishing is a complex business. It is a business because publishers are motivated primarily by profit. It is complex because many people, with very different roles, are involved and because so many factors have to be considered. This is particularly true of coursebook packages, and especially those intended for sale in a number of different countries (the so-called global coursebook).

In this chapter, we explore the process of commercial materials development from two main perspectives: that of the publisher (or those representing the publisher) and that of the writer. **Section 2** briefly describes the development process, with particular reference to the stages and people involved, and **Section 3** discusses the various forms of research that are typically conducted prior to publication. **Section 4** explores the constraints and compromises that determine the final product. **Section 5** presents views, primarily of writers, on teachers as end users of materials.

Accounts of institutional (i.e. non-commercial) materials development can be found in the collections edited by Hidalgo, Hall and Jacobs (1995), Tomlinson (2003a), Alexander (2007), Harwood (2010a), Tomlinson and Masuhara (2010a) and papers by, for instance, Carroll and Head (2003) and St Louis, Trias and Pereira (2010).

## 2. The development process

Publishers of ELT materials make most of their money from coursebooks, dictionaries and grammar books. While they remain open to approaches (unsolicited proposals) from prospective writers of other types of materials, as far as coursebooks are concerned, the major publishers at least tend to play safe by commissioning new series from writers they know or – as a less expensive option – publish new editions of popular series.

Central to the development process on the publisher's side is a person normally known as the commissioning editor or project development editor (not to be confused with the desk editor or copy editor, who carries out the detailed work on the manuscript when it is submitted). As described by Wala (2003a: 58), the project development editor 'operates as the fulcrum of a materials development project, maintaining balance and ensuring that the project continues to progress towards publication. The editor functions as a filter and a crucial contact between content originated by the writers and its expression through layout, design, illustration, marketing and promotion'. As this description implies, the editor supervises a team including one or more desk editors and a designer, but also coordinates the project from its inception through to the post-production phase.

In the case of a new coursebook project, the inception phase involves market analysis and planning. Writers will then be invited to submit proposals and these will be sent out for review. Once a proposal has been approved (and this may take some time) and a contract issued, writing can begin in earnest. During this period, there will be frequent contact between the writer(s), the editor and others in the production team, especially the designer, and the materials revised. Sample sections of the materials will be sent out for review and piloting, visits made to the main market(s) and further revisions made. The end is in sight. Proof copies of the print materials will now be produced for checking by the authors. Changes made, the first copies will then be sent out to bookshops and journal reviewers, and the promotional talks and visits will begin.

Wala (2003a) makes the telling point that 'A coursebook is the way it is because of what it has to do' (p.60), what it has to do being to fulfil a particular role in a particular context. Seen in this light, if a book fails it is because it was either inadequate or inappropriate for that context. The implications for careful research are clear.

## 3. Pre-publication research

### 3.1 Market analysis

The thinking that lay behind an Austrian company's decision to publish *Focus on Modern Business* for upper-secondary business schools in that country is described as follows:

> First and foremost, the market size of Austrian upper secondary business schools is quite big. Secondly, the government-imposed limit on the price of a book for this market is relatively high. In addition, competition was weak and a new syllabus was to become effective exactly when volume one was to be published. Finally, market research made clear that teachers – they decide which book is used in school – were longing for a new textbook. As a consequence, expected sales figures and estimated profit were quite high. (Pogelschek, 2007: 101)

This example of market analysis highlights such factors as potential sales (related to size of market and likely demand), profit margins and market share. Market analysis may, of course, go beyond this to look at specific characteristics of end users (teachers and learners). Describing the market for conversation materials in American English in Japan, Richards (1995) notes that because speaking skills are not assessed in the Japanese university entrance examination there is little demand for conversation skills books in schools. The main markets will therefore be junior colleges, universities and private language schools, where 'teachers are often native-speakers of English, some of whom have little or no training' and 'others may be Japanese teachers, with varying levels of English proficiency' (p.95). In this particular case, the publisher had already decided that it wanted to publish 'in order to help it maintain its position as market leader in the area of conversation texts for the Japanese and related markets' (p.96). The main question therefore concerned what was needed. To answer this question, information was collected in a number of ways from a number of sources: from classroom teachers in Japan, Taiwan and Korea; publishers' marketing representatives; consultants (experienced teachers in the kinds of institutions where the new materials were most likely to be used); and learners, whose views were accessed via the consultants.

Broadly speaking, then, market analysis indicates whether there is a large enough potential market for a book to make its publication potentially profitable and what the nature of that market is likely to be. The wider that potential market is, the better, of course. As Amrani (2011) puts it, publishing 'is about developing materials which offer the highest possible return on investment without compromising essential minimum customer expectations' (p.273).

## 3.2 Writer research

The kinds of research writers carry out will depend on their prior knowledge of the market and the nature of the materials. Where the market is unfamiliar and the potential rewards seem large enough, this kind of planning research may be a lengthy process. Greenall (2011) notes that during the first four or five years of the development of a series of books for Chinese junior middle and senior high schools (a huge market), a great deal of time was spent in discussions with Chinese editors, publishers and professors about 'the kind of English that China would need for the 21st century' and researching 'the traditions of teaching and publishing in China'.

The need for such research to involve contact between writers and classroom teachers is emphasized by Wala (2003b), who points to an inherent tension between curriculum planners, syllabus designers and textbook writers, all of whom offer *proposals* for action, and the teachers faced with implementing these:

> Syllabus designers and curriculum planners are located in the future.... They work with ideals[,]... abstracts[,] ... objectives [and] outcomes in mind.... Teachers, on the other hand, are mired in the present. They must teach today's learner, in today's classroom, within today's curriculum, system and school environment. For the teacher, the syllabus is the theory and the textbook is the manual that will enable the practice. Teachers work with a textbook developed a few years ago in hand and the practical realities of the situation staring them in the face. Such is the location from which teachers will evaluate materials. Materials developers occupy a kind of twilight zone – materials must answer present-day teacher needs for tomorrow's class with a view to meeting the goals of education for the future. Given these different and distinct locations, it is important that the materials development process allows for dialogue ... (Wala, 2003b: 157)

Writers might also consult the professional literature or research language use. When planning his books on conversation skills, primarily for the Japanese market, Richards (1995) looked at existing conversation books and the literature on conversation strategies. Many writers these days would use the internet to check word frequency and concordances to ensure that examples reflect real language use. The internet is also an ideal source of texts. 'The days of the files and boxes full of yellowing newspaper articles and magazines saved for future use are over in a world where "google" has become an accepted verb' (Prowse, 2011: 167). Web texts also have the advantage that they can easily be saved and edited (Sharma, cited in Prowse, 2011).

## 3.3 Obtaining feedback

### 3.3.1 Reviewers

Publishers use reviewers at different stages of a project and for different purposes depending on the nature of the project. In the case of an unsolicited proposal, reviewers will be asked to comment on pedagogic value and commercial potential, and negative reviews will lead to a polite rejection. Commissioned projects will be handled very differently. The first complete draft of the first level of Richards's conversation skills books was sent out to seven reviewers (Richards, 1995). The editor summarized their comments, pointed out that the Japanese market was 'flooded with books based on a functional syllabus', and added his own thoughts:

> The units . . . that are functionally organised (e.g. Places and Directions, Cities and Places, Leisure and Entertainment) for me were the least interesting. The units that are based on topics that are really interesting to students (*Music, Movies, Television, On Vacation*) are . . . the most in line with where the market is right now.

> The direction the manuscript needs to go in is clear: more topic-based units, more real world content and more focus on the world of the students . . . There are several key topics that are missing: dating, travel, customs, careers, environmental issues, campus life, student lifestyles, dos and don'ts in other countries. Some of these are more appropriate for Level 2. Others can be the focus of existing units. (Editor cited by Richards, 1995: 106–7)

The decision was taken to reduce the number of units from 20 to 15 and to write some entirely new units. Richards estimates that 60 per cent of the material in the second draft was new.

Technological developments mean that communications between publisher and reviewer are now much faster than in the past, thereby speeding up the development process. Materials can now be sent out for review in PDF form or Word digital files as e-mail attachments and comments returned in the same way, often using the track change facility in Word. Advances in desktop publishing also mean that the materials sent out for review are much closer to their finished state.

For coursebook materials, reviewers will include experienced teachers who are able to assess how well the materials would work in their contexts and academics, whose views may be sought from a particular theoretical or research perspective. Both of these types of reviewer would be sent basic background information in the form of a rationale and list of contents together with a small quantity of materials and asked to complete a feedback sheet (Amrani, 2011). Being in a standard format, this can then easily be compiled into a single report.

## 3.3.2 Piloting

Given the costs involved in textbook production, one would expect publishers to minimize the risk by piloting (or field testing) draft materials before going into full production. Yet Richards (1995: 100) notes: 'I can think of several major textbook series which were published in recent years involving development and production costs of at least half a million US dollars each, which proved to be failures shortly after publication', the reason in each case being the same: 'both publisher and author failing to do their homework – failing to consult the end users to see if the kind of textbook they were planning really suited the needs of teachers and learners.'

Pogelschek (2007) admits that 'hardly any research was considered' when producing *Focus on Modern Business* for the Austrian market. No piloting was carried out; nor was there any consideration of 'the question of authority in texts and textbooks; different teaching styles; the attitudes of teachers towards textbooks; possible images and roles of textbooks; [or] the design process of educational material' (p.103). This is not to say that no research took place: 'typical topics discussed with authors and advisors were the thematic areas, the length of texts, the types of exercises, the sequence of contents', but there was no deeper consideration of the rationale for any of the proposals made. 'There seemed to be a tacit agreement to produce *Focus on Modern Business* as all the textbooks before' (p.104). One reason for this was time pressure. Even without the kinds of research Pogelschek lists, the time period from first idea to production of first copies was 49 months, that is, 4 years, and to get a head start on the market, the book had to be published at the same time the new syllabus was released.

The distinction between review and piloting is very clearly articulated by Donovan (1998: 186):

> Topics and content, as well as the exercises and tasks themselves, can only really be judged when the materials are actually in use. A contents list which might look prosaic and predictable can come to life in the actual material through the skill of the writers in selecting or constructing suitable texts and tasks. Only by using these in class will we know if they actually appeal to the learners, are relevant to their needs, and stimulate their interest and involvement.

Piloting benefits publishers and authors (and their material) in a number of ways. It is, for example, a way of raising the profile of a new product in the marketplace through piloters or reviewers who are known to be trendsetters; it is also a way of raising awareness within sales development teams and encouraging them to get some of their potential customers involved to ensure that what is produced takes their needs into account (Amrani, 2011). Most obviously, it is an opportunity to 'validate' materials (Donovan, 1998). Feedback through piloting is sought on two levels: that of how well it seems to suit the key features of the target context and meet learners' interests and needs and, on a more micro level, how well specific activities worked.

*Cambridge English for Schools* (Cambridge University Press) was piloted during the 1990s on approximately 5,000 learners in a number of different countries over a two-year period, because it represented a significant financial investment. For the publisher, as we have seen, time is also an important factor. Though it might have been desirable to pilot a complete level (one year's material) in the same institution(s), the distribution of parts of the materials across pilot centres was a means of speeding up the process.

Donovan was describing ELT publishing in the mid–late 1990s. Writing some 13 years later, Amrani (2011) notes that 'the world of ELT publishing [then] . . . was a different place' (p.267), one of the differences being the relative importance attached to piloting – 'whilst this remains one of the ways in which materials are evaluated, it is no longer the main way that publishers do this' (ibid.). Reasons for this change include the fact that the timeframes for materials development are shorter (now two to three years rather than four or more previously); 'course content, approach and task' design may be dictated by standards such as the Common European Framework or exam syllabuses; and digital materials need to be in more or less final format if they are to be properly tested. 'The challenges facing the ELT publisher today are less to do with modifying fundamental materials design for main course development and more to do with how to blend and marry topics or formats into existing well-established core course content' (p.268).

Piloting these days, according to Amrani (2011), typically involves piloters incorporating a small amount of the pilot material into their normal teaching programme, making notes on the pages of the material, and keeping a teaching diary. They are asked for their comments on what went well and less well (and why), on the order of activities, the clarity of exercise rubrics and timing, what questions students asked, and whether anything needs to be added. The editor then collates this feedback into a comprehensive report. A version of this, with the editor's suggestions, is then sent to the writers. One weakness of this kind of piloting, as Amrani points out, is that the kind of experienced teachers who volunteer for pilots may only represent a minority of those for whom the materials are intended. This argues for other forms of input into the development process.

### 3.3.3 Visits (observation, focus groups, discussion)

Prowse (2011) notes that the projects he has worked on as a writer have involved repeated visits to the market by authors and editors while a project is under development and during the writing process. These visits typically include 'classroom observation of lessons in a range of schools and locations, discussions with students about their interests, individual and focus group discussions with teachers, meetings with educational advisers and planners, and discussions with methodologists and teacher trainers working in the market' (pp.166–7).

Amrani (2011: 290) gives a helpful insight into the conduct of a focus group:

> The techniques a facilitator uses are prompt questions to initiate discussion and probe questions to explore deeper-held beliefs and reactions. A common situation would be a general prompt question such as: *'Do you like any of these units?' 'Unit 3'*. This would then be followed by wh-questions such as: *'What specifically do you like about it?' 'It's the way it's structured'. 'Why do you like the structure?' 'Because it has a clear warm-up activity, presentation activity, grammar activity, vocabulary section, skills activity and review and nice workbook activities'. 'When would you use the workbook activities?' 'As homework'. 'Why don't you like the other two units?'*

Focus groups offer the opportunity not only for easy interaction between facilitator and teacher, they are also a way of gauging how the group as a whole feels about important issues, issues in some cases raised by individuals rather than the facilitator (Amrani, 2011). To overcome logistical issues, they can also be organized remotely (Prowse, 2011).

Visits have always continued after publication, for promotional purposes. They now serve the further purpose of collecting feedback on the materials in use in order to inform the development of future editions (Prowse, 2011).

## 4. Constraints and compromises

### 4.1 Time and money

Publishers do not take the decision to publish lightly. While they may accept that it is desirable to engage in certain types of publishing for the sake of their reputation and a balanced list, the decision to publish textbooks is, as Pogelschek (2007: 100) acknowledges, 'most often commercially and operationally oriented'. A textbook is a major commitment in terms of both time and money. As far as time is concerned, one of the key variables is the nature of any piloting and another may be the need to obtain Ministry of Education approval. Time will also be a factor when a new syllabus is to be introduced (Wala, 2003b) in a target market or when a publisher knows that competing publishers are bringing a similar product to market (Richards, 1995). Publishers accept that in the commercial world a successful product will soon be imitated; it is therefore important to be first in order to ensure a larger market share. A number of decisions affecting the final look and feel of the materials will also be determined by a publisher on financial grounds: in particular, the relationship between production costs, anticipated sales price and predicted sales. Since the number of sales is the one variable the publisher cannot control and sales price will to a large extent be limited by the need to stay competitive, publishers will try to control the third variable, production costs, in order to maximize profit while maintaining quality and competitiveness. These considerations will influence, for example, book length and size, type and number of illustrations, paper quality and the provision of additional components (workbook, test book, CD, etc.).

Tomlinson, Dat, Masuhara and Rubdy (2001) surveyed eight courses for adults (two from each of four major publishers), and a similarly focused review was conducted several years later (Masuhara, Hann, Yi & Tomlinson, 2008) of a single coursebook package from each of eight publishers. Both reviews were particularly critical of design features. Tomlinson et al. (2001) comment that some of the courses they reviewed were 'cluttered and dense, with too much text crammed onto each page and not enough white space to provide relief and clarity'; there was also 'a lack of clear separation and sequencing' on the page (p.89). Masuhara et al. (2008) reached a similar conclusion, three of the eight books they surveyed being judged 'cluttered and busy'. They also considered the illustrations in the coursebooks 'unimaginative' and, comparing these with those examined by Tomlinson et al. (2001), wondered:

> Where are the aesthetic paintings, simulated documents (e.g. papers, paperbacks), cartoons, and intriguing illustrations which created interesting discussions and useful activities? The illustrations seem to be smaller and more functional. Even headings and icons seem to have become smaller and more insignificant. (Masuhara et al., 2008: 303)

Where they are available, Teacher's Books can be an invaluable resource for the inexperienced teacher or the teacher using a coursebook for the first time. The most useful type of Teacher's Book will be one which provides not only suggestions for adaptation but also ideas for additional activities (Tomlinson et al., 2001: 91). Design is also important. All but one of the eight Teacher's Books reviewed by Tomlinson et al. (2001) were judged to be 'unattractive in appearance and poorly designed' (ibid.).

What such reviews suggest is that the linked pressures of time and money may mean that compromises are made, compromises which also involve writers.

## 4.2 *The writer's perspective*

Writers, like publishers, hope that what will be produced will make money. After all, they have invested a great deal of time and effort. However, it is probably fair to say that the financial return is not their main or only motivation. Authors are 'generally concerned to produce a text that teachers will find innovative, creative, relevant to their learners' needs, and that they will enjoy teaching from' (Richards, 2001: 14); perhaps one day they will even encounter a student 'who says with a big grin on his face, "I learned English from your book"' (Prowse, 2011: 172). Bell and Gower (1998) write: 'We wanted to produce something that gave us professional satisfaction and was academically credible to our colleagues, something we could be proud of' (p.146). For Harmer (in Prowse, 2011: 171–2), coursebook writing arises from:

> . . . a genuine wish to provide material that will brighten any class; a desire to offer reliable material for the most put-upon teacher; a matter of excitement and compromises; an act of creativity that all too often seems suffocating and doomed. But when, against all the odds, and in the light of linguistic and methodological constraints, you actually manage to make something that you know will work, the feeling is fantastic. It's not actually that much different from teaching; we don't always teach great classes, but when we do we want to shout it from the rooftops. That's what it's like on the rare occasions when coursebook writers get it right.

First-time writers may also feel they have something to offer that is groundbreakingly different:

> Our material, originally written in the late 1980s, was free of graded grammatical syllabuses. In fact, it was free of virtually any conventional constraints with respect to unit length or template. We believed in providing rich language input and engaging tasks. Our units were not fettered by templates but steered by our feelings about what would be interesting material for students to work with. We felt that different topics might require different amounts of time to cover in an interesting way. They did not all merit the same treatment in terms of number of pages per unit, number of activities, etc. (Mares, 2003: 136)

What Mares and his co-author had failed to realize was that they were attempting to enter a world 'which operated according to well-established principles, the most important being that publishing is a business and businesses are run for profit' (ibid.). It took some time for them to come to terms with the fact that the publisher might, after all, know best:

> For a number of years we struggled with the tension that existed between writing materials we believed in and materials someone else believed would sell. We, like the publishing houses, were interested in innovation and principled pedagogy; however, our perspectives were different. The principled pedagogy that we believed in required teachers to belong to a particular teaching generation whose education and training had been fuelled by SLA research findings. We were, in fact, addressing a very limited market. We heard that information before we fully internalised it. Our convictions were stronger than our pragmatic sense. . . . (ibid.)

As the later part of this quotation illustrates, beginner writers' expectations of their audience may well have to be tempered by publishing realities. As Mares (2003) adds: 'I was not writing for non-native teachers with low confidence in their command of the English language, but in the world of "the market" these teachers make up a sizeable slice' (p.131). Eventually, he and his co-author understood that compromise is necessary but takes various forms, 'from complete cop out involving the surrender of most beliefs to principled choice made for the common good within a sound pedagogic framework. We feared the former before understanding that the latter was an acceptable alternative' (ibid.). Given the predictable mismatch between their preference for a free-flowing approach and publishers' liking for standard unit and page formats, one compromise was in the area of design. They therefore 'accepted the need for a template' but settled on 'a varying template within a consistent page limit'; they also agreed that 'listening scripts should be limited to a certain number of lines' and 'grudgingly tried to work with the notion of "white space" . . . [,] a user-friendly page where all stages in any given activity are transparent and doable' (p.137).

Other writers have also commented on the potential for tensions concerning book design. Bell and Gower (2011: 140), for instance, question the preoccupation with page formats and unit standardization:

> We . . . have heard designers severely criticise the design of successful books and praise the design of books that are not thought by teachers to be well designed. Does it matter to a teacher whether there are one, two or three columns on a page and whether a unit is a uniform length in its number of pages? Maybe it is important to some teachers, but in our experience, what matters more is that it is absolutely clear on the page where things are and what their purpose is and that the balance (and tone) of visuals and text is right for their students.

An experienced coursebook writer sums up the difference in perspectives of designer and writer as follows: 'the designer . . . wants the design to be aesthetically pleasing and you want it to be pedagogically effective' (contributor to Prowse, 2011: 161).

Illustrations can also be a source of frustration for writers. If the work is to be illustrated, writers will be asked to supply the designer with an 'artwork brief' (or 'artbrief'), a description of what is needed. If this includes photographs, these will often be sourced from a picture library, and a choice may be offered; if drawings are required, then one or more illustrators will be involved. The same coursebook writer comments drily:

> . . . any one illustrator can either read or draw. So either s/he reads your artbrief carefully and takes care to observe it, in order to produce a boring pedestrian illustration that your seven-year-old could have done; or s/he produces a wonderful illustration that will really draw your learners in and make the page striking and attractive . . . but the learners won't be able to do the corresponding exercise because some of the elements of the illustration are wrong or missing. . . . You can't assume anything with an illustrator. If you say 'desert scene', it is best to specify that there should be no igloos in it. If you don't and you complain about the igloos in the art rough, you will be told it is your fault. Learning to write a tight artbrief may be the most difficult subskill of the EFL writer's trade. (anonymous coursebook writer cited in Prowse, 2011: 162)

Ideally, there will be give and take between designers and writers. Sometimes illustrations may need to be cut in order to allow sufficient space for a series of linked activities; on other occasions, the reverse may be the case. The criticisms made in the reviews of Tomlinson et al. (2001) and Masuhara et al. (2008) suggest that the right balance is not always found.

## 4.3 The stamp of Ministry approval

Compromise may also be involved when textbooks are required to meet Ministry of Education approval. In Austria, for example, as Pogelschek (2007) explains, the state subsidizes textbook purchase (parents pay 10% of the cost) and imposes a limit on the total amount that school-age learners can be expected to spend on textbooks each year; publishers therefore have to work within these limits in pricing their books. As in many other countries, the state also sets criteria which school textbooks must meet, and requires manuscripts to be submitted for approval. Wala's (2003b) account of preparing a lower secondary school textbook for approval in Singapore draws attention to the tight deadlines that publishers often need to work to; in this case, the total time from the publication of the Ministry syllabus to submission for approval was only one year; approval then took six months, after which further revisions were required. In the example of the Austrian publication described by Pogelschek (2007), the process from submission to preliminary approval – involving feedback from Ministry to publisher, revision and resubmission – took nine months. Describing the first ten years of a textbook project in China, Greenall (2011) writes: 'we had to submit the seventeen main coursebooks to the Ministry of Education for approval. About forty books, including teachers' books and supplementary material, had to be ready for the start of the 2006 school year'. It had taken five years to get this far; he does not say how long it took to approve the books.

Price and time may not be the only issues. In Austria, for instance, according to Pogelschek, the criteria used in evaluation are relatively open and can therefore be interpreted subjectively, and members of the evaluation panel, who are nominated by the Ministry, 'do not need to have any expertise in textbook evaluation' (p.102). In Indonesia, one of the criteria for the approval of school textbooks is 'security':

> the content of the books should be in line with and not contradictory to *Pancasila* [the state philosophy], UUD 1945 [the 1945 constitution], Government policies, national unity and security, laws, regulations, ethics, and that the content not exploit the sensitive issue of SARA (ethnics, religions, race and intergroup relations). (Supriadi, 1999, cited in Jazadi, 2003: 145)

Among the evaluators are representatives of the Armed Forces Headquarters, the National Defence Institute and the Office of the Attorney General. Jazadi (2003) comments: 'it is impossible to know the bases on which the officials involved make their judgments', but 'they may not be overly concerned with pedagogic issues' (p.146).

In China, as Greenall (2011) discovered, some of the criteria for approval are explicit and others less so:

> The Chinese Ministry of Education imposes many requirements on the grammar, vocabulary, pronunciation and the social and cultural content. Our final course design had to work within these constraints, as well as to have a storyline, and to be interesting and motivating for the schoolchildren.

As far as vocabulary was concerned, the Ministry had produced a wordlist of some 3,500 words which needed to be taught and practised. Meeting this requirement involved 'trying to write an exciting dialogue for teenagers which included such disparate words as *Ottawa, dumpling, goldfish* and *shabby*'. The writing team also had to take into account Chinese views of what is appropriate in materials for school children. Greenall notes:

> Only positive moral values and role models could be portrayed, respect for parents and older people is maintained at all costs, and negative feelings about, for example, upcoming exams is unacceptable. More specifically, there were certain words which, if we included them in a reading passage, would be questioned. These included not only the most obvious ones, such as *human rights*, *Taiwan* or *God*, but also names, places and events. Apparently innocent (to a westerner) words, such as *change, exile, boss,* needed to be treated with care, and even the word *communism* would have attracted attention to the context in which it was used.

## 4.4 The nature of compromise

Compromise can take many forms. From a writer's perspective, as we have seen, this may well be in the area of design, and in particular the constraints of book length and format. Although writers will normally try to write to agreed length and format, this is not easy. 'Overmatter' (too much material) means that cuts have to be made; 'undermatter' (not enough material to fill a page) that more has to be written. Cuts, especially at a late stage, can be painful for writers. As Bell and Gower (2011) note, 'Lack of space caused us great frustration at the editing stage when we saw many of our practice activities disappear or get pruned. We had to make a decision whether to cut back on whole activities or cut back on the number of items within an activity' (p.148).

Like Greenall (2011), Bell and Gower (op. cit.) found that they had to avoid certain topics:

> In terms of content we realised we could not please everyone. We did compromise and not include some texts we would have used with our own [United Kingdom, private language school] students, on the grounds that they would not go down well in such and such a country. We did not want to fight shy of sex and so on, but found ourselves doing so and being expected to do so. (Bell & Gower, 2011: 149)

This nervousness of 'taboo' subjects can result in material seeming very bland. Tomlinson et al.'s (2001) review came to the conclusion concerning one course that it was 'in many ways the stereotypical middle-of-the-road language course which is unlikely to disturb or delight anybody, and is therefore likely to sell well' (p.94). This situation may be changing. Masuhara et al.'s (2008) more recent review found that 'some courses do make attempts to include a more realistic portrayal of life and some controversial or serious topics, such as war and history, from different perspectives' (pp.300–1).

Other compromises, for Bell and Gower, related to methodology (where they had hoped to break away from a traditional presentation-practice-production approach, but were only able to realize this partially in the lower level – intermediate – of their two books) and recordings. Although they compromised by using actors for some recordings, others were authentic. The response from some markets outside the United Kingdom was that some of the authentic texts were too difficult. They reflect: 'we wonder now whether we should have compromised more. . . . Perhaps we should have made more of them semi-scripted – or at least made the authentic ones shorter and easier and built in more "how to listen" tasks' (p.149).

A particular issue for Bell and Gower was how their books would be used. Their conception was that the materials would be mediated by teachers. They were therefore reluctant to prescribe methodology by making exercise rubrics too specific ('should you ever say "Work in groups" when the teacher may want to do an exercise in pairs, or "Write these sentences" when the teacher may want the students to say them?') (p.147). Above all, they saw the materials as a resource to be used flexibly: 'it was important that teachers should feel they could move activities around, cut them out or supplement them according to need', one source of supplementary materials being the Workbook accompanying the course. However, feedback revealed that 'some teachers felt they had to cover everything in the book in the order presented' (ibid.) and that many students would not have Workbooks. In later editions, they were able to provide additional photocopiable practice activities in the Teacher's Book, thereby putting into practice 'the principle of aiming to supply teachers with a resource to help them build up *their* programme (p.148, emphasis added).

## 5. Teachers and learners as end users

### 5.1 *The distance between*

Having conducted an analysis of the sales potential of a new book, and been reassured as to its profitability, an international publisher will try to orient the book towards the groups and needs identified and focus their marketing efforts accordingly. There are various difficulties with this approach, however: needs across the main target markets may vary greatly, or publishers may seek to increase profits by selling into new markets for which their books were not primarily intended, or those responsible for ordering books are not fully aware what they are getting. The result may be that the end users, teacher and learners, are faced with materials that are palpably inappropriate, as this quotation from Jolly and Bolitho (2011: 108) illustrates:

> It's a very nice book and very lively, but in the section on 'processes' for example all the exercises are about unusual things for our country. We are a hot country and also have many Muslims. The exercises are about snow, ice, cold mornings, water cisterns, writing and publishing EFL books and making wine. I can tell you I can't do making wine and smoking pot in my country! (experienced school teacher from the Ivory Coast)

Jolly and Bolitho comment: 'the further away the author is from the learners, the less effective the material is likely to be' (p.128). The distance referred to here is not simply physical distance, of course, but experiential and psychological distance.

Wala (2003a) makes the point that in the process of planning and development, editors and other materials developers must ask the following questions of coursebooks:

- How do learners (and teachers) use coursebooks?
- How is the coursebook structured for use?
- What is the context in which the coursebook will be used?
- What dimensions of context have an impact on coursebook use?
- Which aspects of the coursebook and its use will be affected by particular dimensions of the context?
- What view of the world, of English, of learning English, of the teacher and of the learner is presented explicitly and implicitly by the coursebook? (Wala, 2003a: 62–3)

Where there is a serious mismatch between context and materials the fault lies ultimately with whoever decided to purchase the book. Ironically, this is often not the individual teacher who has to use the book. The teacher from the Ivory Coast quoted above is clearly a victim of a decision made by someone else. Bell and Gower (2011: 136) put the blame on 'misguided management', but also note that management is 'frequently encouraged by marketing teams and distributors' to adopt materials which are patently unsuitable, and Masuhara and Tomlinson (2008) draw attention to the fact that materials sold into markets outside English-speaking countries may have been *piloted* in very different (e.g. United Kingdom) institutions. We might draw an important, if apparently rather obvious, conclusion from this: that teachers ought to have a voice in deciding which materials are to be used (a point taken up in later chapters) but that if the decision is taken by someone else that person needs to be qualified to make an informed judgement.

## 5.2 Choice

Writing as a publisher's editor, Wala (2003a: 59) states that a textbook is 'a collection of choices . . . from a variety of options'. What she probably means by this is that a textbook is the result of the multiple decisions made at each stage of the development process, by publishers, by writers, or by both. However, a rather different interpretation is that textbooks offer choices, primarily to teachers, through the suggestions made in the Teacher's Book and/or the resources – including, in some cases, linked online resources – that are made available. Although the materials may include components that learners can access independently (e.g. a grammar reference section or a vocabulary list in the textbook) learners are not normally offered a choice between different activities or the opportunity to decide which level of exercise to attempt. However, in *Right Track*, Book 1 (Adrian-Vallance & Edge, 1994) teacher and learners are offered choices between, say, a communicative activity and language awareness work, or between pronunciation, writing and 'learning to learn' activities (Edge & Wharton, 1998). *Landmark* (Haines & Stewart, 2000) also offers choices for learners in its Speaking Personally sections (Tomlinson et al., 2001); and the Norwegian English-language textbook *New Flight*, Book 8 (Bromseth & Wigdahl, 2006) contains not only supplementary reading texts representing a higher level of challenge than the core texts intended for all students but also exercises which are colour coded for difficulty (Lund & Zoughby, 2007). These are exceptions. In the main, the assumption seems to be that it is the teacher who will provide the options, and the teacher, in turn, may be relying on the textbook/Teacher's Book for ideas.

## 5.3 The necessity for teacher creativity

From the textbook writer's perspective, as we have seen, it also seems to be a given that teachers will understand and accept that they cannot just use the materials as they are. They have to be creative (Bell & Gower, 2011). Cost or design constraints can limit what is included in the student's book. 'A good teacher's guide will supplement materials with useful alternatives and adaptations, but where this does not happen or a teacher does not have the teacher's guide, *adaptation will become part of the creative dialogue between teachers and published materials*' (Islam & Mares, 2003: 135, emphasis added). The writer's original manuscript may also have been pared down to broaden its suitability. 'As a consequence, much of the "flavour" and creativity of the author's original manuscript may disappear. In using textbooks, therefore, *teachers have to put back some of the creativity that may have been lost in the process of textbook publication*' (Richards, 2001: 14, emphasis added).

Bell and Gower (2011) also emphasize the importance of teachers adapting materials:

> With international materials it is obvious that the needs of individual students and teachers, as well as the expectations of particular schools in particular countries, can never be fully met by the materials themselves. Indeed, most users seem to accept that what they choose will in many ways be a compromise and that they will have to adapt the materials to their situation.
>
> . . . In other words, contrary to many current arguments about the inhibiting role of coursebooks, international course materials can actually encourage individualisation and teacher creativity rather than the opposite. The better Teacher's Books will . . . suggest pathways . . . and urge teachers to cut, adapt and supplement the material for their context. Everything depends on the relationship that a user, in particular a teacher, has or is allowed to have with the material. Coursebooks are tools which only have life and meaning when there is a teacher present. They are never intended to be a straitjacket for a teaching programme in which the teacher makes no decisions to add, to animate or to delete. The fact that course materials are sometimes treated too narrowly – for example, because of the lack of teacher preparation time, the excesses of ministry or institution power, the demands of examinations, or the lack of professional training – should not be a reason to write off global coursebooks. (Bell & Gower, 2011: 137–8)

Not everyone would agree that 'coursebooks . . . only have . . . meaning when a teacher is present' – should they not also have meaning for students using them outside class time? Bell and Gower's main point here, however, is that teachers have an important role to play in 'animating' the materials (to use their word), in bringing them to life, making them meaningful and relevant. To do this, they need to make their own creative decisions about how to use the coursebook, and what other materials to use, based on their knowledge of their learners. Whether this actually happens will depend partly on an individual teacher's attitude: 'the relationship that . . . a teacher . . . has . . . with the material'. Does the teacher see the material as the writers do, as a tool, or treat it more like an instruction manual, for example, or even a holy book, to be followed faithfully (McGrath, 2006)? Another factor, of course, as Bell and

Gower acknowledge, is that teachers do not operate in a vacuum ('the relationship that . . . a teacher . . . *is allowed to have* with the material'), a reference to 'excesses of ministry or institution power'. The constraints under which teachers operate are a central theme of Chapter 8.

We turn now, however, to the professional literature, and the views expressed there of how teachers might be expected to interact with materials.

# CHAPTER THREE

# The professional literature

> There is inevitably a subjective element in textbook selection, but we can seek to minimise this.
>
> (McGrath, 2002: 53)
>
> . . . a boring book will remain boring if all the teacher does is plod through the material exactly as it is on the page.
>
> (Prodromou, 2002: 27)

## 1. Introduction

Chapter 2 dealt with the development of commercial materials from the perspectives of publishers and textbook writers and the ways in which teachers as end-users figure in their thinking. In this chapter, the focus shifts more directly to the teacher. The views expressed here – about teachers and materials – come from what might be broadly conceived of as the professional community, which is made up of all those who actively contribute to debate about the teaching and learning of English and not just the 'academic' community referred to by Maley (2001). Many of these contributors occupy more than one role: as teachers but also textbook writers, or teachers and teacher educators, and some combine all three of these roles. Teachers who speak at conferences or write for teachers' magazines and journals are also assumed to be a part of this professional discourse community.

The point was made in Chapter 1 that teachers have two broad responsibilities in relation to materials: to evaluate them and to (re)design them. As we shall see in this chapter, the evaluative function is not confined to materials selection. It also applies at a number of points and in a number of ways in the process of course delivery. It is therefore relevant to all teachers, including those who have no influence over the materials they use. Design, similarly, is not a single discrete stage or operation, but encompasses activity ranging from relatively minor forms of adaptation, prior to and during lessons, to the creation of whole courses. The processes of evaluation and design are also logically and practically interrelated: for example, evaluation may reveal a need which can only be filled by redesign, and any new design must itself be evaluated, and if necessary further refined. The general expectation expressed in the professional literature, then, is that teachers will adopt a critical and creative stance in relation to materials, and that this will manifest itself in several very specific ways. **Section 2** deals with the role of the teacher in relation to course design, **Section 3** with materials selection, and **Section 4** with materials adaptation, a process in which evaluation and design are inextricably linked. **Section 5** focuses on supplementation, that is, the choice or development of materials to be used alongside a core textbook, and **Section 6** on the design of original materials. **Section 7** returns to the theme of evaluation – in this case, in-use and post-use evaluation in the context of the teacher as reflective practitioner; and **Section 8** summarizes the arguments for involving learners in both materials evaluation and design.

## 2. The responsibility for course design

A traditional linear course design process, as outlined in Masuhara (2011: 246), would include five main stages: needs analysis, goals and objectives, syllabus design, methodology/materials and testing and evaluation. More recent models tend to be cyclical, consider constraints, and allow for evaluation – as distinct from testing – to feed into and modify the model at any of the previous stages (see, for example, Graves, 1996); moreover, as Graves (1996) points out, these 'stages' may be more realistically viewed as 'a framework of components that overlap both conceptually and temporally' (p.5). Masuhara's concern, however, is to draw attention to the difference in the relationship between syllabus design and materials in the traditional model (Model X) and Model Y, the situation experienced by 'many practitioners . . . all over the world' (ibid.), which is described as follows:

> First, the teachers and administrators draw up a very general profile of a particular class and learners. In this profile the characteristics of the learners are defined in terms of the learners' preference for a course

and the levels of their proficiency based on the tests administered at the beginning of the course. The goal of teaching is usually represented in the name of the course (e.g. First Certificate Preparation Course, Oral Communication 1).

Materials selection holds a crucial position in the second stage of the course design sequence; the teachers and administrator select from commercially available coursebooks the one suitable for the class defined in the initial stage. The stages such as needs analysis, objectives specification, syllabus design and selection of methodology which Model X presupposes to happen prior to materials selection are assumed to have been taken care of by the producers (e.g. materials writers and publishers). (Masuhara, 2011: 246–7)

In this scenario, Masuhara argues, early 'crucial stages' (needs analysis and objectives specification) of the course design in Model X have been allowed to pass from the hands of teachers and administrators to materials producers – or, as Byrd (2001) puts it, when no clearly articulated curriculum aims have been formulated, the book is allowed to shape the design of the course. There is widespread agreement in the literature that responsibility for course design cannot be delegated to a textbook, however comprehensive that textbook may appear to be. Now it can be argued that in many contexts textbooks are written to suit a Ministry syllabus and that since public examinations are based on this syllabus there is no reason (or freedom) for teachers to do anything other than conform to it, or its embodiment in the form of a national textbook or an approved textbook. However, syllabus documents embody general expectations about what will be taught, not how learning objectives will be achieved; moreover, they make no allowance for local conditions. It falls to the teachers within an institution, therefore, to plan courses which are based on the official syllabus but also take into account learners' existing knowledge, needs, wants and likely rate of progress. The selection of suitable materials then becomes a stage in the course design process rather than dictating the design. Yalden (1987) expresses the consensus view: 'A syllabus should be, in the first instance, a statement about content, and only in the later stage of development, a statement about methodology and materials' (p.87) (see also, Johnson, 1989; Graves, 2000; Woodward, 2001; McGrath, 2002; McDonough & Shaw, 2003).

The degree to which teachers are willing or able to take an active role in planning courses will depend in large measure on their attitudes, training and experience. The same considerations will also affect the extent to which the materials control what goes on in the classroom. As Byrd (1995b) points out:

> Some teachers seem to have few techniques for analyzing the resources offered them by textbooks. Some teachers simply start at the front of the

text and teach as much of the book as they can in the time allowed by a course. Other teachers report bafflement over making choices among sets of exercises. Still other teachers seem bemused if not amused by the suggestion that they should read a textbook all the way through prior to teaching from it. (p.7)

Graves (1996) has argued that the kinds of decision-making involved in planning and teaching lessons are actually a 'microversion' of planning and teaching courses: 'A teacher's expertise at the level of planning and teaching lessons is thus both part of and similar to the overall process of course development' (p.4). This apparently simple analogy is actually hugely important because it suggests that experienced teachers already have the basic expertise to design courses. In institutions where course design is delegated to the book, this expertise is not tapped, the inexperienced are left to their own devices and the situation described by Byrd prevails. Where the truth of Graves's statement is recognized, course design is by contrast a dynamic, democratic and professionally enriching process.

## 3. Materials selection

### 3.1 The materials evaluation cycle

Much of what has been written about materials evaluation deals with coursebooks and most of what has been written about coursebook evaluation is broadly concerned with processes and criteria which can help the evaluator decide whether a coursebook is *likely* to be suitable for a particular context of use. Ellis (1997) makes an important distinction between this kind of pre-use or 'predictive' evaluation and post-use or what he calls 'retrospective' evaluation, that is, evaluation based on experience of having used a book or other materials and assessing the effects. Other writers have argued that there is also a need to evaluate materials while they are being used ('in-use' evaluation or 'whilst-use' evaluation – see, for example, McGrath, 2002 and Masuhara, 2011). McGrath (2002, chapters 1 and 9) presents a 'cyclical' approach in which the data gathered at each stage – pre-use evaluation, in-use evaluation and post-use evaluation – feeds into the next stage and may ultimately lead to the modification of the evaluation process itself.

Materials selection (predictive evaluation) is discussed in Section 3.3 with particular reference to the selection of coursebooks, and in-use and post-use evaluation in Section 7.3. First, however, we turn to the difference between materials analysis and evaluation.

## 3.2 *Materials analysis and context analysis*

### 3.2.1 Materials analysis

Materials analysis is concerned with getting inside a book (Graves, 2000), discovering what is there (Littlejohn, 2011). As the term suggests, its purpose is descriptive–analytical rather than evaluative. Its importance lies in the fact that 'beyond the most basic level, the concern is to understand what assumptions and beliefs lie beneath the surface and what effects can be anticipated' (McGrath, 2002: 22). It may, of course, be a preliminary to evaluation, both when selecting materials and prior to using them.

Littlejohn (2011) proposes an analysis at three levels:

1 *What is there* (objective description)
2 *What is required of users* (subjective analysis): focus on tasks, their content, what the learner is expected to do and who with
3 *What is implied* (subjective inference): deducing aims, principles of selection and sequence, teacher and learner roles and demands on the learner's process competence (i.e. ability to draw on knowledge, skills, abilities and attitudes.)

(based on Littlejohn, 2011: 185)

When materials selection is the main concern, such a process offers, Littlejohn argues, a thorough means of testing the claims made by publishers and textbook writers. It might also serve, he notes, other purposes: for instance, to identify the causes of dissatisfaction with existing materials, and as a form of continuing professional development, especially when teachers are developing their own materials.

### 3.2.2 Context analysis

Materials analysis is, of course, only one of the types of analysis that need to precede textbook evaluation, the other being context analysis. Context analysis involves consideration of the *macro* context (factors relating to, for example, the role of English in the country and its language policy, the syllabus, examinations, cultural and religious considerations) and the *micro* context where the materials will be used (factors relating to the institution, course, teachers and learners) – see McGrath (2002) for an overview of macro and micro factors which draws on various sources. Graves (2000) differentiates clearly between analysis of materials (in this case, a textbook) and context analysis, but also explains why textbook analysis is also desirable after a textbook has been selected:

> There are two facets to understanding how to use a textbook. The first is the textbook itself: 'getting inside it' so you can understand how it is constructed and why. The second is everything other than the textbook: the

context, the students, and you, the teacher. The second facet is important, because when you evaluate a textbook, you generally use the lenses of your experience and context to evaluate it, and I think it is important to be aware of those lenses. The first facet, getting inside the textbook, is important so that you know *what* you are adapting or supplementing. The second facet helps you to be clear about what you are adapting it *to*. (p.176)

## 3.3 Selecting a coursebook

The importance of choosing an appropriate coursebook was emphasized in Chapter 1 (Section 3.3.1). However, in many situations teachers do not themselves choose the coursebooks they use. Byrd (2001) points out that while teachers at the tertiary level in the United States of America and elsewhere can often determine the materials to be used, in other settings selection decisions may be taken by administrators or committees; and in centralized systems there may be a requirement to use a national textbook series, thus precluding choice altogether. Nevertheless, 'teachers can sometimes influence the decision-making process. [This] is not just a matter of pedagogical knowledge but also of political skill' (Byrd, 2001: 416). No advice is given on how to acquire the political skills referred to, but the pedagogical knowledge needed to contribute to informed textbook selection is certainly available in the professional literature, as we shall see in the remainder of this section.

### 3.3.1 Methods

A number of writers have argued for a two-stage approach to coursebook selection. Given the pressures typically operating in educational institutions, this may seem a luxury. However, when several possible coursebook packages are being assessed, if the least suitable materials can be quickly discarded or 'filtered out' at the first stage, this allows more time for closer scrutiny of fewer materials in the second stage (Grant, 1987; McGrath, 2002).

Suggestions for the first stage are similarly motivated, but differ somewhat in their details and have distinctive labels applied to them by their originators. They include the 'flick' test (Matthews, 1985), involving a quick flick through the materials to assess their overall attractiveness and likely appeal to learners; 'impressionistic overview' (Cunningsworth, 1995) based on surveying the publisher's 'blurb' on the back cover, the contents page, and then a quick skim through the book taking in organization, topics, layout and visuals; and 'external' evaluation (McDonough and Shaw, 2003) focusing on the back cover, publisher's blurb, introduction and table of contents. 'First-glance' evaluation (McGrath, 2002) combines a set of *Yes/ No* questions and a flowchart procedure (pp.33, 37); and the CATALYST test (Grant, 1987), in which the acronym stands for Communicative? Aims? Teachability? Available add-ons? Student interest? Tried and Tested? (p.119), requires rather more judgement, and therefore more time.

The method most frequently advocated for the second stage, involving a closer scrutiny, is that of the checklist. Checklists are a means of making evaluation criteria *explicit*, thereby providing a 'common framework for decision-making'; they ensure that *systematic* attention is paid to all aspects considered to be important; and information is recorded in a manner that is *cost effective* and in a format that is *convenient* for purposes of comparison (McGrath, 2002: 26–7). Cost effectiveness and convenience in particular are merely potential strengths, of course. Whether a particular checklist actually realizes this potential will depend on its format (see Section 3.3.3, below).

The best known published checklists are probably the following: Tucker (1975), Cunningsworth (1979, 1984), Daoud and Celce-Murcia (1979), Williams, D. (1983), Matthews (1985), Breen and Candlin (1987), Grant (1987), Sheldon (1988), Skierso (1991), Ur (1996) and Harmer (1991). The most detailed of these is Skierso (1991), although Cunningsworth (1995) contains checklists relating to a variety of aspects. Other examples include Bruder (1978), Haycraft (1978), Williams, R. (1981), Byrd and Celce-Murcia (2001) and Brown (2007) – an adaptation of Robinett (1978). McElroy (1934) is an interesting example of an early checklist (or what he calls 'a score card'). Checklists accessible online include Peacock (1997a) and Garinger (2002). Coleman (1985), Cunningsworth and Kusel (1991) and Gearing (1999) all focus specifically on Teacher's Guides – see also Skierso (1991). Extracts from a number of checklists can be found in McGrath (2002). Ansary and Babaii (2002), Riazi (2003), Mukundan and Ahour (2010) and Karamoozian and Riazi (nd) all review checklists from different periods. Gomes de Matos (2000) argues for interdisciplinary checklists.

## 3.3.2 Criteria

Checklists intended for detailed evaluation are typically organized into a number of sections which correspond to major areas of focus. For example, that of Grant (1987) contains 30 specific questions (or microcriteria) organized under three more general questions (or macrocriteria): 'Does the book suit your students?', 'Does the book suit the teacher?' and 'Does the book suit the syllabus and the examination?'; and that of Byrd (2001) similarly focuses on the fit between materials and (1) curriculum (2) students and (3) teachers. Garinger (2002) contains four categories: (1) program and course (2) skills (3) exercises and activities and (4) practical concerns; and Richards (2001b) suggests five: (1) programme factors: reflecting the concerns of the programme (2) teacher factors: reflecting teachers' concerns (3) learner factors: reflecting learners' concerns (4) content factors: concerned with content and organization and (5) pedagogical factors: concerned with method and the design of activities and exercise types. Many checklists allocate categories to specific aspects of language, differentiating between language skills (e.g. speaking, writing) and language systems (e.g. grammar, pronunciation) and include a catch-all category headed 'Practical considerations' or 'General' to cover considerations such as price, durability and availability if these have not been assessed by a stage 1 checklist. For many checklist designers, this kind of conceptual mapping is a convenient starting point for more detailed thinking about specific criteria, but a reverse operation, working from beliefs and specific criteria, has also been advocated (Tomlinson, 1999).

One problem with the criteria developed at a particular point in time is that they may not be entirely appropriate some years later, as one can see if one compares checklists produced in the 1970s, say, with those developed in the 1990s (for discussion, see Riazi, 2003 and Mukundan & Ahour, 2010; and for examples, McGrath, 2002). Contexts also differ, of course. What this means, in broad terms, is that 'different criteria will apply in different circumstances' (Cunningsworth, 1995: 2). We cannot simply take an existing checklist and reuse it without careful scrutiny as to its relevance. Tomlinson and Masuhara (2004: 9) emphasize, for example, the need to consider 'local' factors, which – in addition to the kinds of institutional and learner/teacher-specific factors likely to be included in any checklist – might include the need to prepare learners for examinations and the availability of target-language exposure outside the classroom environment. They also point out that the range of materials which form a part of modern coursebook packages argues for the inclusion of criteria relating to each of these elements (i.e. media-specific criteria), and Bahumaid (2008) makes the rather similar point that different criteria are likely to be relevant to the evaluation of a conversation skills book, say, as compared to a coursebook. Examples of more narrowly targeted checklists include Ioannou-Georgiou (2002) for software, Karamoozian and Riazi (nd) for reading skills books and Reinders and Lewis (2006) for self-access materials.

Roberts (1996), in the course of an admirably cool and incisive look at checklists, observes that contexts are so different that there is only academic interest in checklist comparison. 'While some of the criteria they embody may be relevant to one's own teaching/learning situation, perhaps their most valuable aspect is that they stimulate thought about the system of evaluation and the modus operandi to be adopted' (p.381). Let us turn, therefore, to systems and modus operandi.

### 3.3.3 Format and processes

Ease of use and economy of time and effort are key considerations in both stages, but particularly so at Stage 1, if a two-stage procedure is adopted. On this basis, McGrath (2002, in press), for example, argues for a limited number of *Yes/No* questions and a flowchart process in which there is an option to exit if one or more key criteria are not met.

More generally, format concerns the following:

- whether the checklist contains an introductory section in which basic information (e.g. author(s), publisher, date of publication, components, price) is recorded
- whether it is intended to be used for the evaluation of a single book/package or comparison
- whether it is intended to be self-explanatory or accompanied by notes explaining criteria
- how criteria are framed (e.g. in the form of statements or questions)
- whether criteria are grouped into sections
- if questions are used, whether these are closed or open
- the form of response (e.g. *Yes/No* or other fixed verbal response; number on a scale; free verbal response)
- whether additional comments are encouraged
- whether results can be quantified (e.g. by adding up numbers).

In most situations, comparison will be involved and, as noted above, economy in terms of evaluator time and effort will be important factors. Although the presence or absence of specific elements can be assessed using a *Yes/No* format, judgements of quality require a scale. These considerations argue for a closed-response numerical format (i.e. a rating scale). Individual criteria can also be weighted using another scale to allow for distinctions to be made between criteria felt to be more/less important. Subtotalling of section scores facilitates easy comparison of different sets of materials across sections as well as indicating relative strengths and weaknesses. Space for comments at the end of subsections allows respondents to explain their responses or draw attention to features not covered by the criteria. Both rating and weighting scales are used by, for example, Tucker (1975), Daoud and Celce-Murcia (1979), Williams (1983) and Skierso (1991), though Tucker uses the term 'rating' for what others have called 'weighting'. There is critical discussion of various aspects of format in Roberts (1996) and McGrath (2002).

Issues of format are essentially technical: they are concerned with arriving at a design which is fit for purpose. Logically, decisions about format should follow discussion of criteria (Section 3.3.2), and just as decisions about criteria need to take account of what those who will use the materials (teachers and learners) want from them so too decisions about checklist format need to take account of those who will use the checklist and the processes involved.

Similar criteria apply to the design of checklist criteria as to the design of any research questionnaire. For example, each item should be framed in such a way that only one concept or proposition is addressed, that its meaning is transparent and that the response format is appropriate. Issues with any of these have an impact on reliability. In order to achieve economy in checklist design but overcome any possible problems with transparency, the designers of some materials evaluation checklists have felt the need to provide additional briefing notes to try to ensure that respondents fully understand what is intended. Within an institution, a Key of this kind is useful as a point of reference, but an introductory discussion – of the need for systematic materials evaluation and the approach proposed – is likely to be both preferred and more effective than simply presenting a *fait accompli*. If criteria have already been specified in a prior stage, this can be followed by consideration of how individual criteria should be weighted (a possibly lengthy process, but one which would encourage teacher 'buy-in') and followed by a 'practice' session with materials already in use or known to the teachers. Any widely divergent responses would reveal any obvious remaining differences in understanding of key concepts and, following clarification, checklist items, format or briefing notes could be tweaked to eliminate these. Daoud and Celce Murcia (1979) have suggested that materials under consideration be assessed by three experienced teachers; others favour the involvement of all teachers who will use the materials (for further discussion, see, for example, Skierso, 1991; Chambers, 1997; McGrath, 2002).

## 3.4 Lesson planning and materials evaluation

Lesson planning also involves materials evaluation. Whether planning a series of lessons or a single lesson, teachers take account of learners' *current* knowledge and skills, the *desired* level of knowledge and skills (as described in a syllabus, for example) and the materials available (which will often include a textbook). Experienced teachers also draw on their experience (of teaching, of teaching similar learners, of using the materials). While some will refer to copies of previous lesson plans which they have annotated to show how well activities worked and what modifications they made to procedures and timing, others may rely on a few scribbled notes and some on just a mental plan. In contrast, inexperienced teachers are advised to make a detailed written plan. Senior (2006) distinguishes between this latter kind of 'planning' and the 'preparation' more characteristic of experienced teachers.

Whatever form it takes, lesson planning involves consideration of the kinds of input and activity needed to achieve the desired learning outcomes and how these should be sequenced. When a teacher is working with a coursebook, the teacher will evaluate the book for its potential to contribute to the learning outcomes (see, for example, Acklam, 1994 and Byrd, 2001, for checklists of some of the general questions that might guide an interrogation of the material). This evaluative scrutiny will lead to decisions concerning what can be used without any kind of change, what not to use, what should be replaced, and what needs to be changed. If, following this process, the teacher decides that supplementary resources (e.g. material from other books, authentic texts or online sources) will be needed, the same set of evaluative decisions would logically be repeated in relation to these resources. Sections 4 and 5 discuss these processes in more detail.

That is not the end of evaluation as far as lesson planning is concerned. Lesson plans are, after all, not set in stone. Harmer (2007) makes the point that teachers should not pursue a planned activity 'simply because it is in the plan' (p.367). Plans have to be evaluated – and, if necessary, modified – in the course of implementation, as well as at a less pressured point after the lesson (see Section 7.3); and where the plan or the improvised plan involves materials adaptation, the appropriateness or otherwise of the adaptation needs to form part of that evaluation.

# 4. Adaptation

## 4.1 *Defining adaptation*

The consensus in the professional literature seems to be that whenever teachers working with a coursebook or other material omit something, add something or change something, they are adapting those materials. This may be a useful starting point for discussions of adaptation, but a more helpful definition – one that could be used to analyse or guide teachers' practice – would need to answer the following four questions:

- *Why should we adapt?*
    - The answer that emerges from the literature is that coursebooks are written for everyone and therefore no one, and the same point can be made of any published materials. Adaptation is

thus an attempt to tailor materials so that they are a better match for a specific learning context (see Sections 4.2 and 4.3).

- *What should we adapt?*
  - Anything (language, level, context, content, procedure) – see Section 4.4. Graves (2000) points out that much of what has been written about adaptation is at the level of the activity and therefore rather narrow, and that teachers also adapt at the levels of unit and syllabus. Where new material is added, this will be treated as supplementation (Section 5).

- *How should we adapt?*
  - A general answer would be the one given above: by omitting, adding or changing. A more specific answer would explain what 'adding' and 'changing' mean in operational terms (see Section 4.5). It would also make reference to the principles influencing particular decisions (see Section 4.6). Some forms of adaptation require very little effort; others involve time, knowledge and skill.

- *When should we adapt?*
  - Adaptation can be both a part of lesson planning (proactive) or an instinctive response while a lesson is in progress (reactive). With experience, teachers may become better at reactive adaptation, but teacher education can open their eyes to the range of proactive possibilities open to them (Sections 4.5 and 4.6) and thereby help them to plan more effective lessons.

## 4.2 The importance of adaptation

The importance of adaptation is widely acknowledged. Richards (2001b: 5) states: 'The ability to . . . adapt commercial materials . . . is an essential skill for teachers to develop', and Prodromou (2002) points out:

> A textbook does not teach itself . . . It is the teacher, in collaboration with the class, who brings the material to life. . . . a book that is considered mediocre for whatever reason can be transformed into motivating material by an enthusiastic and imaginative teacher but a boring book will remain boring if all the teacher does is plod through the material exactly as it is on the page. (p.27)

For Islam and Mares (2003), adaptation is necessary even when the coursebook is appropriate for the context:

> In many cases, the teacher using published materials in any given classroom is not involved with creating the materials and may have little to do with adopting the materials for her institution. However, even when the classroom teacher selects the book, knows every student in the class well, and is using materials designed specifically for the context they are in, she will still *have to* adapt the materials either consciously or subconsciously. (Islam & Mares, 2003: 86, emphasis added)

The belief that teachers – at least experienced and good teachers – *do* adapt materials is also widespread, and can be supported by observational evidence. Hutchinson and Torres (1994: 325) refer to two teachers in Torres's PhD study, at that time in preparation:

> ... teachers and learners do not follow the textbook script. Most often teachers follow their own scripts by adapting or changing textbook-based tasks, adding new tasks or deleting some, changing the management of the tasks, changing task inputs or expected outputs, and so on. Moreover, what is also clear from the study is that the teacher's planned task is reshaped and reinterpreted by the interaction of teacher and learners during the lesson.

Islam and Mares (2003) make a similar distinction between 'pre-planned' and 'spontaneous' adaptation: 'Whether pre-planned or spontaneous, materials adaptation is an integral part of the success of any class' (p.86).

Some commentators refer to 'good' rather than 'experienced' teachers, perhaps implying that experience does not of itself lead to this kind of responsive, creative teaching. Madsen and Bowen (1978: vii), for example, say: 'The good teacher is constantly adapting', and their depiction of such a teacher neatly captures the intricate negotiation involved: 'The good teacher is . . . constantly striving for congruence among several related variables: teaching materials, methodology, students, course objectives, the target language and its context, and the teacher's own personality and teaching style' (p.ix). The influence of the teacher's own preferred teaching style is also recognized by, for example, Senior (2006) and Richards (2001b).

> No matter what form of materials teachers make use of, whether they teach from textbooks, institutional materials, or teacher-prepared materials, they represent *plans* for teaching. . . . As teachers use materials, they adapt and transform them to suit the needs of particular groups of

learners and their own teaching styles. These processes of transformation are at the heart of good teaching and enable good teachers to create effective lessons out of the resources they make use of. (p.16)

## 4.3 The purpose of adaptation

Adaptation, it is generally agreed, helps to make materials meaningful and interesting for learners. Saraceni (2003: 77) states that the purpose of adaptation is to render materials 'more relevant and effective'; and Prodromou (2002) provides examples to show how adaptation can cater for heterogeneity and bring materials to life by making tasks 'more engaging, achievable, memorable' (p.29). As Madsen and Bowen (1978) point out, adaptation is not necessarily a form of criticism of a text: 'even when a text[book] is well written, it may not be completely compatible with the instrumental aims, student level, or teaching style in a given school or classroom' (p.viii).

McGrath (2002) summarizes the purposes of adaptation as follows:

> 1. To make the material more suitable for the circumstances in which it is being used, i.e. to mould it to the needs and interests of learners, the teacher's own capabilities and such constraints as time, or, as McDonough and Shaw (1993: 85) put it: 'to maximize the appropriacy of teaching materials in context, by changing some of the internal characteristics of a coursebook to suit our particular circumstances better';
>
> 2. To compensate for any intrinsic deficiencies in the material, such as linguistic inaccuracies, out-of-datedness, lack of authenticity (Madsen & Bowen 1978) or lack of variety (Tice, 1991). (p.64)

The circumstances in which the material is being used include, of course, the macro environment and the micro environment of the institution (syllabus, tests, course features) referred to earlier. By maximizing the appropriacy of materials, McGrath adds, we can hope to stimulate learner motivation, which in turn will lead to 'a classroom atmosphere more conducive to learning' (ibid.).

## 4.4 Focus

Adaptation typically focuses on any one or any combination of the following:

- *language* (the language of instructions, explanations, examples, the language in exercises and texts and the language learners are expected to produce)

- *process* (forms of classroom management or interaction stated explicitly in the instructions for exercises, activities and tasks, but also the learning styles involved)
- *content* (topics, contexts, cultural references)
- *level* (linguistic and cognitive demands on the learner).

In relation to language, for example, adaptation would have three main concerns: to ensure that learners are exposed to samples of language which are accurate, up-to-date, authentic and relevant – and that can therefore serve as models for their own production; that this input language is at a level which is appropriate for learners; and that exercises and activities provide opportunities for learners to use language which is likely to be useful to them. Adaptation related to language, carrier content or classroom management (whether an exercise is written or spoken, for example, or done individually or in pairs) all stem from a teacher's judgement of what is best in a particular set of circumstances for a particular group of learners. Groups are composed of individuals, however, and a recognition of the need to cater for individual differences lies behind forms of adaptation focusing on both process and level.

## 4.5 Procedures

One of the simplest descriptions of adaption techniques is offered by Cunningsworth (1995), who states that teachers *leave out, add, replace* and *change*. However, as will be evident from Table 3.1, other writers use a headache-inducing variety of alternative terms and categorizations. **Leave out** is not only paraphrased as *omit, delete* and *reject*, but distinctions are made within this category (*reduce, subtract, abridge*) and within that of **addition** (*extend, expand, extemporize, exploit*). **Changes in order or organization** are variously described as *reordering/reorganizing/restructuring/resequencing*, and other forms of change are either listed as separate techniques (e.g. *replacement*) or grouped together according to the writer's individual preference (see, for example, Richards, 2001a; McGrath, 2002).

Establishing what is common in all this diversity may be difficult, but it is not an idle academic exercise. As noted in Chapter 1, we might expect that all teachers, as they gain in experience and confidence, will adapt in minor ways. However, many may need to be made aware that other forms of adaptation are also desirable and, where expertise and time are likely to be needed, persuaded and helped to acquire that expertise, either within their institutions or as part of a teacher education programme. Achieving consistency of terminology may be difficult, but we need to be able to at least describe the adaptation techniques that can be used. What follows is an attempt to provide such a description based on three basic categories – omission, addition and change, and a limited number of sources.

**Table 3.1** Adaptation procedures: Same or different?

| | | | | |
|---|---|---|---|---|
| Cunningsworth (1995) | leave out | add | replace | change |
| Harmer (2007) | omit, reduce | add | replace | reorder, rewrite |
| Maley (2011) | omit | add | replace | reduce, extend, rewrite/modify, reorder, branching |
| Graves (2000) | delete | add | reorder, change | |
| McDonough & Shaw (2003) | delete, including subtract and abridge | add, including expand and extend | simplify, modify (including rewrite and restructure), reorder | |
| Richards (2001a) | delete | add | reorganize or modify content, modify (change) or extend tasks, address omissions | |
| McGrath (2002) | reject | add: extemporize, extend, exploit | change: including change to language, contexts and content, procedures and classroom management; restructure | |
| Tomlinson & Masuhara (2004) | minus: delete, subtract, reduce | plus: add, expand | zero: modify, replace, reorganize, resequence, convert | |

*Omission* refers to the decision:

- not to use a whole component of the material (McDonough & Shaw's quantitative *subtracting* and qualitative *abridging*; Tomlinson & Masuhara's *deletion*)
- not to use part of a component (*subtraction*, as defined by McDonough & Shaw and Tomlinson & Masuhara)
- not to use material in class, but to set it as homework (McGrath – no specific term suggested).

*Addition* can take at least six different forms:

- examples, explanations, paraphrases offered spontaneously in response to a predicted or perceived learner problem (McGrath's *extemporization*)
- more practice or test items of the same kind (McGrath's *extension*)
- increase in the length, depth or difficulty of a text or activity (Tomlinson & Masuhara's *expansion*)
- creative use of the material in ways not intended by the writer (McGrath's *exploitation* and perhaps Maley's *extension*)
- the provision of alternatives to an existing activity or different pathways through the materials (Maley's *branching*)
- new material (e.g. text, activity) (McDonough & Shaw's *expansion*, Tomlinson & Masuhara's *addition*).

Three major types of *change* (or modification) have been identified:

- rearrangement: typically involving resequencing
- replacement
- rewriting: including both minor and more ambitious changes.

For a fuller discussion, see McGrath (in press).

## 4.6 Examples of adaptation

Examples not only offer some relief from analytical discussion, they are also a way of testing the adequacy of the conceptual frameworks that are proposed. Here, then, are two examples which may serve both purposes. They concern the handling of dialogues.

### Example 1

When a recording of a coursebook dialogue is not available, a teacher may feel obliged to read the text aloud. Graves (2003) recalls a colleague who made ingenious use of a plastic bow to indicate whether the speaker was female (bow held in hair) or male (bow held to throat to simulate bow tie); an alternative, as she notes, is to use glove puppets.

### Example 2

Appel (1995) describes his own use of glove puppets as follows:

I occasionally did my own dialogues. All it required was reading the dialogue in the book, checking on the new words, and two glove puppets known to the class under the names Tony and Ilona. Tony and Ilona became our companions. They were good fun for everybody because they could say all the things authors and editors of nationally used textbooks would never dare to put into a dialogue. (Appel, 1995: 119)

Example 1 conjures up, for me, a vivid mental image of a jolly-looking male teacher skipping to and fro to represent the two characters and deftly switching his brightly coloured plastic bow from hair to throat; and Example 2 conjures up a picture of the two mischievous puppets apparently chatting with each other, perhaps even about the teacher, and bright-faced children hanging on every word. These are the kinds of fun-filled moments that can make the language of a textbook much more memorable for the students concerned. On a more mundane note, Example 1 is an illustration of adaptation as change (specifically, what McDonough and Shaw (2003) call *restructuring* and McGrath (2002) refers to as a *change in procedure*). Example 2, on the other hand, seems to be closer to what McDonough and Shaw term *rewriting* (also a form of change), but for McGrath (2002) would be *exploitation* (a form of addition). Further examples – to provide more light relief or to test the framework – can be found in, for example, Mosback (1984), Grant (1987), Graves (2000, chapter 9) and McGrath (2002, chapter 4).

## 4.7 Principles

The changes made to materials in the process of adaptation are usually justified by reference to one or more principles. The principles most often referred to or implied are summarized below.

Materials need to:

- be perceived as relevant by learners (localization)
- be up-to-date (modernization)
- cater for differences in learning styles (individualization)
- encourage learners to speak/write about themselves and their own experiences (personalization)
- engage the whole person (humanizing)
- be appropriate to learners' level/offer an appropriate level of challenge (simplification/complexification/differentiation)
- be varied (variety).

## 4.7.1 Localization

On the face of it, *localization* applies particularly to the use of global materials and to two aspects of these: the language syllabus(es) and the cultural content. As noted earlier, an expectation expressed in the professional literature is that teachers will make materials-related decisions on the basis of their assessment of, inter alia, learners' needs. It therefore follows that if using published materials, they will (1) use only those parts of the materials that they judge to be relevant and (2) provide additional materials if they feel the published materials are inadequate. McDonough and Shaw (2003) use the example of pronunciation coverage in a global textbook to illustrate both of these processes. The materials provide systematic coverage of a range of potential pronunciation problems (e.g. vowel contrasts, voiced/voiceless contrasts, phonemes), and the teacher working with a monolingual group in a specific context applies the principle of what we might call *linguistic localization* when they (1) choose not to deal with phoneme contrasts that are not problematic for their students and (2) provide additional practice of those phonemes or phoneme contrasts if that provided by the book seems insufficient. The same principle would obviously apply to other aspects of the language.

As far as cultural content is concerned, it seems to be widely accepted that learners should be able to relate to contexts, content and characters in materials. It has therefore been suggested that teachers using global materials which contain culturally unfamiliar, alien or inappropriate elements should – according to what we might call the principle of *cultural localization* – replace these with local equivalents. At the level of an example or an exercise, replacement might simply involve substituting one noun (e.g. name of fruit, vegetable, animal, sport) for another or one place name with another. The same principle applies to pictures of people or places and maps which are used as the basis for practice. An alternative option may be omission, but in the case of spoken and written texts which 'carry' language important for the syllabus but deal with or refer to topics felt to be inappropriate this is not really possible – and finding or creating suitable replacement material may not be very easy.

Practicalities and cultural taboos apart, the whole concept of relevance and cultural localization is somewhat problematic because it assumes that teachers are in a position to make judgments for their students. If all reference to people, places and events outside students' experience is to be replaced or deleted, does this not deprive students of information and knowledge that might possibly be of interest or value to them? A thoughtful compromise suggested by Altan (1995) is that while input might include reference to the wider world, student output (i.e. what students are asked to say or write) might focus on the world they know.

### 4.7.2 Modernization

Compared to some of the principles included in this section, *modernization* appears relatively unproblematic. It refers to change in either of two aspects of materials: language – where this appears not to reflect current usage and can therefore no longer serve as a model for student production; and content – whether, for example, illustrations, facts and topics seem inaccurate or inappropriate because they are old-fashioned. Minor language points can be dealt with by a brief teacher comment, and out-of-date content can be replaced (by teacher or learners) or used as a focus for class discussion.

### 4.7.3 Individualization

McDonough and Shaw (1993: 87) define *individualization* as 'addressing the learning styles both of individuals and of the members of a class working together'. On a simple level, this just involves teachers ensuring that activities are not always conducted in the same way. Students might also appreciate being offered what Maley (2011) calls 'branching' choices – for instance, as to whether they work individually or in pairs/small groups, or the form in which they present their work on a task (a cartoon strip, a role play, a written narrative).

### 4.7.4 Personalization

Personalization is a form of materials exploitation in which the student is encouraged to engage with the material on an individual, personal level. Graves (2003) offers a simple example: 'I remember observing a high school French teacher teach telephone numbers using the examples in the textbook. The students were bored and inattentive. By simply asking them to use their own telephone numbers, she would have made the material more relevant and motivating' (p.235). Prodromou (2002) illustrates the concept by comparing the use of the same (invented) textbook example by a teacher (characterized as 'Mr Plodder') who does no more than work through the text as it is with what a more imaginative teacher ('Miss Spark') might do with the same material. The invented text is in the form of a leaflet taken from a British department store which illustrates, describes and gives prices for household appliances such as irons and cookers. Whereas Mr Plodder works through the text, asking the accompanying comprehension questions and explaining any difficult words, Miss Spark begins with a pre-reading warm-up, asking learners to picture the rooms in their own flat or house, make a note of the household appliances they contain, and then decide which were most and least expensive. Essentially, then, personalization enables students to draw on their own experience in order to express ideas in the target language. As Woodward (2001: 57) suggests: 'students can write or speak about how the stimulus is similar to or different from them, what the stimulus reminds them of, if they have ever . . ., what they would do if . . ., etc.'.

### 4.7.5 Humanizing

Tomlinson (2003b) explains the need for humanizing coursebooks as follows: 'I've suffered countless . . . coursebooks (including some I've written myself) which have needed humanizing because they didn't engage the learners I was using them with and because they didn't manage to connect with the learners' lives' (p.163). The purpose of humanizing, then, is to enable learners 'to explore their capacity for learning through meaningful experience' through helping them 'to connect what is in the book with what is in their minds' (ibid.). Meaningful experience would include opportunities 'to learn through doing things physically, to learn through feeling emotion, to learn through experiencing things in the mind', being involved 'intellectually, aesthetically and emotionally' (p.162). Tomlinson's examples of humanizing a coursebook include getting students to draw a version of a coursebook text, produce an extended version of a text using a local context, and writing 'inner speech monologues' of the characters in a coursebook dialogue (pp.165–6). See also Rinvolucri (2002).

### 4.7.6 Simplification/complexification/differentiation

*Simplification* patently refers to attempts to make materials easier for learners; *complexification* to increasing the level of difficulty; and *differentiation* to catering for learner differences – typically in proficiency level, although the term can also cover differences in learning style (see *individualization,* above) and multiple intelligences (Gardner, 1983, 1999). As regards simplification, McDonough and Shaw (2003) and Tomlinson (1998b) both warn against the simplistic assumption that the omission of 'difficult' words and phrases will necessarily make a text easier to understand, and Darian (2001) provides a brief, illustrated discussion of simplification in relation to specific language features. The examples he gives of abridgement, which involve deletion and some paraphrase, also raise issues concerning the relationship between information deletion and the purpose of and audience for a message. Prodromou (1990) and McGrath (1994) describe techniques for providing an appropriate level of challenge for learners with, respectively, different levels of proficiency and confidence (see also Hubbard, Jones & Wheeler, 1983; Prodromou, 1992b; Tice, 1997).

### 4.7.7 Variety

One of the criticisms of coursebooks noted in Chapter 1 was their unrelenting repetitiveness (Harmer, 2001). Graves (2000) points out that students need both the security of repetition and variety. Their need for security can be met by using the same procedure for listening activities, for example, for some time, but once they are familiar with this procedure interest can be added by occasionally varying it. Tice (1991), who complains of 'the textbook straitjacket', suggests a number of ways of introducing variety.

### 4.7.8 Principles, practice and theory

The dividing lines between some of these principles are perhaps a little blurred. *Individualization*, in particular, might be subsumed under *differentiation* (with its broader meaning) or *humanizing*. As more accounts of adaptation are published, these lines may become clearer, the list of principles may expand or principles may be combined. Islam and Mares (2003: 89), commenting on the four principles listed in McDonough and Shaw (1993) – localization, personalization, individualization and modernization – suggest what they see as further objectives of adaptation. These include 'add real choice' (by allowing learners to choose how they want to learn – 'Style matching' or try a different approach to learning – 'style stretching'); 'cater for sensory learner styles'; and 'provide for more learner autonomy'. All of these might conceivably form part of a fully thought-out commitment to *individualization* or *differentiation* in its broader meaning; catering for sensory learner styles also echoes Tomlinson's description of 'humanizing'. The same kinds of categorization issues are raised by Helgesen's (nd) argument for adapting activities to incorporate opportunities for learners to plan what they will say/write. Helgesen's examples, which cater for different sensory styles in the ways suggested by Islam and Mares, include mind mapping, guided visualization, drawing pictures of events (real or imaginary) prior to talking about them and mental rehearsal (think first about content, then about form). The advantages, it is claimed, are reflected in increased fluency, complexity and accuracy. Is the planning-stage principle underlying Helgesen's suggestion novel or are his ideas simply examples of the kinds of expansion or extension discussed earlier in relation to adaptation as addition? Saraceni (2003) has pointed out that 'adapting materials seems to be a relatively underresearched process' (p.73), and one has to agree. The examples given above are a helpful reminder that practice and theory can form part of a virtuous circle that begins at either point: principles can and should be derived from practice as well as from theory.

## 4.8 Summary and conclusion

At the end of such a long section, a brief summary may be helpful.

Materials adaptation is necessary and natural. It is realized through evaluative-creative decisions that lead to three processes: omission, addition and change. These processes can be justified by reference to one or more principles (localization, personalization, etc.). More research into these principles is desirable. Where the gap between the teacher's assessment of what is required and what published materials actually provide is small, adaptation will be minimal. However, if the teacher has very different objectives from those on which the materials are based (Saraceni, 2003) or holds different beliefs about how a language should be learnt and taught from those reflected in the materials (Mares & Islam, 2003), the attempt to achieve the kind of congruence referred to by Madsen and Bowen (1978) will be much more difficult. Conclusion: careful selection procedures will not eliminate the need for adaptation, but they can reduce it. The same holds true for supplementation.

# 5. Supplementation

## 5.1 Defining supplementation

Very little has been written about supplementation as a design process. It tends to be merely listed as one form of adaptation or referred to in discussions of the use of authentic materials. Where it is mentioned as a separate process, the point is simply made that it should happen. Garinger (2002), for example, notes: 'Every instructor should supplement the textbook with self-created materials or materials from other sources that reflect the unique needs of the class'.

In what is currently the most wide-ranging discussion of supplementation, McGrath (2002) offers the following definition:

> Supplementation . . . stems primarily from the recognition of a deficit: it is an attempt to bridge the gap between a coursebook and an official syllabus (or statement of aims), or a coursebook and the demands of a public examination, or a coursebook and students' needs. (McGrath, 2002: 80)

The deficits referred to here concern knowledge or competence: that is, they are gaps between what students need to know or be able to do and what is provided in the coursebook. A broader view, which takes account of learner motivation and mood, would see supplementation as also having the potential to bridge an affective gap. McGrath (2002) adds that both lesson-initial warm-ups and activities designed to lift the mood of a class, 'can serve their affective purpose *and* relate to the topic of the lesson' (p.81).

Certain forms of adaptation may also be intended to serve very similar purposes, but whereas adaptation involves working with existing material, such as a coursebook, supplementation involves introducing something new (McGrath, 2002). Adding additional items to an exercise to provide more practice would thus be one form of adaptation (extension) and asking additional questions about a coursebook text would be another form of adaption (exploitation); providing an additional exercise, on the other hand, whether copied from another source or devised by the teacher, would be supplementation. On the basis of these examples, the difference may seem small and relatively insignificant. It is not. There are, in fact, quite important implications for the ways in which teachers view published materials and their own skills as well as for their workload. It is usually easier and quicker to add to something that already exists than to find or create something new. This is even more obvious when supplementation is on a larger scale, as with the provision of new texts and accompanying tasks. The notion of a continuum of scale stretching from very simple forms of adaptation at one end to more extended forms of supplementation can also be seen in Samuda's (2005) discussion of task design. This distinguishes between task adaptation or 're-design' '(tweaking, adjusting and adapting existing materials to suit particular needs), which may entail small changes to the surface details of a task (localizing names and places for instance) or larger changes to elements of its internal structure (changing the order of steps for enacting the task, for example)' with 'unique' design work – 'the development of new tasks from scratch' (Samuda, 2005: 235), where the latter refers to the design of both one-off, supplementary tasks and a series of tasks.

## 5.2 *Starting points*

Long-term planning and careful scrutiny of the materials available in relation to course goals may enable some forms of supplementation to be prepared well in advance of their use. Often enough, though, needs emerge as a teacher gets to know a class – for example, through poor progress test results (alternative form of presentation and/or more practice required!) or student questions (see, for example, Jolly & Bolitho, 2011).

Getting to know a class is not simply a matter of being able to predict how they will cope with materials but also how they will respond. When teachers realize at the lesson-planning stage that if they only do what is in the book students will be very bored, they need to come up with an alternative or inject something extra to add interest or fun. With this in mind, many teachers are subconsciously on the look-out for materials which will enable them to revitalize a class imminently in danger of falling asleep or provide absorbing input or a thought-provoking prompt for the expression of personal ideas. As McGrath (2002) has noted, the discovery of such materials – which need not be designed for teaching, and might be a piece of realia, for example, or a picture, cartoon, YouTube clip or text – is typically accompanied by one of two reactions: 'I could use this with Form 3' or 'I could use this to practise X'. In both cases, the material is a starting point, a stimulus that can be developed for teaching purposes. McGrath (2002) terms this 'concept-driven' (i.e. ideas-driven) design to distinguish it from the often laborious search for material to fill a specific linguistic need. Text-based, and task-based syllabus designs, neither of which starts from a linguistic syllabus, are more deliberate and more elaborated versions of the one-off concept-driven activity or lesson. Arguing for a text-driven approach, for example, Tomlinson (2011c) writes:

> . . . deriving learning points from an engaging text or activity is much easier and more valuable than finding or constructing a text which illustrates a predetermined teaching point. . . . If the written and spoken texts are selected for their richness and diversity of language as well as for their potential to achieve engagement, then a wide syllabus will evolve which will achieve natural and sufficient coverage. If the materials are constrained by an external syllabus, then a text-driven approach with constant reference to a checklist . . . is the most profitable approach. (p.175)

## 5.3 Forms of supplementation

Supplementation can be in the form of materials taken from an existing source (e.g. another textbook, a practice book or test book, authentic print materials, the internet, in-house materials) or specially created by the teacher. In the case of any of these types of existing material, the same expectation applies as for coursebooks: that is, teachers will select from and, using the techniques described in Section 4, either adapt the materials in order to improve upon them and make them more suitable for their own students or exploit them for pedagogic purposes. A supplementary exercise might thus be adapted in any one of a number of ways (e.g. by giving it a title, simplifying the instructions, changing or adding items, etc.); and words might be deleted from a song, a cartoon cut up into separate frames and exploitation activities (not necessarily in the form of comprehension questions!) devised to accompany an authentic text from a newspaper or magazine.

Accuracy-focused supplementary material might deal with any of the language systems and be intended to raise awareness, practise or test. Oral drills and worksheets containing transformation, gap-fill or multiple-choice sentence-level exercises are not the only option. Songs, concordance lines and other texts can be used to raise awareness of aspects of language use, for example, and games can be exploited to practise specific phonological and grammatical features. Surprisingly little attention has been given to worksheet design. However, McGrath (2002) devotes several pages to this topic, Hughes (2006) draws attention to simple ways of improving on worksheets, and Tomlinson and Masuhara (2004) give more general advice on instructions, illustrations and design and layout. On visual design, see also Wright (1976) and Ellis and Ellis (1987).

Increased access to materials via the internet means that authentic materials are also widely used to supplement coursebooks. Criteria for the selection of written and spoken texts are discussed in, for example, McGrath (2002), Tomlinson and Masuhara (2004) and Berardo (2006). Lamie (1999) gives examples of supplementation using three types of material: games, texts from other textbooks and authentic materials (magazines, films and TV advertisements); and the use of authentic materials is also discussed by, inter alia, Peacock (1997b). McGrath's (2002) account of supplementation includes what he calls 'the real': authentic materials, concordances and the internet – the latter as both a source of materials and a medium of interaction; numerous references to other sources are also provided (pp.137–8). Tomlinson (2011d) draws attention to the various possibilities for autonomous student learning that have emerged as a result of new technology. Wraight (nd) provides a list of useful website resources (see www.c-english.com/files/effectiveuseofthetext_awraight). Additional references are given at the end of Section 6.

It is perhaps worth emphasizing that supplementation need not involve the preparation of materials by the teacher. Appel (1995), whose outspoken puppets Tony and Ilona were referred to earlier, describes how he used a model of a London cab (known as Black Taxi) to stimulate his young German pupils to reuse creatively language they had already encountered:

> Originally ... meant to introduce the word *taxi*, it quickly developed a personality of its own. The class had long and deep conversations with Black Taxi. I held it up in front and asked if there were any questions. The 11-year-olds were remarkably clever in using bits from the questions I had asked them at the beginning of the lesson along with bits from the book for drawing out the conversation with Black Taxi. When one of the kids asked Black Taxi 'Have you got any children?' his question led to an ingenious two-page homework showing Black Taxi's family tree. (p.119)

We come back to learner involvement in materials development in Section 8.

## 5.4 Sharing the load

Since finding and adapting or developing original materials can be very time-consuming, collaboration is desirable. Where several teachers are using the same basic coursebook and agree on the gaps that need to be filled, for example, a coordinated plan can be prepared which draws on individuals' knowledge of suitable resources and/or allocates specific responsibilities for finding or devising materials that can then form part of a shared bank (McGrath, 2002).

# 6. Developing original materials

As we saw in Chapter 1, some commentators believe that teachers need to be capable not only of adapting published materials and of supplementing using existing resources but also of creating their own original materials. Block (1991), who feels that 'for at least part of the time, teachers should replace the commercial course book with a contribution of their own' (p.213), sees this as just one dimension of reflective practice:

> Materials development is simply one more element within the larger concept of teachers taking responsibility for what happens in their classes. If we are to be reflective practitioners in the field of ELT, we need to consider all aspects of our teaching. I believe that preparing our own materials is one of those aspects. (p.216)

Block puts forward three reasons for what he calls do-it-yourself (DIY) materials design: (1) *contextualization* (teacher-prepared materials are likely to be more relevant and interesting than coursebook materials, which are prepared for a general audience); (2) *timeliness* – in that teacher-prepared materials will be more topical and (3) '*the personal touch*' will be appreciated by learners. Anticipating concerns about the time involved, he argues that the time investment is worthwhile if materials are reused, but that sharing of materials among teachers is desirable.

Developing Block's argument, Howard and Major (2004) give four reasons why teachers may wish to take on the task of materials development. Two of these echo Block's reasons: (1) *contextualization* (teacher-prepared materials can achieve a better 'fit' than commercial materials) and (2) *timeliness* (teacher-prepared materials can respond to local and international events: 'the teachable moment can be . . . seized' (p.102)), the other two reasons being: (3) *individual needs* (teacher-prepared materials can build on L1 skills, ensure that texts and activities are at a suitable level and adopt an appropriate organizational principle or focus) and (4) *personalization* (teacher-prepared materials can take account of learners' interests and preferred learning styles). However, they go on to list both a number of possible pitfalls and six factors to be considered. 'Time' occurs in both lists. Logistical considerations are mentioned under pitfalls in relation to 'physical organisation and storage', and under the factors to be considered as 'resources and facilities'. The 'quality' of the materials, physical and conceptual, is seen as a possible pitfall; and this also has its counterpart under the factors to be considered in 'personal confidence and competence'. One of the conclusions of the authors is that 'however passionately one may believe in the advantages of teacher-designed materials, the reality is that for many teachers, it is simply not viable – at least not all of the time' (p.103). However, they also quote Harmer's (2001: 7) view that 'the good DIY teacher, with time on his or her hands, with unlimited resources, and the confidence to marshal those resources into a clear and coherent program, is probably about as good as it gets for the average language learner'. Harmer chose to frame his point in positive terms but he is expressing exactly the same caveats about time, resources, confidence and competence.

For teachers who feel able to meet these requirements, guidance is available in a variety of forms. Howard and Major's paper includes 10 guidelines for developing effective materials. Other design guidelines, sets of principles and suggested criteria for judging effectiveness can be found in, for example, Breen and Candlin (1987), Hutchinson and Waters (1987), Crawford (2002), Tomlinson and Masuhara (2004), Tomlinson (2010a, 2011b), Jolly and Bolitho (2011); and, for self-access materials design, Dickinson (1987) and Sheerin (1989). Nunan (1988a) offers both principles and illustrations of these; and McGrath (2002) draws on a number of sources to illustrate how materials development can be made more systematic. Maley (1998) lists 12 procedures for exploiting 'raw' texts and providing variety. These are: expansion, reduction, media transfer, matching, selection and ranking, comparison and contrast, reconstruction, reformulation, interpretation, creation, analysis and project work; appendices give examples of techniques that can be used with each procedure, and then show how the techniques can be applied to short texts. Woodward (2001) gives further brief illustrations of Maley's procedures. Young (1980), Low (1989) and Nunan (1991) discuss further design options. Byrd (1995a), Hidalgo et al. (1995), Graves (2000), Richards (2001a), Harwood (2010a), Tomlinson and Masuhara (2010a) and Tomlinson (2011a) all contain helpfully detailed accounts of materials development; Graves (1996) draws on six such accounts in a perceptive analytical study of course development processes. Maley (2011) describes what he calls 'scissors and paste' and process approaches to materials development. Tomlinson (2011a) contains two papers on technological developments.

Whether teachers should be *trained* to create original materials is a question we will return to in Chapter 4. At this point, it is perhaps sufficient to repeat the conclusion of Hutchinson and Waters (1987), who saw this as 'a last resort, when all other possibilities of providing materials have been exhausted' (p.125).

# 7. Teachers as reflective practitioners

## 7.1 Reflective practice

Schön's (1984) discussion of the reflective practitioner and Wallace's (1991) argument for a reflective approach in English language teacher education established the foundation for the now widely accepted view that reflection on practice is a defining characteristic of teacher professionalism. This belief underpins the view of teacher roles outlined in this chapter. Reflective teachers will take into account all the relevant factors in the context, but then determine their goals and design their course. If they are expected to work with a coursebook and to use specific parts of the coursebook, they will make up their own minds about how to use, adapt and supplement the material. They will also reflect on their decisions.

## 7.2 Innovation and experimentation

One of the implications of the discussion above of adaptation and supplementation is that teachers will not be content simply to use coursebooks as they are, but will be actively looking for ways to get as much out of them as they possibly can, and then bring in additional material to bridge any gaps that they have identified.

Evaluative coursebook-based lesson-planning along these lines is one form of reflective practice. The adjustments made during a lesson (Schön's 'reflection-in-action') are another. Reflection after the event (Schön's reflection 'on action'), on what went well and less well, and what further changes might need to be made to materials or procedures (or any other aspect of the lesson plan) completes this phase of the reflective cycle.

In the quotation below, Broudy (nd, cited in Graves, 2000: 168) reflects on the experience of teaching a unit of materials she has designed herself:

> I still like most of the materials I developed for this module. However, they are only a resource, to be selected or adapted as it seems appropriate. I must remember that it is not the materials themselves, but what the students do with them that is important.

She adds:

> On my first go-round, I interpreted sequencing to mean that every lesson plan should be perfectly planned out and timed. However, such preciseness makes the lessons too materials-centered and thus too rigid. Classroom management is important; good pacing and time use are essential for enjoyable, effective learning. However, as Stevick (1980)

points out, there needs to be a proper balance between teacher control and student initiative. (Broudy, nd, cited in Graves, 2000: ibid.)

The concluding sentences in both of these quotations underline the need for flexibility in materials, and in the materials designer a willingness to let go. Jolly and Bolitho (2011) include in their 'materials writer's kitbag' the following items: 'phials containing small doses of courage and honesty enabling writer to throw away materials that do not work or cease to enchant'. Another phial needed is perseverance, admirably illustrated in Lackman's (2010) painstakingly critical reflection on the four versions of an activity that led up to the procedure he was satisfied with. Tomlinson's (2011d) assertion that 'We need to innovate and experiment if we are really to find out how we could make language-learning materials more effective' (p.439) was made in the context of a discussion about cooperation between universities and publishers, but it applies equally to teachers and their own classrooms.

## 7.3 In-use and post-use evaluation

In their conclusion to a discussion of adaptation, Tomlinson and Masuhara (2004: 18) state: 'adapting materials can help you produce materials that you want to teach because you enjoy teaching them. If whilst-use and post-use evaluation can be included in the process, you can feel confident that your students are enjoying your adapted materials and that they are learning the target language successfully'. There is no guarantee, of course, that evaluation will reveal the kind of positive results Tomlinson and Masuhara seem to be promising, but there are two reasons why in-use and post-use evaluation are necessary: (1) if we do not evaluate the response to and effectiveness of materials, we have no way of knowing if they were a suitable choice, and (2) evaluation can provide information which enables us to improve upon the materials and/or the way in which they were used. It follows that in-use and post-use evaluation have a place in reflective practice. Indeed, we might expect that teachers who take the trouble to adapt materials, provide supplementary materials and develop their own materials will naturally reflect on how successful these appeared to be and, if necessary, modify them further in the light of experience (for discussion and examples of the revision process, see, for example, Lynch, 1996; McGrath, 2002; Jolly & Bolitho, 2011).

Logically, coursebooks should be subject to the same process. Coursebook selection, discussed in Section 3.3, may be seen as the end of one phase of evaluation, but as Cunningsworth (1995) and others have argued in-use and post-use evaluation are also important. Ellis (1997) has pointed out that retrospective evaluation should be seen not just as a means of evaluating the specific materials that have been used; it is also 'a means of testing the validity of a predictive evaluation, and may point to ways in which the predictive instruments can be improved for future use' (p.37). McGrath (2002) and Masuhara (2011) both describe a range of procedures and processes for systematic in-use and post-use evaluation. These include the involvement of learners.

## 8. The role of learners in materials evaluation and design

Discussions of learner-centred teaching frequently make the point that learners should have some input to decisions about not just what they should learn and how they should learn but also what they should learn through or with – that is, materials. On one level, this might mean no more than consulting learners – for example, about their interests or preferred activity-types (for very different approaches, see, for example, Spratt, 1999 and Johansson, 2006). Feedback on materials can also be elicited from learners either at the point of selection or while materials are being used (see, for example, Breen & Candlin, 1987; Peacock, 1997b; Davis, Garside & Rinvolucri, 1998; McGrath, 2002). In such cases, learner input is used as a contribution to teacher decision-making.

A rather different kind of relationship is implied by one of the tasks that readers of Wright (1987) are encouraged to try out. This involves learners planning and continuously evaluating their own course. Having first gathered information on any syllabuses, prescribed materials and tests relevant to the group, the teacher asks learners to respond to the following set of prompts:

**Objectives**: What do you want to achieve?

**Evaluation**: How do you want to be evaluated?

**Working modes**: How would you like to work in the class – with your friends or with the teacher leading class activities?

**Activities**: What sorts of activity and language learning activity do you want to do?

**Materials**: What sorts of learning materials would you like to work with? Textbooks/Newspapers and books in English/Magazines/Tape recordings of native English speakers? (Wright, 1987: 141)

Learners are subsequently expected to set learning objectives, choose working modes, learning materials and activities and keep a running record of what they have done (for more general discussion of negotiated (process) syllabuses, see, for example, Nunan, 1988b; Tudor, 1996; and Breen and Littlejohn, 2000).

As regards materials, the suggestion has also been made that learners be asked to produce materials that can be used for teaching. Allwright (1978) lays a logical basis for this on the grounds of teacher overload and learner under-involvement (see also Clarke, 1989). Deller (1990) and Campbell and

Kryszewska (1992) are book-length accounts of implementing this idea. Perhaps inevitably, individual published reports of classroom experiments tend to be positive (see McGrath, 2002 for a review). Based on these reports, McGrath (2002) offers the following unequivocal conclusions concerning the benefits of learner-generated materials:

> When learners are actively and creatively involved, motivation is increased; such activities as peer teaching (including correction) constitute a valuable and valued learning experience and can contribute to group solidarity. There are also benefits for the teacher. Monitoring learners as they discuss and prepare materials raises the teacher's awareness of individual or general difficulties. Some of the material is potentially re-usable with learners in other classes. Teacher-preparation time is reduced. And because there will always be an element of unpredictability, the classroom is a more interesting place for the teacher as well as learners. (p.178)

Current research in Singapore involving approximately 100 (mainly primary-school) teachers (McGrath, forthcoming) is investigating what work on learner-generated materials actually requires of the teacher in terms of preparation and troubleshooting, and whether teachers feel the effort involved is really worthwhile.

In the course of previous sections, our focus has gradually shifted from materials provided for the teacher to the teacher as a provider (through adaptation, selection or development) of materials. Learners were always present, but only as a reference point. The writers referred to in this section conceive of a more active role for the learner, one in which the learner is not only a critical consumer but also, potentially, a provider of materials. For this to happen, however, both teachers and learners have to be persuaded of the benefits of a readjustment of traditional roles. We return to this topic in Chapter 7.

## 9. Summary

Most of the teacher roles discussed in this chapter can be grouped together under one of two headings: **teacher as evaluator** (selection of textbooks and other materials; lesson planning decisions, including selection/omission, adaptation and supplementation; in-use evaluation; post-use evaluation) or **teacher as designer** (course design; adaptation of textbook and other materials; original materials design). As we saw in Section 8, however, **responsibility for materials evaluation and provision might also be shared with learners.** The next chapter considers what this view of teacher and learner roles might mean for teacher education.

# CHAPTER FOUR

# Teacher educator perspectives

> Where's the coursebook? It's in the wastebasket.
> (Harmer, 2001: 5)
>
> Teacher training in ESL/EFL seems to be more concerned with teacher creation of materials . . . rather than with training in effective textbook use.
> (Byrd, 1995b: 7)

## 1. Introduction

As we saw in Chapter Three, teachers are expected to possess the awareness, knowledge and skills needed to fulfil roles relating to materials at what are potentially two levels of responsibility:

- to design a course; this involves the selection of materials and the evaluation of the course as a whole
- to plan, deliver and evaluate lessons within an overall course design; this involves adaptation and, conceivably, supplementation and materials writing.

In practice, the responsibilities for course design and coursebook selection (where there is a choice) often lie with an institutional manager (e.g. Head of Department) or a small group of teachers. Many teachers may therefore not have the freedom to design their own courses or select the materials on which courses are based. It is nevertheless seen as desirable that they should know enough about these processes to make a contribution to decisions if there is an opportunity to do so. At the level of lesson planning, however, all teachers are considered to have a responsibility to evaluate and select from such materials as are available and, if necessary, adapt and supplement them. Some may also feel the desire – or need – to develop original materials to supplement prescribed materials or as an alternative to available materials. The range of competences required at even this second level of responsibility is unlikely to be acquired simply through experience – at least not in the first year or two of teaching. Given the importance of materials in language learning and teaching, this constitutes a powerful argument for a sustained focus on materials evaluation and design within both pre-service and in-service teacher education programmes.

In one or more of their several forms, materials are, of course, inevitably a focus of teacher education. For instance, a typically practical pre-service course may include a demonstration of how to organize boardwork, how to draw stick figures or how to make and use flashcards to teach and practise vocabulary. During a theoretically oriented course on Methodology, at pre-service or Masters level, on the other hand, recorded materials in the form of drills or communication games may be used as illustrations of specific methods. Or in a module on Curriculum Planning or Syllabus Design, the final two or three sessions might be devoted to implementation, in the form of materials selection and design. Each of these references to materials is valid in the context given. Language teachers need an awareness of how technology (including the use of the board – be it blackboard, whiteboard or interactive whiteboard) can be used to present language and provide for effective practice. They should also understand that teaching materials are based on particular theories (and beliefs) about the nature of language and how it is best learned; and they may be interested to know where materials selection or design fit into a curriculum planning model. However, what the designers of teacher education programmes need to bear in mind is that technology, like the materials which it is used to present, is no more than an aid to learning; that for a pre-service trainee, a knowledge of language teaching history is less important than familiarization with the materials used in schools; and that even on a Master's course, the time spent selecting and/or designing materials within a course on Curriculum Planning will probably be more directly relevant to most participants' day-to-day work than all the other sessions put together. If teachers are to acquire and develop the range of skills referred to in Chapter Three, then a more integrated and systematic approach is needed; in short, a component dedicated to materials evaluation and design.

This chapter discusses just two of the many issues involved in designing such a component: the specification of objectives and content, and how this might differ for pre-service and in-service programmes, and the predictability or otherwise of course participants' work contexts. Sections 2–4 address the first of these issues. **Section 2** considers whether coursebooks ought to be a focus of teacher education and the implications of a positive answer to this question. The obvious alternative to coursebook-based teaching is for teachers to prepare their own materials, and **Section 3** deals with the question of whether training in materials development should be included in a non-specialized teacher education programme. **Section 4** is also concerned with programme scope, in this case the relationship between instructional technology and materials evaluation and design. **Section 5** argues that, while work contexts should be taken into account where possible, teacher roles provide a more logical starting-point for course design. Reference will be made throughout to the teacher education literature, but the conclusions offered are my own.

Chapter Ten contains a detailed practical discussion of how the objectives discussed here can be realized.

## 2. Aims and content of a materials evaluation and design component

### 2.1 Introduction

To judge from the discussion of teacher roles in Chapter Three, teacher education in materials evaluation and design might embrace all of the following:

- course design (including, as a first step, context and needs analyses)
- selection of coursebooks and other materials
- effective coursebook use (lesson planning, adaptation)
- sourcing of supplementary materials
- materials writing (supplementary materials and stand-alone materials)
- in-use and post-use materials evaluation
- learner involvement in materials evaluation and design.

However, teacher education courses vary in length and level. They prepare participants, who differ in innumerable ways, to teach learners of a particular age or no particular age in a specific context or no specific context. What this means is that in any particular context teacher educators have to make decisions about what to include and what to emphasize. At pre-service level, in particular, one of these decisions concerns coursebooks.

## 2.2 The coursebook issue

The attitude of teacher educators towards the use or otherwise of coursebooks in language learning will have a profound influence on whether – and if so, how – these are treated within a teacher education course. This section starts from the anti-coursebook view (i.e. the view that coursebooks should not be used in language teaching–learning and therefore have no place in teacher education) and its related vision, of the teacher as course/materials developer. It then presents the arguments for the pro-coursebook view (in this case, the justifications for a focus on coursebooks in teacher education) and what this might encompass.

### 2.2.1 The anti-coursebook view

Coursebooks have come in for considerable criticism from language teachers, as we saw in Chapter One, with the result that some opt not to use them even when they have the opportunity to do so. On some teacher education courses too, the mere mention of a coursebook may be anathema. Harmer (2001) recalls interviewing teachers who had done four-week training courses at International House, London in the 1970s and early-mid 1980s. One claimed that he had been told that it was 'a sin to use a coursebook'; another recounted that it was only when he started to work in another school that he realized that some institutions used coursebooks. The extent of the negativity towards coursebooks is amusingly illustrated by another example from Harmer (2001:5):

> I once knew a teacher trainer who held up a coursebook in front of his trainees and said 'Do you know what the only good use for one of these is?' When they looked blankly at him he dropped it into the wastebasket. 'The only good use for a coursebook,' he said, pointing downwards, 'is as a visual aid: Where's the coursebook? It's in the wastebasket.'

The real punchline follows: 'Since the book had been written by the trainer's school director, this may not have been the most tactful thing he ever said . . .' (ibid.).

A more recent version of the same attitude to training can be seen in a paper by Thornbury (2000), who was referred to earlier as the founder of the Dogme in ELT movement. Thornbury describes how he and a fellow trainer determined to 'wage war on materials-driven lessons'. Materials, in this case, were not simply coursebooks: 'Photocopies were proscribed; the OHP was banished . . . Real talk, usually relegated to the bookends of the lesson proper, had to form the lesson core. And the teacher had to talk – not at the students or even to them – but with them'. The trainees in this case were teachers on post-experience Diploma courses and might therefore be assumed to be better capable of coping than those in Harmer's anecdote, and the motive – to increase communicative interaction between teacher and learners – was laudable. However, to deliberately deprive teachers and learners of potentially helpful aids seems not only perverse but also an abuse of power. Crawford (2002) quotes a contributor to an online forum who felt that 'a teacher's decision *not* to use a textbook may actually be "a touch of imperialism" . . . because it retains control in the hands of the teacher rather than in the learners' (p.84).

What we have here, in effect, are striking personal examples of the divide between (some) teacher training institutions and schools (whether in the private sector or the state sector). Recent research in Australia summarized in Horsley (2007) of initial teacher education courses in a variety of subjects found that these included compulsory courses on information and communication technology (ICT) and how to incorporate this into lesson activities, whereas 'all students reported that they received no training or instruction in the use of teaching and learning materials and textbooks' (pp.252–3). Ironically, 'the technology rich environment in university teacher education contrasted significantly to the lack of ICT infrastructure in many schools' (p.254), and in preparing their lessons the student teachers 'used school texts far more than other resources' (p.253). Most tellingly, in one of the key documents also surveyed as part of the research, a 500-page review carried out for the state of Victoria (*Step Up, Step In, Step Out*, 2005), there was no mention of teaching or learning materials.

Horsley's conclusion sets out seven key propositions. All have general relevance for ELT and seem worth quoting in detail:

1 **Teacher education discourages the use of textbooks:** One consequence of this 'ideology' is that institutions do not make available to student teachers the range of published resources used in schools. This means that, in advance of their practicum, they are unlikely to receive a 'systematic introduction to adapting and modifying textbooks for groups with diverse learning abilities and cultural backgrounds' (p.255). Note that the argument relates to textbooks and not a specific textbook. The concern is with generic, transferable skills. An institution need not therefore have copies of a vast range of textbooks, but trainees do need an opportunity to familiarize themselves with a variety of textbooks and other materials.

2 **Lack of school textbooks in teacher education courses contributes to perceptions about teacher education being disconnected from schooling:** Textbooks are used in schools because they reduce preparation time. However, in their teacher preparation courses, student teachers do not learn how to use them. They thus have a steep learning curve under time pressure. This point applies even

if trainees have had some exposure to textbooks, but they will presumably approach an unfamiliar book with more confidence if they have some insight into how textbooks are organized and what is expected of them.

3 **Teacher education students use textbooks in schools significantly during practicum experiences:** Studies of teacher education in general have shown that between 75 and 85 per cent of student teachers use textbooks when developing units of work and planning lessons (Loewenberg-Ball & Feiman-Nemser, 2005). 'One of Loewenberg-Ball's students expressed the view that "even though I was trained to be critical of textbooks I had no alternative" (p.192). Another remarked that "teaching and planning all day long . . . is an overwhelming task" (p.193)' (Horsley, 2007: 256). Textbooks embody professional experience, pedagogical content knowledge which, as yet, student teachers do not have: 'the topics, activities and approaches that experienced teachers have found useful in promoting teaching and learning with students' (ibid.).

4 **Teacher education students use school textbooks to learn requisite knowledge:** For student teachers, a textbook can provide quick access to students' level and the kinds of work they have been doing. 'Textbooks provide new teachers and beginning teachers with a guide to the depth and breadth of knowledge required, the concepts involved, the key points that students need to learn and the level at which the lesson needs to be developed' (p.257). As noted earlier, for non-native speakers of English who lack confidence in their own proficiency, they serve as a valuable support; and for both non-native speakers and native speakers, they also indicate how the language can be broken down, integrated, and sequenced in order to facilitate learning and provide opportunities for practice.

5 **Resourcing lessons is a fundamental aspect of teaching:** 'All classroom tasks, activities and teaching and learning strategies are based on resources and materials, and are not independent of them. . . Teaching and learning resource selection, procuring and accessing is a fundamental aspect of teaching' (pp.256–7). Teachers need to know what materials are available, and be able to justify their selections. If access to the internet is available, guided browsing and evaluation of websites should also form part of this resource familiarization process.

6 **Teacher education neglects textbook pedagogy:** The term 'textbook pedagogy' was coined by Lambert (2000, cited in Horsley 2007: 258) to refer to 'the way teachers use texts in the classroom, how they access and adapt texts, and how they create a context for their use' (p.258). Logically, teacher education should introduce student

teachers to these processes, rather than relying on their learning through experience.
7 Textbooks and teaching and learning materials are changing: 'Textbooks have continued to evolve and change and have become more complex' (p.259). This is certainly true of ELT textbooks, as we have seen earlier. This is, of course, an argument for training which focuses on textbooks, as noted above, rather than a single textbook.

## 2.2.2 The alternative to a coursebook: write your own materials!

In the Australian context, as described by Horsley, trainees had access to textbooks in the practicum schools but had not been trained in how to use them. In other contexts, the anti-textbook view extends to the practicum context as well. Highlighting the contrast between her school and College of Education experiences in Hong Kong, Yuen (1997) writes about her own introduction to teaching:

> In Chinese 'study' means 'read the textbooks'. From the first day I went to school, I had to bring my textbooks. Throughout my school years, I learned with textbooks. It was not until I entered the College of Education that I was told not to use textbooks, and I had to design and produce my own teaching materials during teaching practice.

This will no doubt strike a chord with many teachers.

Commenting on what lies behind this pressure to produce original materials and writing about (American school) teachers and teacher educators in general, Loewenberg-Ball and Cohen (1996) make a number of important points:

> . . . [teacher] educators often disparage textbooks, and many reform-oriented teachers repudiate them, announcing disdainfully that they do not use text[book]s. This idealization of professional autonomy leads to the view that good teachers do not follow textbooks, but instead make their own curriculum. Advocates of this view, which is consistent with American individualism, acclaim teachers who create original materials and lessons. Textbooks, and the commercial and political constraints that shape their production, are viewed as a conservative influence (Ben-Peretz, 1990). Curriculum materials are seen to constrain and control both knowledge and teaching (Apple and Jungck, 1990; Ball and Feiman-Nemser, 1988), limiting students' opportunities to learn (Elliott, 1990). Teachers who invent lessons are said to be creative and imaginative. This hostility to text[books]s, and the idealized image of the individual

professional, have inhibited careful consideration of the constructive role that curriculum might play'. (Loewenberg-Ball & Cohen, 1996: 6, square brackets added)

What is striking here is the reported strength of feeling of those opposed to textbooks, expressed in the words 'repudiate' and 'hostility', and their promotion of the 'creative and imaginative' individual, as a bulwark against the 'conservative' and 'constraining' influences of commercial curriculum materials. Loewenberg-Ball and Cohen's own attitude to these views comes through clearly in their use (and repetition) of the word 'idealized' and, indeed, the negative connotations of 'disparage' and, towards the end of this extract, 'inhibited'; the force of 'disdainfully' in particular leaves us in no doubt that, for these writers, the spurning of coursebooks is sheer arrogance.

O'Neill (1982: 105) recounts a relevant anecdote, an interesting case of ESP at one remove. He had just spent three weeks in a German shipyard teaching English to German technicians who would then instruct Iranians in the maintenance and repair of submarines, and was handing over to his replacement, 'a young intelligent teacher' fresh off a course in applied linguistics at a British university:

'My God, you haven't been using a coursebook, have you?' he said, when he saw my notes. It was as if one doctor trained in the latest medical techniques had discovered that a colleague had been bleeding one of his patients with leeches. Indeed, I had been using a textbook for one central part of the course. My replacement believed that this was inherently wrong. His objections boiled down to the fact that he didn't want the people he was teaching to know what he was going to do the next day. 'It takes away the element of suspense. Besides, I don't like using other people's materials. It's so uncreative!' he exclaimed.

There is an important difference, of course, between an individual teacher taking the decision not to use a coursebook, with all that this implies by way of additional preparation and a possible negative reaction from learners, and teacher educators forbidding their trainees to use coursebooks, which flies in the face of reason. If coursebooks are being used in the schools where trainees do their teaching practice, it makes sense (and is less disturbing for the students) if they make use of these coursebooks. Novice teachers, and especially non-native speakers of English who lack confidence in their own language proficiency, find reassurance in the support that a coursebook can provide. On courses for more experienced teachers, there might be good reasons for encouraging teachers to write their own materials, but little justification for insisting that they do so. Even excellent teachers are not necessarily capable of writing good materials, as Johnson (2003) discovered when running a materials writing course for Italian teachers of English.

## 2.3 The pro-coursebook view

Let us be clear. The arguments for including the study of coursebooks in pre-service and in-service teacher education courses are not the same as those for using coursebooks in language courses. Whatever their own views, teacher educators owe it to participants who may use coursebooks from choice or necessity to consider how they might be used (more) effectively.

### 2.3.1 Coursebooks and pre-service courses

Coursebooks are widely used and, as noted above, can provide much-needed support for the beginning teacher. Senior (2006) tells the story of a trainee teacher who was diagnosed by her trainers as suffering from 'text avoidance syndrome'. As reported by the trainee, 'their argument was, "The people who wrote the textbook are the experts. Why are you recreating the wheel? They've done the hard work for you, they're the brilliant ones who have been in the industry forever, Just use their knowledge." Which is true – I mean, I'm a new teacher, so what do I know about it' (Senior, 2006: 49).

To deal with coursebooks only incidentally on pre-service courses or not to deal with them at all is to sell the trainee short. Trainees need to know what coursebooks can offer, what their limitations are, and how they differ, ideally through exploring them analytically. They need to learn how to use them as teaching aids, minimizing or compensating for their limitations and exploiting their strengths. Teacher education can provide the guidance to help them to do this and the awareness, knowledge and skill to make choices for themselves, one of which may be not to use a coursebook. Harmer (2001: 9) argues: '... examination of issues surrounding the design, choice and use of coursebooks ... illuminates just about every theoretical and practical issue which trainees need to examine'.

At pre-service level, a related issue is whether participants can – and therefore should be asked to – evaluate published materials. Brumfit and Rossner (1982: 129) are in no doubt that they cannot and should not:

> Until experience has been gained working with other people's materials, within other people's syllabuses, decisions about what are and are not good materials and syllabuses can only reflect the external views of those who train, rather than the internal feelings of students/teachers themselves.

In Chapter Three, a distinction was made between materials evaluation and materials analysis. As far as short pre-service courses are concerned, materials analysis might be concerned with, for example, helping trainees to understand how textbooks are constructed, and to identify the beliefs and principles on which they are based. On longer pre-service or in-service courses, it might be wider-ranging and go much deeper (see, for example, Littlejohn & Windeatt, 1989; Ellis, 2011; Littlejohn, 2011). Evaluation, on the other hand, is concerned with making judgements about, for instance, whether we *agree* with the beliefs and principles on which the materials are based (Breen & Candlin, 1987), on whether there is *a good match* (Hutchinson & Waters, 1987) between materials and our analysis of needs in a specific context, and on whether one set of materials appears to be *more suitable* for that context than another.

According to Brumfit and Rossner, trainee teachers do not have the experience to make judgements about the strengths and weaknesses of materials or their potential suitability for specific contexts. However, at the point when trainees begin teaching practice and have to plan lessons which take account of their students, this argument loses some of its force. As trainees gain awareness of students' needs, we would expect them to take progressively more evaluative decisions as regards materials (e.g. whether an explanation needs to be paraphrased or supplemented, whether different or additional examples are necessary, whether to use this exercise or activity or whether to adapt or replace it).

Training in textbook use also extends to consideration of the need for supplementation. Where this consists of borrowing from existing sources (e.g. other textbooks, online sources), this may seem relatively unproblematic for an experienced teacher: having identified a specific need, the teacher locates potentially suitable source material and uses it unchanged or adapts it following the procedures and principles discussed in Chapter Three (Section 4). However, beginner teachers may have little or no knowledge of what suitable sources might be and where to find them. It therefore follows that familiarization with as wide a range of resources as possible should form part of any pre-service course.

Whether trainees should also be introduced to systematic procedures for the selection of coursebooks and other materials (as envisaged in Chapter Three, Section 3) should not depend simply on what will be expected of them in their future teaching context. The point was made in Chapter Three that even if teachers are not in a position to take decisions, they may still be able to influence them. It therefore seems preferable to provide trainees with some evaluation tools and experience of using them rather than leave them to fend for themselves.

## 2.3.2 Coursebooks and in-service courses

Teachers with experience of using coursebooks will have views about what they like/dislike and what they want in a coursebook. If they use supplementary materials, they will probably also know what they look for in such materials. They may nevertheless feel the need for help in selecting coursebooks and other materials more systematically. This can obviously be combined with awareness-raising concerning new materials (which might include potentially useful websites).

A shift away from coursebook dependence can be seen very clearly in this account by a Singaporean teacher:

> In the first few years in my teaching career, I was totally dependent on the course books. I was obviously course book-led. I would teach my students from page 1 to the next. Each lesson was carried out step-by-step. I would start by reading the passage aloud followed with lessons on grammar items and so on. There was really no need to source for supplementary materials, to adapt or differentiate the lesson since everything is provided. Needless to say, there was no differentiated instruction since the course book is a one-size-fits all. I am almost embarrassed to admit that I was very contented with the way things were. Whatever I was teaching in my class was duplicated in the 5 to 6 other classes in my level. There was a sense of security for us beginning teachers. I don't feel we should be too hard on ourselves for the way we were as novice teachers.
>
> However, after a couple of years of having that Instructional Manual by my side, I started to deviate. I started going to class with newspaper cutouts, brochures, and even maps of Sentosa [an island close to Singapore] for the lessons. I started to depend less and less on the course books. If the aim of the lesson was to teach pronouns, I will teach it. I made sure that I 'covered the syllabus' albeit my own way. (Asmoraniye Shaffie, 2011)

In her first few years of teaching, this teacher was teaching by the book, literally. This gave her a sense of security, and her students no doubt also felt secure in the knowledge that they were being thoroughly prepared for any tests. However, as the writer came to realize, textbooks are simply aids to achieving course goals. As she gained in confidence, she made less use of the book.

This was clearly a positive development. The teacher had taken control and was selecting authentic materials which she felt would appeal to learners. If this kind of development can be predicted as teachers gain experience, is training in textbook use really necessary? Teacher educators are in no doubt that it is. Richards's (2001b:16) views are typical: 'teachers need training and experience in adapting and modifying textbooks as well as in using authentic materials and in creating their own teaching materials'. Teachers can be expected to develop some strategies for adapting and supplementing textbooks to meet learners' needs, but teacher education can accelerate the process (and perhaps make teaching–learning easier). In-service teacher education can also raise awareness of a wider range of possibilities and encourage reflection on alternatives to practices that have become habitual.

In the example above, the teacher expresses a preference for authentic materials in preference to the coursebook. There will be occasions when this is clearly the right decision, but there will also be occasions when coursebook materials can be adapted with relatively little effort. In-service teacher education offers opportunities to explore such options and develop new skills.

For teachers using coursebooks, one of these skills is the development of supplementary materials. There is arguably a qualitative gap between the kind of borrowing-based supplementation discussed above in relation to pre-service courses (which on in-service courses can have its counterpart in pooling recommendations and discovering new sources) and the development of original supplementary materials, whether these are in the form of a worksheet, text-based activities or larger-scale projects. Materials writing is discussed below, in Section 3.

Teachers need not shoulder the whole burden for supplementary materials preparation, of course. The argument has been advanced (see Chapter Three, Section 8) that learners should be involved in supplying supplementary materials. This is not a new idea, but it is not one that has been widely discussed in the professional literature. In-service courses would seem an ideal context for discussion of the pros and cons, for consideration of such issues as the preparation of learners for a new form of autonomy, and – if time and circumstances permit – for small-scale experimentation and feedback.

## 3. Materials writing revisited

The impression given by the more fanatical opponents of textbooks is that teachers face an *either/or* choice (almost a moral choice) between using a textbook and writing one's own materials. This is not the case: teachers can use a coursebook *and* write their own materials. Coursebook-based teaching is a continuum from frequent to less frequent coursebook use, with opportunities for autonomy and creativity ranging from minor forms of adaptation to extensive supplementation.

In this section, we are concerned with both writing as a form of coursebook supplementation (e.g. the preparation of worksheets or text-based activities) and the writing of more ambitious – and potentially stand-alone – materials. As discussed in Chapter Three (Section 6), these might range from a single thematic unit to a component on a skill such as writing but fall short of the development of a whole course.

There are, naturally enough, differences of opinion within the teacher education literature as to whether courses (pre-service or in-service) ought to equip participants to write their own materials.

Let us begin with those who are opposed to the idea of teachers writing materials. Allwright's (1981: 6) view that teachers and textbook writers fulfil complementary but distinct roles because they have different kinds of expertise has already been quoted. Brumfit and Rossner (1982) are a little more open to the idea of trainees writing materials but nonetheless quite guarded:

> *Materials construction* (which does not, of course, require specialized training) is something which can grow out of dissatisfaction with existing materials (used in personal teaching experience), and *is inappropriate as a goal for initial training.* (Again, we should emphasize that we are not objecting to the writing of materials during initial courses, in order to enable trainees to understand some of the problems of materials design. We are concerned with the idea that teachers can or should leave initial training courses able and willing to base much of their teaching on materials they write themselves.) (Brumfit & Rossner, 1982: 129–130, emphases added)

There is an acknowledgement here that exercises in materials writing can raise trainees' awareness of 'some of the problems of materials design'. Brumfit and Rossner would probably also concede that if trainees are dissatisfied with the materials they are asked to use on teaching practice, they need to know how to make appropriate changes to these materials (omission or other forms of adaptation) or know where to find something to supplement what is available – and agree that these kinds of knowledge and awareness ought therefore also to form part of an initial training course. Where they seem to draw the line is between materials writing conceived largely as an awareness-raising activity and the expectation that student teachers should be capable of *originating most* of the materials they will need for teaching.

What is most striking about the quotation, however, is the opening statement: 'Materials construction . . . does not require specialized training'. As we saw in Chapter Three (Section 6), there is now a growing body of literature offering principles and practical advice for language teachers on the topic of materials development and there are also specialized courses, short and long, providing such training (see, for example, Tomlinson, 2003c: 446, 456, 460). Perceptions within teacher education of teacher roles have also changed, as can be seen in the reference in the quotation below to action research as a component of teacher education programmes:

> It is not until teachers have attempted to produce their own materials that they finally begin to develop a set of criteria to evaluate materials produced by others. Only then does the full range of options, from blind acceptance of other materials, through adaptation and supplementation, to the production of 'purpose-built' materials, become clear. The process of materials writing raises almost every issue which is important in learning to teach: the selection and grading of language, knowledge of

learning theories, socio-cultural appropriacy; the list could be extended. And . . . the current emphasis on action research in teacher education programmes needs to be backed up by the establishment of *materials writing as a key component on initial training courses* and a regular feature of in-service training programmes. (Jolly & Bolitho, 2011: 129, emphasis added)

By initial training courses, Jolly and Bolitho are presumably referring to longer courses (e.g. one-year postgraduate certificates or three-to-four-year BA/B.Ed programmes), where trainees have the opportunity to go through the 'full range of options' described in the quotation, assess what is needed during their practicum, and then write and try out their own materials, adapted or specially written. (For discussion of an in-service BA module based on such principles, see Al-Sinani, Al-Senaidi and Etherton, 2009.)

Support for such writing is, of course, essential. In the quotation below, Samuda (2005) is writing specifically about teachers developing their own tasks, but her comment is equally applicable to any form of materials development:

initiatives towards localized materials production . . . rest on the assumption that the addition of task design to the teaching repertoire is essentially unproblematic, either because it is assumed that teachers have already acquired the relevant design skills to develop tasks . . . or because it is assumed that task design is a non-specialist activity that is easily picked up on the side. (Samuda, 2005: 236)

Underlining the lack of a foundation for such assumptions, she cites Tsui's (2003) example of a teacher who had 'never considered the question of how to design the task in a way that would make it necessary for the students to collaborate for task completion' (p.174, cited in Samuda, 2005: 236) and who did not have 'any principles on which to base her judgment of whether the activities [were] well designed' (p.219, cited in Samuda, ibid.). This example has extra force given the explicit expectations of the Hong Kong Ministry of Education, referred to in Chapter One, that teachers *should* design tasks for their learners.

A further argument advanced for incorporating materials writing into courses – and this applies particularly to in-service courses – is that the use by teachers of materials with which they feel uncomfortable ('teaching against the grain') 'leads to dissatisfaction, a loss of confidence and learning failure' (Jolly & Bolitho, 2011: 129). Such feelings are minimized, Jolly and Bolitho suggest, if teachers are helped to produce their own materials. Moreover, since this process involves teachers 'teaching themselves' it is a form of professional development. We should note here the implicit assumptions that teachers, pre-service and in-service, have a level of language proficiency such that they can write materials which offer an appropriate model for their learners or that their tutors can provide editing/proofreading help.

While it may be true that attempting to develop materials makes one much more aware as an evaluator (Brumfit & Rossner, 1982; Jolly & Bolitho, 2011), it also makes sense for that writing to be contextually motivated. When teachers other than those involved in teacher education programmes decide to write materials, it is usually for one of two reasons: either they are dissatisfied with the materials they are using – the point made by Brumfit and Rossner (1982) – or no suitable materials are available for the purpose they have in mind. If teacher educators take teacher realities seriously, this argues for all materials development within teacher education programmes to be preceded by an evaluative activity of some kind (e.g. identification of a learner need, evaluation of a piece of material). We might therefore envisage a cyclical process in which initially both evaluation and design tasks are very limited and very focused (e.g. at the level of a language exercise), but gradually become larger and more complex.

This kind of systematic accretive approach might be appropriate at pre-service level, but at in-service level there may be another possibility. If teachers have been producing their own materials – for example, worksheets, progress tests – and/or exploiting authentic texts, and are willing for them to be used as input to discussion, these examples can provide an ideal starting-point not only for exploring what is being done and what is possible but also for consideration of other key aspects of organized teaching and learning: aims, methodology, syllabus and the beliefs and theories that underlie these. (See Breen, Candlin, Dam and Gabrielsen (1989) for an interesting account of a long-term in-service programme in which materials 'provided a doorway into wider and more important pedagogic issues' (p.114)). Even if teacher-made materials are not available, it is difficult to imagine a situation in which experienced teachers would not be exercising some degree of autonomy towards the published materials they are using, and discussion of why and how they have exploited or adapted a particular fragment of a book they are using could ultimately lead in the same direction.

We might conclude that training in materials writing is desirable for a number of reasons, some of which are process-related. For instance:

- it stimulates the examination of beliefs and theories concerning teaching and learning
- it prompts consideration of principles which underlie lesson design as well as materials design
- it raises awareness of evaluation criteria
- it enhances teachers' ability to meet learners' needs
- it provides opportunities for professional development.

Materials writing is, however, just one of the 'full set of options' mentioned by Jolly and Bolitho (2011). It is the most demanding, for obvious reasons. In some teacher education contexts, moreover, its relevance might be questioned. Paradoxically, as Byrd (1995b) has pointed out: 'Teacher training in ESL/EFL seems to be more concerned with teacher creation of materials . . . than with training in effective textbook use' (p.7). In contexts where textbook use is required, expected or prevalent, it therefore seems logical that training in adaptation and supplementation should be prioritized and that (unless the Ministry says otherwise, or teachers themselves see this as a need) within non-specialized courses on materials evaluation and design materials writing is presented to teachers as an option rather than an obligation.

## 4. Materials and instructional technology

One way in which publishers seek to improve their product (and keep a step ahead of their competitors) is to make use of new technology, but to use these new materials effectively teachers have to know how to use the technology. For practising teachers, in-service workshops may be organized and ongoing (in-house) support provided. In large institutions offering pre-service teacher training in a range of disciplines, there appear to be three options: (1) a generic course on instructional technology and a separate subject-specific course on materials evaluation and design; (2) two separate subject-specific courses; (3) a single course which combines the two. Let us compare two examples of option 3.

The Ministry of Higher Education (YÖK) in Turkey requires all universities, public and private, to include a course on Educational Technology and Materials Development in their programmes for future English language teachers. This course should contain:

> Concepts of Instructional Technology, characteristics of various types of Instructional Technology. Role and use of Instructional Technology in teaching. Identification of technology needs in the classroom and school. Appropriate planning and management of the use of technology. Using technology to develop 2D and 3D materials, developing teaching tools (worksheets, activities, slides, visual media tools such as DVD, VCD, smart boards,and computer-based tools). Analysing educational software, evaluating teaching tools of varying quality. Internet and distance education, principles of visual design, research pertaining to the effectiveness of teaching materials. The state of Instructional Technology for teaching in Turkey and other countries (translation).

As interpreted by Bilkent University, for example, this is a course about 'the use of technology in teaching: computers, visual teaching aids and all other interactive materials. The production of such materials by student teachers, and the evaluation of these materials when used in teaching'. It is taught for 3 hours a week over 14 semester weeks (Margaret Sands, personal communication).

The time allocated to this course (a total of 42 hours) bears witness to the importance attached to it. As the syllabus indicates, moreover, this is not intended to be simply an illustrated lecture series on how to use a variety of teaching aids. Reference is made to needs-identification, the use of technology to develop teaching materials, the analysis and evaluation of software and other teaching tools, as well as to concepts, principles and research. Taught by a tutor with first-hand knowledge of the school settings in which trainee teachers will find themselves and the kinds of teacher-produced materials that might be useful, a course based on this syllabus would be a helpful form of preparation; and, in the Bilkent version at least, the requirement that student teachers produce their own materials and evaluate these during teaching practice ensures that there is an applied dimension to their learning. One would hope that students would also be encouraged to consider the pros and cons of high-tech, low-tech and no-tech teaching, assess the appropriateness of one form of technology for a specific purpose against another – and devise strategies for coping when there is a power cut.

Now compare this with the treatment of materials and ICT in Table 4.1. This is taken from Unit 4 ('Planning and resources for different teaching contexts') of the 5-unit syllabus for courses leading to the award of the Cambridge ESOL Certificate in Teaching English Language to Adults (CELTA).

**Table 4.1** Extract from CELTA syllabus

| Syllabus content | Successful candidates can: |
|---|---|
| 4.4 The selection, adaptation and evaluation of materials and resources in planning (including computer and other technology-based resources) | a. select and evaluate materials and resources (including use of technology)<br>b. understand the need for and begin to put into practice with due regard for the provisions of copyright, the adaptation of resources and materials to meet the requirements of specific groups of adult students |
| 4.5 Knowledge of commercially produced resources and non-published materials and classroom resources for teaching English to adults | develop a basic working knowledge of some commercially produced and non-published materials and classroom resources for teaching English to adults |

University of Cambridge ESOL Examinations (2011: 10).

Courses offered by Cambridge-approved centres must be based on the syllabus and consist of a minimum of 120 contact hours, including a minimum of six hours' observation of experienced teachers and six hours of assessed practice teaching. They are intended for those with little or no ELT experience or with some experience but little training. A concern for materials evaluation and design runs through all the awards offered by Cambridge ESOL – see http://www.cambridgeesol.org/sector/teaching/index.html.

Unit 4 as a whole is assessed through lesson plans, observed teaching and an assignment. The first few criteria for the assessment of teaching practice are as follows:

(4a) identifying and stating appropriate aims/outcomes for individual lessons

(4b) ordering activities so that they achieve lesson aims/outcomes

(4c) *selecting, adapting or designing materials, activities, resources and technical aids appropriate for the lesson.* (CELTA syllabus, p.15, emphasis added)

These criteria are noteworthy for three reasons. First, they imply a particular approach to lesson planning, one in which lesson aims/learning outcomes are determined first and materials selected subsequently, as a way of achieving these aims (as recommended in Chapter Three). Second, we might note that while adaptation is expected the use of 'or', in 'adapting *or* designing materials', indicates that design (or what we have earlier referred to as 'supplementation' and 'materials writing') is an alternative to adaptation and not a requirement of every lesson. And third, 'materials, activities, resources and technical aids' are grouped together as means which enable outcomes to be achieved. The CELTA syllabus and assessment criteria and the Turkish syllabus both express pedagogical expectations, but these are rather different. Moreover, the Turkish syllabus is weighted towards technology and the development of teaching tools using technology, whereas the CELTA syllabus appears to prioritize materials adaptation (though design is also mentioned) and awareness-raising concerning resources. Two further points of comparison concern the scope of the two syllabuses and the time available. The CELTA syllabus contains an additional section (Unit 5.4) on the use of teaching materials and resources, but is nevertheless clearly much narrower in scope than the Turkish syllabus. Doubts might be raised in relation to both syllabuses about the time allocated to materials. Within the CELTA syllabus, Sections 4.4–4.5 and 5.4 represent only a small part of the 120 contact hours; as regards the Turkish syllabus, it seems possible that the technological tail will wag the materials dog. All courses operate under time constraints, however, and this simply points to the need for continuing education in materials evaluation and design, both formally organized and self-directed.

## 5. Training context and teaching context

In the previous section we looked at an extract from the CELTA syllabus. Courses based on this syllabus are typically taught intensively over a four-week period. Trainees on such a course, at a language school in London, for example, might be aged between 20 and 60, say, of any nationality, and with potentially very different educational backgrounds and work experience, and the course would usually provide a daily mixed diet of input and teaching practice with multilingual groups of young adults – and frenzied preparation every evening for teaching the following day. In this situation, teacher educators must try to balance support tailored to teaching in the *training* context with generalized preparation for teaching beyond the course. This may turn out to involve teaching children (as well as or instead of adults) in mixed-nationality groups in the United Kingdom or in a country where groups of learners are monolingual.

What this scenario reveals is that the starting-point for such 'open access' pre-service courses cannot be a defined context. It can only be a specification of the roles that teachers need to play and the knowledge, skills and awareness that they need to fulfil these roles. Teacher educators in other contexts also have to prepare trainees for the unpredictable. González Moncada (2006), for instance, points out that student teachers following an undergraduate programme at the Universidad de Antioquia in Colombia may, after graduation, find themselves working in an institution bursting with technological resources or with no resources at all. Asked how trainees might be better prepared for materials use on teaching practice, a teacher in the first kind of environment suggested: 'You should expose students to the use of multimedia software and the adaptation of Internet pages', whereas his counterpart working in a very poor neighbourhood argued: 'As a student [teacher] one needs to learn to work with nothing. I cannot ask my students to buy a textbook, a dictionary, or to get some money to pay for copies. I just have the board and chalk. It's very hard to be creative under these circumstances. I wish student teachers could visit my school and face the reality of displaced people who have nothing' (González Moncada, 2006: 10). González Moncada's principal conclusions are that student teachers need: 'to be exposed to real school contexts [and] face the limitations . . . experienced in regular English classrooms'; to have 'longer and deeper training in the use of technical and non-technical materials'; and to 'be acquainted with different possibilities to make adequate choices' (p.11). A more general conclusion, which takes account of variation in teaching contexts, might be that the syllabus for a pre-service teacher education course in materials evaluation and design should be based on a specification of core teacher roles vis-à-vis materials, as discussed in this chapter, but at the same time equip trainees to cope flexibly with a variety of predictable constraints (a point we return to in Chapter Eight).

When teachers have experienced one or more specific teaching contexts and have a sense of their own needs, they expect to take away from a course not just new knowledge and useful insights but also practical ideas that can be applied. Writing of postgraduate programmes in English-speaking countries, Canniveng and Martinez (2003) make the claim that teacher educators on such courses do not take participants' contexts and previous experience into account: 'General criteria related to materials development, evaluation and adaptation is usually fed to the trainees but there is little time paid to the process of how to develop personal specific criteria to suit the trainees. As a consequence, the trainees do not always engage in self reflection' (p.483). Teacher educators who teach on such courses and endeavour not only to gain an understanding of participants' work-contexts but also make use of tasks which encourage individuals to reflect on how general principles and procedures can be applied or adapted in their own contexts will no doubt feel irritated by such unsupported assertions. They might also argue that a legitimate aim of a postgraduate programme is to equip participants for possible changed responsibilities commensurate with their new knowledge and skills – and their shiny new qualifications (Tomlinson & Masuhara, 2003).

# 6. Summary

The argument advanced in this chapter is that language learning materials are such a key element in the teaching–learning encounter that consideration of their selection, use and design cannot be consigned to the periphery of a teacher education programme, narrowly constrained within wide-ranging courses dealing with curriculum/syllabus or method, or labelled as optional: materials evaluation and design should be a central (core) component of both pre-service programmes and post-experience postgraduate programmes. The chapter has furthermore suggested that at pre-service level aims and content should be related to predictable teacher roles. A number of these roles cluster around the use of effective use of textbooks. It therefore follows that textbooks should normally be a focus, but opportunities should also be provided to explore other resources. Trainees may not go on to use textbooks, but they will use materials. They therefore need to know how to source alternative materials, evaluate them, exploit them fully and, if necessary, modify them and supplement them. On in-service courses, the starting-point where possible should be the materials teachers are using, including those they have produced themselves, and teachers' views of their own needs, such as guidance in systematic materials evaluation procedures or materials writing.

This is the last of our three external perspectives on teacher roles and the end of the final chapter in Part One. We turn now to the perspectives of teachers and learners. Among the questions that we might carry with us from Part One are the following:

- What do teachers see as their responsibilities in relation to materials and learners?
- What do teachers and learners feel about coursebooks?
- How are coursebooks selected?
- Do teachers use coursebooks critically and creatively?
- Do teachers involve learners in materials selection, evaluation and design?

**PART TWO**

# Teacher and learner perspectives: 'Practice'

# CHAPTER FIVE

# How teachers evaluate coursebooks

> Most private and state schools choose coursebooks based on what publishers offer and make available; in some cases, the donation of a computer becomes more of a determining factor than a suitable procedure for evaluating and selecting coursebooks.
> (Inal, 2006: 20, describing the situation in Turkey)
>
> In all schools, the majority's view would naturally win and the conflicts would be resolved in this way. Usually no voting was needed and the decision came from negotiation or persuasion.
> (Law, 1995: 105, describing the selection process in Hong Kong secondary schools)

## 1. Introduction

The professional literature on coursebook evaluation presents compelling reasons why teachers should take coursebook selection seriously and approach it systematically (see Chapter Three, Section 3). One of the most obvious reasons is that coursebooks are normally an investment, in more ways than one: 'Students work with the textbooks for just one year, whereas . . . teachers work with them year in and year out' (Fredriksson & Olsson, 2006: 22). Recommended selection practices include the use of a checklist and the involvement of all those who will use the chosen book, including learners. More broadly, the literature also argues that the evaluation process should not be simply predictive, that is, stop at the point of selection, but continue in the forms of in-use and post-use (retrospective) evaluation. Although the primary focus of this chapter is on the evaluation of coursebooks, the same principles hold good for any materials.

Section 2 reviews a number of retrospective evaluation studies – that is, research in which teachers were asked to evaluate the coursebooks they had used on the basis of criteria supplied by the researchers. Section 3 then presents a variety of accounts which illustrate how coursebook selection procedures differ across contexts. Section 4 reports on studies exploring teachers' own evaluation criteria. Finally, Section 5 considers whether in-use and post-use evaluation appear to be taken seriously.

## 2. Retrospective evaluation studies

It is perhaps natural that the introduction by a Ministry of Education of a new official textbook series should prompt independent evaluation studies. After all, it is in the national interest that these books should promote effective teaching–learning. Moreover, any negative findings are more likely to inform the revision of future editions than might be the case with a global coursebook package, unless the feedback comes from a major market.

Alamri's (2008) evaluation of the sixth grade English language textbook for boys in Saudi Arabia, introduced in 2004, starts from just these premises. The researcher also points out that this first book in the series has particular significance since it represents pupils' first contact with English and is thus 'the building block for primary English language education' (p.2).

The study was narrowly focused on the Riyadh Educational Zone, but sought to include the whole population (127) of teachers and supervisors in this area. A 64-item questionnaire based on a number of sources was used with items grouped into 12 categories (e.g. Topic Appropriateness; Teaching Strategies). Responses were elicited using a 4-point Likert scale, where 4 indicated strong agreement and 1 strong disagreement. The combined response rate for completed questionnaires was 81 per cent (93 teachers and 11 supervisors).

On the basis of a statistical analysis by category, Alamri singles out Teaching Strategies as the category provoking most dissatisfaction, commenting that the majority of respondents felt the textbook to be 'outmoded' as far as teaching methods and learning strategies are concerned: 'an overwhelming majority maintained that the book is teacher-centered, does not allow for student participation and quite effectively constrains any, and all, opportunities for class activities which would promote the teaching and learning of English' (pp.81–2) – a rather damning conclusion.

Other categories provoked very mixed views. For example, varying levels of satisfaction were expressed with three of the four criteria under Topic Appropriateness, five of the six criteria under Skills Development, all three criteria under Teachability and all four criteria under Flexibility. Although no explanations are offered for responses which are sometimes distributed across the whole range from Strongly Agree to Strongly Disagree, one might speculate that in some cases this is because the items contain more than one proposition, in other cases because respondents are interpreting concepts (such as 'integrated skills' or 'communicative') in different ways.

Examples of the 13 individual features generally felt to be weak, judged by mean scores (based on the combined response of teachers and supervisors) below 2.50, are shown below, in rank order from lower to higher:

- The topics allow students to think creatively (Topic Appropriateness)
- The illustrations stimulate students to be creative (Design and Illustration)
- The methods used allow students to talk more than teachers (Teaching Strategy)
- The book caters for different levels of formality (Flexibility)
- The methods used are student-centred (Teaching Strategy)
- The book provides communicative exercises and activities that help students carry out communicative tasks in real life (Practice and Testing)
- Listening material is well recorded, as authentic as possible, and accompanied by background information, questions and activities (Skills Development)

In respondents' judgement, then, the topics *did not* allow students to think creatively, the illustrations *did not* stimulate students, etc. Overall, supervisors tended to give more positive ratings than teachers. We might surmise that this was because they had not taught from the book themselves and were therefore unaware of some of the weaknesses. If only teacher ratings had been used, then even more individual criteria would have been judged unsatisfactory.

On the face of it, this study would seem to be of purely local interest and of most relevance to the Ministry and coursebook writers. This may be true as regards the specific findings. One might argue, however, that such studies also have value for the teachers and supervisors concerned, in prompting reflection on aspects of the materials that they might otherwise not have thought about and in offering an outlet for feelings that might otherwise not have been expressed. From a broader perspective, moreover, the study and others like it have significance as examples of systematic attempts to research the match between a proposal for teaching–learning (embodied in a textbook package) and the judgement of the suitability of that proposal by those with intimate knowledge of the circumstances in which it needs to be implemented. Researchers with similar objectives will no doubt wish to give careful attention to the design of this and similar studies by consulting the original sources.

Al-Yousef (2007) offers a rather different motivation, the criticisms of teachers and students, for his study of the third grade (intermediate) textbook in the same series, introduced in 2005:

> Some argue that the ... CB is overloaded with too many new vocabulary items, and others claim that it is too difficult for learners. Some teachers' and supervisors' criticisms included a mismatch between content to be covered and the time allotted for English lessons. This stance was noticed from personal communication with some colleagues, as well as from the online messages posted by teachers and supervisors in several educational forums. (Al-Yousef, 2007: 3)

Although Al-Yousef's study was similar in scale to that of Alamri as far as the teacher and supervisor respondents were concerned, it was much broader in its geographical scope, drawing on informants from 30 cities and villages all over Saudi Arabia (79 teachers, 8 supervisors and 8 teacher-supervisors who were unemployed at the time of the survey); it also elicited feedback from students (88). The main data collection instrument, referred to as a Textbook Evaluation Tool (TET), which was based on Cunningsworth (1995) but customized for the purpose of the study, contained 50 items in statement format divided into 14 categories and used the same 4-point Likert response scale as Alamri. The students were volunteers recruited from the researcher's own classes.

Each of the four items rated only by teachers and supervisors attracted a generally negative response. These ranged from a mean of 1.88 for the Teacher's manual to 1.74 for grading and recycling. In general, the students rated the book more highly than the teachers/supervisors, an exception being their reaction to the treatment of phonology. Table 5.1, which is a selective and reorganized version of Al-Yousef's Table 30 (p.85), shows the highest and lowest mean scores for the students; aggregated teacher/supervisor means are shown alongside for comparison.

The differences were statistically significant in all but the last (supplementary material) of these categories.

What do these differences between the ratings of students and teachers/supervisors tell us? Well, perhaps students were less aware – of what they needed to know, or of how this could be presented – and therefore less critical. On a more general level, and bearing in mind that any score below 2.5 should be interpreted as a negative judgement, we can see that, despite

**Table 5.1** Student and teacher/supervisor means on selected items

| Item | Student mean | Teacher/supervisor mean |
|---|---|---|
| Visuals | 2.84 | 2.56 |
| Content | 2.74 | 2.48 |
| Vocabulary | 2.69 | 2.15 |
| Grammar | 2.57 | 1.98 |
| Study skills | 2.53 | 2.25 |
| Phonology | 1.98 | 2.22 |
| Supplementary material | 1.97 | 1.70 |
| **Mean of means** | **2.44** | **2.09** |

the mildly positive reactions from students to the first five items in the table, the means of means suggest that, overall, the materials appealed to neither students nor teachers. While this may suggest that insufficient attention had been paid to students' needs and teachers' beliefs, we should not be too hasty to jump to this conclusion. It is possible, for instance, that the materials were innovative and that teachers had not been adequately trained in their use. This would inevitably have had a negative effect on teacher ratings and a knock-on effect on student ratings.

A number of other studies have used questionnaires or checklists to explore teachers' views of commercial textbooks. Kayapinar (2009), for example, reports on a survey carried out in the academic year 2006–7 of English teachers in 25 high schools in Turkey. Fourteen of the schools were using one global textbook package (*Opportunities*), and the other 11 another package (*New English File*). Ninety-four teachers completed a 76-item questionnaire and another 40 took part in interviews. Unfortunately, perhaps for reason of space constraints, neither the original questionnaire nor the detailed findings are included in the appendices to the paper; moreover, the discussion of the questionnaire findings is based on the combined responses of all the teachers, despite the fact that two different packages were being used. Nevertheless, the negative tendencies reflected in the results are of some interest. For instance, the teachers felt that the packages provided insufficient support for independent learning; that pronunciation was not treated as systematically as it might be; and that more reinforcement of vocabulary would be desirable. Unsurprisingly, given that the two coursebook packages are intended for the global market, the teachers pointed out that though the target language culture is always or usually presented, that of (Turkish) students is rarely or never illustrated.

The interviews obviously allowed teachers to express their views more forcefully. They commented that students would not be able to transfer language items related to specific cultural events such as Hallowe'en or going to church to other contexts, and this would affect their motivation to learn these items; and that the packages severely limited their freedom as teachers:

> . . . the particular coursebooks do not expand their teaching repertoire. On the contrary, they narrow down their teaching repertoire because there is almost nothing to do except for following the books.
>
> They sometimes decide in English circles to supplement the books with workbooks but they hardly do it in the classroom because they should do it in a rush or leave some of the exercises. (Kayapinar, 2009: 75)

The strongest theme to emerge from the interviews is that, in the view of these teachers, such global textbooks cannot adequately meet local needs. One teacher commented dismissively that the authors were 'just writers in dark rooms with internet connections', and respondents were agreed that 'experts in national universities' (ibid.), with their awareness of local needs, would be able to create more appropriate materials.

This conclusion is at odds with that of Çakıt (2006), who made use of a questionnaire to study the attitudes of 336 Turkish students to the ninth grade (high school) textbook produced by the Ministry of National Education. Eight teachers were also interviewed. Students were negative about the appearance and interest level of the materials. Teachers commented that exercises, tasks and activities were too difficult and that texts were too lengthy and linguistically complex, with the result that students had no desire to read them. There was insufficient recycling, too little attention to the development of learner autonomy, and no provision for differences in learning style. Teachers also felt that there was too much material for one year's work. Çakıt's findings emphasize the importance of incorporating learner needs analysis into the process of materials evaluation: 'The teachers pointed out that the aims and objectives of 'New Bridge to Success 3' are quite in line with the ninth grade English course syllabus [. . .]; however the needs, aims and interests of the students are totally neglected in both' (p.139). The dissertation is also of interest for the fact that it contains mini reviews of a number of studies of in-house materials used in Turkish universities.

Although the motivation for the study reported in Litz (2005) was very different, it was also concerned to evaluate a specific book, in this case the global textbook 'English Firsthand 2'. Before this was 'arbitrarily introduced' by the administration of an unnamed South Korean university as a 'mandatory textbook' for 'high-beginners' classes in the EFL programme teachers had been using 'a variety of "in-house" materials' (p.10), and, as Litz makes clear, the teachers were clearly not pleased by the university's decision. He notes drily, 'it was decided by the teaching staff soon thereafter that a research project needed to be initiated in order to determine the overall pedagogical value and suitability of this book towards this important component of the university language program' (ibid.).

The study took place at the end of the academic year 2000–1, the first year in which the textbook was used. A specially designed 40-item questionnaire with a 10-point response scale was administered to all 8 teachers working on the course and an abridged version of this (25 items) to 500 students, all aged 22 or over. Items receiving the most positive response, as reflected in the mean teacher ratings, were items 9, 12 and 37, all of which had a mean of 9 out of 10:

9. An adequate vocabulary list or glossary is included.

12. The teacher's book provides guidance about how the textbook can be used to the utmost advantage.

37. The textbook is appropriate for the language-learning aims of my institution.

The lowest means were for the following, where the mean is shown in brackets:

10. Adequate review sections and exercises are included (6).

19. The tasks are conducive to the internalization of newly introduced language (6).

24 The textbook highlights and practices natural pronunciation (i.e. stress and intonation) (5).

Litz's online report does not make an explicit item-by-item comparison between teacher and student ratings, but in Table 5.2, a number of items have been extracted from the student questionnaire (SQ) and teacher questionnaire (TQ) which might be assumed to relate to issues of direct concern to students. The means are based on a scale of 1 (low) to 10 (high).

The differences are not very clear-cut, but one might argue that there is a weak indication that students are less convinced than teachers about the appropriateness of the book for their needs (items 19, 10 and 14 in the student questionnaire). In fact, in response to a needs analysis survey which accompanied the questionnaire, 44 per cent of the students stated that they did not like using a textbook (the reasons are not given). More

**Table 5.2** Students' and teachers' ratings for specific items

| SQ | TQ | Item | S mean | T mean |
|---|---|---|---|---|
| 13 | 26 | Authenticity of language | 8 | 8 |
| 19 | 32 | Relevance | 6 | 7 |
| 21 | 34 | Interest | 7 | 7 |
| 6 | 15 | Adequacy of communicative/ meaningful practice | 8 | 6 |
| 10 | 21 | Focus on skills I need to practice | 6 | 7 |
| 14 | 27 | Right level for my ability | 6 | 8 |

broadly, however, the survey indicated that both teachers and students were reasonably satisfied with the book. The author's conclusion is as follows:

> Despite a few reservations and shortcomings (e.g. lack of an ESP focus), the teachers felt that EF2 was relatively compatible with the university's language-learning aims (intermediate communication skills) and suitable for small, homogeneous, co-ed. classes of senior Korean students. It was also felt that any superfluous concerns might be alleviated or eradicated through supplementing, modifying and adapting problematic aspects of the book. (Litz, 2005: 34)

The University no doubt felt that its decision had been vindicated.

Retrospective evaluation studies can serve a number of purposes, as we have seen. They can encourage reflection in teachers and thereby enhance their personal and professional development; they can also give them a voice. Most obviously, they point to weaknesses in materials that have emerged as a result of using them, feedback which may lead to revisions in later editions. Al-Yousef's (2007) research employed only four questions specifically for teachers, as compared with the 15 in Litz's (2005) study. However, one common finding was that teachers felt that more review was desirable. The implication is clear: action is needed. If the books do not make adequate provision for review, then teachers must build it in themselves. In Litz's (2005) study, moreover, students were rather less positive than teachers about some aspects of the materials. An initial survey of students' interests, perceived needs and wants can provide useful baseline data for course planning purposes, but feedback on materials use from both students and teachers is a vital instrument in course review and development.

## 3. Selecting coursebooks: processes and criteria

Teachers are not always in a position to choose the book(s) they use. They may be obliged to use a textbook produced by their Ministry of Education or the institution in which they work. Of the 106 Indonesian teachers surveyed by Jazadi (2003), 67 per cent stated that they used the Ministry textbook 'all of the time or most of the time' and a further 27 per cent 'sometimes'. Top-down mandates may be even less effective. Chandran's (2003) interview-based study of 60 Malaysian teachers in urban schools found that most did not use the prescribed textbooks, preferring to use commercially published workbooks instead.

Where there is a choice to be made, various forces may have an influence on selection. Inal (2006) claims that in Turkey 'most private and state schools choose coursebooks based on what publishers offer and make available; in some cases, the donation of a computer becomes more of a determining factor than a suitable procedure for evaluating and selecting coursebooks' (p.20).

Often the decision is taken by someone in authority within an institution. The induction into secondary school teaching of two Thai teachers, Arunee and Sasikarn (both pseudonyms) is described by Hayes (2008). Arunee was given a book and told to use it. Sasikarn had a choice, but no guidance:

> [I was told] Here's your room . . . this is English Department, that's your table . . . this is another coursebook we have for you. This is from last year. Oh this is the pile of books you can choose by yourself which one you are going to teach and then we will order that for students . . . Yes, after that have to, you know, look at the coursebook and then start planning the lessons. ('Sasikarn', cited by Hayes, 2008: 62–3)

As the following extract from an interview with a Lebanese teacher indicates, teachers may be asked for their views about textbooks, but the final decision may rest with a coordinator or even an administrator.

> T: At the end of the year . . . the coordinator comes up with probably maybe say five different coursebooks. 'OK, these are new coursebooks, what do you think of them?' We go home, we browse through them, we like them, fine; we don't like them, we tell her. But it doesn't mean that because we like them they're actually chosen. The administration might tell us, no, it's too expensive or something else . . . We don't even have a meeting about it, we just meet with the coordinator and tell her very informally, 'I like it, this is what it has, it doesn't have, and that's it' . . .
>
> I: Would you describe this process as systematic?

T: No, definitely not . . . [I was] just thrown in – 'What do you think of this book?' And you're expected to know, you are a teacher, you're supposed to know what you should look for. Well, I don't really know. So basically I just use my gut feeling, so to speak.

What comes through clearly in this account is that the teacher, who had approximately eight years' teaching experience, felt that she was being asked to do something for which she had not been prepared (by either her training or the coordinator). What is also striking about the process described is that teachers reported individually to the coordinator; no meeting was arranged at which teachers could exchange views about the competing books.

Fredriksson and Olsson (2006) carried out an interview-based study of four experienced teachers of languages in a Swedish secondary school who had regular monthly meetings. Decisions concerning the choice of textbooks for the following year were made at one of these meetings. The school had been open for only eight years and in that time new textbooks for English had been purchased three times. The teachers felt that the first choice, influenced largely by the recommendation of another school, had been over-hasty. On the second occasion, a teacher had brought in a copy of a book co-written by someone she knew. Following discussion, it was agreed to adopt the book. When, at a later date, another book was suggested, some teachers volunteered to try this out, and the book was then piloted in two classes. The researchers see the different approaches adopted as being indicative of 'how the school's ability to select textbooks has improved' (p.27). The inclusion of a piloting stage certainly seems to have been an advance; however, it might still be argued that in the absence of any agreed explicit criteria the selection process remained unsystematic.

As part of a decentralization process that has taken place in Taiwan, since 2002 junior high school teachers have been free to choose their own textbooks rather than use those produced by the Ministry. Wang's (2005) study of six teachers reveals that they found the process of predictive evaluation using a checklist provided by their coordinator 'a burden', both because it was time-consuming and because they felt ill-equipped in terms of their own expertise. Such feelings of inadequacy are attributed to the fact that 'there is not much professional training on this part' (Teacher 1, cited by Wang, 2005: 80) but may also have been a consequence of the fact that for these junior high school teachers textbook selection was still a relatively new role. Studies conducted by Ie (2003) and Huang (2004), both cited in Wang (2005), suggest that elementary school teachers, by comparison, felt confident in their ability to evaluate textbooks.

The teachers in Wang's study also felt that some of the evaluation criteria that they were expected to respond to were too vague: 'How to give marks to "corresponding to objectives of instruction"? It's a big question. Actually, we just have the general impression' (Teacher 3, cited by Wang, 2005: 87). At the same time, there was a recognition that checklists have a value: 'At the very beginning of evaluating the textbooks, I do not know how to evaluate or what to review. With the checklists, I find there are some items worthy consideration . . . Through using the checklists, we reduce the number of alternatives to two or three sets' (Teacher 1, cited by Wang, 2005: 87). Nevertheless, there is some evidence of an attempt to subvert the process. Two teachers admitted that they engaged in what they referred to as a 'reversed operation', that is, 'We would figure out which version we prefer first. Then we give the marks . . . If I want some version to be selected, I would give higher marks to this' (Teacher 3, cited by Wang, 2005: 87). The implication is that though the checklist may have served a useful purpose initially, it is no longer used to guide systematic decision-making.

Law (1995) carried out a carefully designed survey of all (101) teachers of English in a representative selection of 10 schools in Hong Kong, and followed this up with interviews with four heads of English, known locally as 'panel chairs'. The focus of the teacher survey was on teachers' attitudes to coursebooks, their use of these, and their views on the need for a textbook evaluation model. Specialists from the English unit of the Curriculum Development Institute (CDI) also completed a questionnaire to permit comparison between the 'official' view and those of the teachers. Seventy-one per cent of the teachers had been teaching for at least five years; 54 per cent had a degree and a teaching qualification and 23 per cent a teacher's certificate, that is, almost a quarter were not professionally qualified. Law acknowledges that her own position as an officer in the CDI may have affected the outcome of the interviews, as may the fact that the questionnaires were not anonymous and were collected by panel chairs.

Roughly 10 per cent of the teachers surveyed stated that textbooks were selected by the panel chair, the remainder claiming that all teachers were involved. Nearly all (96%) thought that the selection decision should be taken by teachers. However, a small number of teachers admitted that though they had not taken a very active part in the selection process, they would not have wanted any more active a role, citing as reasons their lack of experience and confidence. Other teachers pointed out that their workload constrained the time they could spend on textbook selection and evaluation. Teachers' recommendations included more formal meetings for discussion of textbooks and the provision of guidelines for new teachers.

Only two chairs held formal meetings to discuss textbook selection and evaluation; prior to these, they would circulate the textbooks under consideration and ask teachers to complete forms or write comments. However, five chairs thought that formal meetings and the records associated with these were too time-consuming and that informal exchange elicited more ideas. The remaining chairs thought both types of discussion were useful and necessary. None of the schools had written guidelines for materials selection. Three panel chairs said they gave teachers general oral guidelines. According to the panel chairs, voting on preferences was generally unnecessary, decisions normally being the result of 'negotiation or persuasion' (p.105). Three panel chairs claimed that there were 'no differences in opinions among their staff as all of them were either obedient, cooperative or compromising' (p.104).

Although some panel chairs clearly had more confidence in the ability of their teachers to make well-informed judgements than others, all but two saw value in training teachers in textbook selection and evaluation and providing them with guidelines. The need for a consensus on such guidelines, underpinned by training, is well illustrated by Law's own ranking experiment. She asked panel chairpersons, English teachers and CDI officers to rank a set of 12 criteria in terms of their importance. A total of 15.8 per cent of the teachers misunderstood the instructions and three stated that all the criteria were equally important. As Table 5.3 shows, there were also differences across groups (see, for example, the means for panel chairs (PC) and English teachers (ET) on the first four items and between these two groups and the CDI officers on items 4, 10 and 11); there was also wide divergence of opinion within subgroups.

**Table 5.3** Relative importance of evaluation criteria (ranking by subgroup)

| | Criterion | PC (*n* = 8) Mean | ET (*n* = 77) Mean | CDI (*n* = 33) Mean | Overall mean (*n* = 118) |
|---|---|---|---|---|---|
| 1 | Be functionally based giving students opportunity for meaningful and appropriate use of English | 4.75 | 3.17 | 3.67 | 3.33 |
| 2 | Appeal to students' interests | 6.50 | 4.21 | 5.67 | 4.47 |
| 3 | Teach the four skills integratively and systematically | 4.38 | 5.32 | 5.33 | 5.24 |
| 4 | Provide good models of language in use | 4.00 | 5.62 | 2.67 | 5.38 |
| 5 | Be appropriately sequenced, e.g. move from controlled to guided to free practice, and move from easy practice to more difficult | 5.25 | 6.16 | 5.67 | 6.06 |
| 6 | Have an adequate coverage of an appropriate range of vocabulary and structures for the level concerned | 5.88 | 6.16 | 6.33 | 6.14 |

**Table 5.3** Contd.

| | Criterion | PC (n = 8) Mean | ET (n = 77) Mean | CDI (n = 33) Mean | Overall mean (n = 118) |
|---|---|---|---|---|---|
| 7 | Have authentic tasks | 6.88 | 6.39 | 7.00 | 6.45 |
| 8 | Teach grammar in context | 6.88 | 6.68 | 6.00 | 6.67 |
| 9 | Combine a good variety of materials and activities | 7.38 | 6.92 | 8.00 | 7.00 |
| 10 | Be in line with the CDC syllabus for English in general direction, purposes and contents | 7.50 | 7.29 | 1.67 | 7.12 |
| 11 | Be easily used and adapted | 7.75 | 7.51 | 11.00 | 7.65 |
| 12 | Provide enough practice for examination purposes | 10.88 | 9.82 | 11.23 | 9.97 |

(Law, 1995: 84)

The fourth column, showing the mean for the entire population, is of course heavily influenced by the number of teachers relative to the much smaller groups of panel chairpersons and CDI officers.

The approaches to selection illustrated above are, of course, only examples of what is a much wider range, but they serve to make three important points: (1) teachers do not always determine the textbooks they use; (2) selection processes tend not to be based on systematic examination of the materials; (3) for the most part, teachers would like to be more fully involved in selection decisions, but be provided with guidelines to support them in this.

## 4. Teachers' own criteria

The importance attached to specific criteria when selecting a textbook was an incidental focus of a study in Spain by Sercu, Mendez Garcia and Castro Prieto (2004) which formed part of an international project investigating the role of culture in foreign language teaching. The researchers presented 35 teachers with experience ranging from 2 to 26 years (mean 11.2 years) with a set of criteria and asked them to tick the six criteria they felt to be most important. No statistics are given in the report, but the results are shown in Table 5.4, in rank order.

**Table 5.4** Criteria used to select coursebooks (by rank order)

| | |
|---|---|
| 1 | The degree to which the book can motivate my students |
| 2 | The degree to which the book is attuned to the level and the age of my students |
| 3 | The fact that additional materials come with the book (Workbook, listening materials, texts, video, etc.) |
| 4 | The degree to which the textbook meets the curricular requirements |
| 5 | The degree of matching between the amount of materials offered and the number of teaching periods assigned to my subject |
| 6 | The quality of the teacher's manual |
| 7 | The amount of cultural information the book offers |
| 8 | The pace of the book, the speed with which the book progresses |
| 9 | The lay-out |
| 10 | The price |
| 11 | The textbook authors' nationality |

(Sercu, Mendez Garcia and Castro Prieto, 2004: 15). Reprinted by kind permission of the authors.

Given the researchers' particular interest in the cultural component, they were dismayed to find this ranked only 7. Teachers were perhaps predictably more influenced by learner factors (1 and 2) and practical considerations (3, 4, 5).

Botelho (2003) also used a criterion-ranking approach to compare the importance attached to specific criteria by Brazilian (34) and non-Brazilian (27) teachers of EFL and ESL (see Table 5.5). The majority of the non-Brazilian group were American, but many had taught in other countries. Seventeen of this group were NESTs. All the Brazilian teachers had teaching experience in the private sector and four had taught in colleges and universities; with one exception all had at least five years' experience. The majority of the non-Brazilian group had experience in ESL contexts; 22 had taught in universities and 14 in state-sector schools. In general, they were less well experienced: 12 had taught for less than five years, and three of these for less than a year.

Comparison of the two rank orders shows that both groups attached importance to the same four categories, but differed in the value they placed on the cultural dimension of a textbook, the guidance provided,

**Table 5.5** Criteria used to choose textbooks (rank ordered by participant group)

| | Braz | Other |
|---|---|---|
| Method/approach/theory | 1 | 2 |
| Activities/exercises (meaningful, communicative) | 2 | 1 |
| Cultural component (no stereotypes, for all cultures, etc.) | 3 | 8 |
| Extra material available (videos, CDs, audiotapes, etc.) | 4 | 3 |
| Layout (colourful, real pictures, well organized, etc.) | 5 | 4 |
| Guidance (teacher's notes, suggestions for supplementing the book, etc.) | 6 | 10 |
| Year of publication | 7 | 5 |
| Price | 8 | 11 |
| Author | 9 | 6 |
| Publisher | 10 | 9 |
| Other: integrated skills, adequate for ss' needs (Brazilian teachers) / American English, explanations, availability, content, length of the book, clarity of text (other teachers) | 11 | 7 |

(Based on Botelho, 2003, Tables 10 and 11: 70)

and – to a lesser extent – the relative importance of price and author. What is also noticeable, however, is that when asked what else they considered when choosing textbooks, the groups mentioned very different criteria (see the final row of the table). The non-Brazilian group listed more of these additional criteria and apparently attached more importance to them than some of the given criteria.

One weakness of the kind of research conducted by Sercu et al. (2004) is that it relies on criteria supplied by the researchers and ignores the fact that teachers may also use other criteria which, for them, are equally or even more important. Provision for the 'Other' category in Botelho's table at least acknowledges that teachers may operate with criteria other than those anticipated by the researcher; however, because these cannot be quantified in the same way their real importance for the group of teachers concerned cannot be established.

Interesting though Botelho's results are, they are inevitably generalizations. A more fine-grained analysis would have been necessary to show whether there were any striking differences related to the nature of teachers' experience or between the NESTs and NNESTs in the non-Brazilian group, or whether teachers with a similar length of experience tend to use the same criteria. Nor were the participants asked whether in evaluating textbooks they relied on their own criteria or used some form of evaluation instrument. This would have been a relevant question because experienced teachers may be reluctant to accept a set of evaluation guidelines or checklist, feeling that they can rely on their own intuitions and knowledge of their students.

The Swedish teachers studied by Fredriksson and Olsson (2006), for example, shared very similar views. For instance, they all saw as important the provision of a CD for students, and wanted this to include the texts from the students' book, a wish apparently shared by students. They felt that this would allow students to listen to the texts as often as they liked and be of particular benefit to students with reading or writing difficulties. A good glossary and a Teacher's Guide were also seen as valuable. The teachers had particularly strong views on texts, and felt that these should be the principal criterion in selection: '[t]he texts have to be authentic, inspiring and catch the students' interest' (p.21) through topics which are 'absorbing, entertaining and modern' (p.22). Teachers' own reactions to the texts were important: 'one reason for choosing a new textbook was that they as teachers were tired of the old texts' (ibid.). Short stories were preferred to extracts from novels – two teachers felt that it was 'pointless to talk about texts you cannot finish reading' (p.21). Datedness – for example, reference to people with whom students were unfamiliar and lack of reference to modern technology – was seen as a cause for concern. Other criteria mentioned by the teachers included visual appeal (use of colour, 'a fresh and modern impression' (ibid.)), suitability for use with a range of proficiency-levels, and integration of student book and workbook (seen as practical).

The conclusion reached by the authors is that 'teachers with some teaching experience subconsciously know what to look for'; nevertheless, not following a checklist 'could increase the risk of missing several aspects' (p.30).

Xu's (2004) interview-based study of six ESL teachers in Canada (cited in Çakıt, 2006) also sought to ascertain what factors teachers consider when selecting ESL textbooks. The teachers' own criteria are summarized as follows:

- Easy-to-access components and content
- Developmental progression
- Relevant, interesting topics
- Canadian content
- Variety of activities

- Sufficient number of activities on same theme
- Up-to-datedness
- Provision for mixed-level class
- Questions to accompany all readings
- Attractive design/layout
- Quality of the language used in the coursebook
- Quality of editing (Based on Xu, 2004: 23, cited in Çakıt, 2006: 58)

Teachers' negative comments on the materials they are expected to use are also revealing. For example, a small minority of the Indonesian teachers in Jazadi's (2003) study commented on the fact that the materials were biased towards students living in one part of the country, and towards urban students of a particular socio-economic level; and the Vietnamese teachers in Tomlinson (2010b) complained about the lack of relevance in the textbooks they were using. Lack of relevance, on several counts, also figures in Chandran's (2003) study of Malaysian teachers. Among the criticisms of Ministry-prescribed textbooks made by the teachers were that the materials were outdated; the layout was conservative and dull; the level was inappropriate for the students with low proficiency and high proficiency; there was insufficient description and practice of grammatical structures; and they did not provide adequate preparation for the examination. Commercial workbooks were seen as preferable because they provided what the Ministry textbooks did not. They were 'more in synch with learners' personal experiences, ideas, beliefs and interests' and 'attractive and colourful'. They contained graded texts and tasks; 'elaborate description of structures and . . . a variety of [practice] activities'; and revision exercises' related to 'the demands of the examination' (pp.165–6).

Teachers' individual criteria also emerged in Wang's (2005) study of Taiwanese junior high school teachers. The appropriateness of the materials for students' level was felt to be of great importance. As one teacher put it: 'I would mainly consider if the textbooks correspond to students' proficiency levels . . . If the textbooks would destroy his confidence . . . You are just using the textbooks to hurt your students' (Teacher 4, cited by Wang, 2005: 84). Another teacher says: 'I would look at the layout first. . . . Then I will check if the themes would appeal to students. Other concerns are the quantity and the sequencing of the syntactic structures. I will examine if it is logical for students to learn easily. Then it comes to the ancillary materials last' (Teacher 2, cited by Wang, 2005: 85). Teacher 6 used similar criteria: 'It's important to have logical sequencing, enough exercises, attractive layouts, appropriate quantity of the vocabulary, and natural context to make students acquire the sentences more effectively' (ibid.).

Wang's study is also interesting for the insights it yields into teachers' feelings about the books they were currently using. For instance, Teacher 6 wishes that textbooks for the third year of junior high schools contained more literary and inspirational texts – 'more articles . . . to cultivate students' minds . . . materials with greater depth and wisdom. I think the textbook could be such kind of leader' and Teacher 5 would like to see a critical dimension: 'Take the computer as an example. I suggest that the textbooks should not only talk about its positive sides but also its negative sides' (both cited in Wang, 2005: 72). Teacher 3 is also concerned about the appropriateness of cultural content:

> . . . when we learn English, could we also explore our own culture in English? For example, we learn another culture through learning their language, Like Christmas or Halloween. Could we also learn our own culture and the things that in our daily lives, such as Moon Festival, Dragon Boat Festival, rice-dumpling or beef-noodle. I think it would interest our students more. I think we have departed from our own culture. Students won't have the chance to use English outside the classroom. I mean let the language be our lives, and let the students have the chance to speak about their native culture in English. (Teacher cited in Wang, 2005: 71)

The same teacher has difficulty in coping with mixed levels in a class: 'The students with high proficiency levels handle the materials very quickly' and get bored because 'we don't have extra time to offer them more advanced materials', whereas 'the low proficiency level students, they just couldn't catch up with their classmates' (Teacher 3, cited by Wang, 2005: 75).

In another interview-based Taiwanese study, Huang (2010) investigated the criteria used to select coursebooks by 19 EFL teachers in 6 institutes of technology. These were then compared with criteria found in 19 checklists published between the 1970s and 2002. The criteria mentioned by the majority of respondents (i.e. 10 or more) are shown below in rank order:

Coursebooks will:

- cater for the four skills (19)
- introduce real-life topics (16)
- match the vocabulary needs and grammatical level of students (16)
- contain a CD-ROM for homework (12)
- have clear page layout (12)
- have rich resources and information in the Teacher's manual (11)
- introduce foreign cultures (10)
- provide the right amount of content for the time available (10)

- be carefully graded (10)

For the most part, these figure among the criteria to be found in most coursebook evaluation checklists, which raises an interesting question. If teachers are already operating with such criteria, do published checklists serve any useful purpose? The answer perhaps lies in the fact that while all 19 teachers in Huang's survey agreed that books should cater for the four skills, there was no unanimity on any of the other criteria. Published checklists make explicit a set of common standards by which

**Table 5.6** Teachers' context-specific expectations of coursebook packages  $n = 19$

| Context-specific features | | Technological resources | |
|---|---|---|---|
| Introduce Taiwanese culture | 9 | Contain a CD-ROM for homework | 12 |
| Provide instructions/ explanations in Chinese | 7 | Contain a test question databank | 7 |
| Provide *short* reading texts | 7 | Contain an accompanying CD-ROM for class use | 5 |
| Meet students' needs in relation to the GEPT exam (a national exam) | 6 | Be accompanied by online learning materials | 5 |

(Based on Huang, 2010)

coursebooks can be judged. Moreover, in order to ensure a reasonable level of comprehensiveness, they contain a wide range of criteria.

There were, however, some differences between the criteria voiced by the Taiwanese teachers and those in the published checklists. These can be attributed to the teachers' expectations that coursebook packages will (1) meet context-specific needs and (2) keep pace with technological developments (see Table 5.6).

The study also serves as a practical illustration of the fact that, although existing checklists can provide a useful basis for materials evaluation and selection, they need to be subjected to careful scrutiny as to their suitability for a specific context and customized, a point made in the literature by a succession of writers ranging from Williams (1983) to Bahumaid (2008).

It will be apparent from the discussion thus far that teachers themselves may have rather different views about the value of checklists, with some experienced teachers at least feeling that they are unnecessary. However, a recent paper by Johnson, Kim, Liu, Nava, Perkins, Smith, Soler-Canela and Wang (2008) makes an important distinction between experience and training. The researchers, who point out that 'empirical studies revealing what experienced textbook evaluators actually do are rare' (p.158), used a think aloud protocol to explore the approaches adopted by three teachers of the same nationality working in the same kind of context (university level in China). The three teachers had been selected for their different levels of experience and training backgrounds: T1 had been teaching for one year, but had had no prior training of any kind and no experience of textbook selection; T2 had been teaching for five years, had a Cambridge ESOL CELTA, and had some experience of textbook selection; T3 had 12 years' experience, a DELTA and a Master's degree incorporating some training in textbook evaluation, and had been a curriculum coordinator and the leader of a textbook-writing project. The three teachers were asked to evaluate the teacher's and student's books of a recently published textbook for possible use in their own teaching context. Not surprisingly, T3 was both the most systematic and the most efficient. As the researchers say, he knew what he was looking for and where to find it. In fact, he looked at only two units of the student's book (4 and 8 out of 14) and compared these with the teacher's book. (T2, by comparison, looked through every page of the first 13 units of the student's book before looking at several units in the teacher's book.) Differences in the three teachers' approaches are characterized as follows:

> T1: 'equates the textbook with a script for lessons and prioritizes the teacher's need for "survival" when evaluating the book'.
>
> T2: 'focuses on the student's needs, although it is their immediate needs of functioning in an English-speaking environment that are of greatest concern'.
>
> T3: 'manages to consider how the textbook fits into a long-term programme of preparation for academic study and how other teachers might relate to it. Also, whereas T1 seems to be looking for a textbook packed with activities to cut short the need for supplementary material, T2, and especially T3, put a high premium on the "jumping off" opportunities that a textbook provides. What for T1 is a lifeline may seem like a straightjacket (sic) for the more experienced teachers'.
> (Johnson et al. 2008: 161–2)

One tentative implication that we might draw from this very small-scale study is that while experience (and particularly experience of textbook selection in a specific context) is valuable, it is not a substitute for training in evaluation. What the last of the quotations above also suggests, however, is that teachers with different levels of experience may not only have different needs as far as materials are concerned but also require different kinds of training and support if they are to evaluate materials for their own teaching.

Teachers in some of the studies reviewed in this chapter would agree with the basic proposition that support (which is, after all, just one form of training) is necessary. The Hong Kong school teachers surveyed by Law (1995) were in almost unanimous agreement that textbook evaluation was necessary. The majority also wanted to be involved in this, feeling that 'it is the duty of teachers to acquire the knowledge and ability to judge textbooks and use them wisely' (p.76). A substantial majority also agreed with the proposition that textbook evaluation was a means of helping them to develop their professional knowledge and judgement. Of particular importance for the theme of this chapter was the view held by over 90 per cent of the teachers, including those who already claimed to use evaluation criteria or guidelines, that there was a need for a common set of accessible evaluation guidelines and that these should be developed by the CDI and teachers working together, a view strongly endorsed by panel chairs.

Sampson's (2009) survey of teachers in a Hong Kong university language centre reached a very similar conclusion. The 41 teachers who completed a questionnaire saw it as their professional duty to evaluate the (institutionally produced) coursebooks they were using and felt confident of being able to do so. Interviews with a representative selection of 11 teachers, however, revealed a rather different picture:

> . . . when asked to outline the steps or processes they took when evaluating a course, the majority were unable to do so. When gently pushed to explain further, the teachers (except for one) admitted that they followed no clear steps when evaluating their course materials. . . all teachers stated that they would welcome a set of evaluation guidelines to help them critically evaluate their course material. (Sampson, 2009: 197)

## 5. In-use and post-use evaluation

According to 77 per cent of the respondents in Law's (1995) study of Hong Kong school teachers, existing textbooks were evaluated retrospectively, at the end of the year, either in a formal meeting (51%) or by informal discussion. Fredriksson and Olsson (2006) report that one of the four teachers in their study usually asked her students to complete a form evaluating the textbook and the other materials she had used, but 'no time [was] set aside for such a procedure and [there were] no [standard] forms to fill in' (p.24). Kang (2003, cited in Wang, 2005) reports that teachers in Taiwanese junior high schools are concerned about the lack of retrospective evaluation.

## 6. Summary and conclusions

Tomlinson (1998c: 341) wrote: 'I have not seen any research which convinces me that teachers and learners actually want what they are being given by the materials they are using... Nor have I seen any research which demonstrates their dissatisfaction'. As this chapter has demonstrated, there is now a limited amount of published research which shows what teachers like (and do not like) about materials or want in them, and Chapter Seven will report on learners' reactions to materials.

When materials evaluation is carried out by researchers it may result in changes being made to the materials (if those in a position to make those changes see the research and feel inclined to act on it). The kinds of evaluation carried out by teachers, on the other hand, really can inform action. Evaluation for selection will determine which materials are chosen, and this decision has important implications for teachers and learners. Evaluation can also identify weaknesses in the material which will require the development of further resources. Given its importance, it is imperative that evaluation for selection purposes be carefully designed and conscientiously implemented. To judge by the evidence reviewed in this chapter, this may be the exception rather than the rule.

The paucity of published accounts of in-use and post-use evaluation by teachers may reflect the much greater emphasis given to evaluation for selection. However, one form of in-use evaluation is, of course, reflected in teachers' decisions to adapt and/or supplement textbooks. This is the topic of the next chapter.

# CHAPTER SIX

# How teachers adapt and supplement coursebooks

> It shouldn't be necessary to adapt every page of a coursebook. If every section needs to be supplemented and adapted, then it's a defective or unsuitable text . . . Too much adapting and supplementing will reduce the effectiveness of the text, and thus the framework of the course will become tenuous.
>
> (Teacher cited in Dunford, 2004: 48)
>
> Often an element of play was introduced, as for example, in the UAE where a child was dressed in baseball cap and sunglasses and given a camera in order to play a tourist. In Italy, the teacher had a 'birthday' hat which a child wore on his/her birthday and where the other children offered imaginary presents while repeating a well-rehearsed dialogue.
>
> (Garton, Copland & Burns, 2011: 15)

## 1. Introduction

The studies reported in Chapter Five and teachers' own personal accounts indicate that few teachers are wholly satisfied with their coursebooks. However, for teachers with little experience and no training in textbook use this raises an awkward question. As a young Taiwanese teacher put it very clearly: 'Should a professional teacher follow the coursebook without missing a single page? Or alternatively, should a good teacher select and modify the content to be more appropriate to the target learners?' (Hsiao, 2010). The point at issue here is what constitutes professionalism and the nature of a teacher's responsibility. Does professionalism reside, this teacher is asking, in following the script he has been given, a script prepared by experts, endorsed by the authorities, and visible to the students with whom it will be used (and, in school contexts, their parents)? Or is it a matter of making one's own judgement about what is needed and acting accordingly? If there is a conflict between doing what one is expected to and doing what one feels is in the best interest of learners, how does one resolve this conflict? This dilemma can be even more extreme when the book in use focuses on the development of language skills but the teacher has to prepare learners for a high-stakes examination, such as a school-leaving/university entrance exam, which tests knowledge of language systems.

As we saw in Chapters Two to Four, textbook writers, teacher educators and other commentators are united in their view that teachers *should* adapt materials, both those they are given and those they source themselves. Three forms of adaptation are suggested, omission, addition and change, and guidance is available both in the Teacher's Books accompanying coursebooks and in the professional literature in the form of examples accompanied by commentaries. When a lack has been identified, supplementation is also seen as necessary. Research evidence indicates that 'curriculum adaptations' resulted in language learning gains and stimulated interest in classroom learning, whereas 'material transmission' had no such effects (Shawer, Gilmore & Banks-Joseph, 2008: 6).

In this chapter, we consider the extent to which teacher practice appears to be in line with these expectations. **Section 2** looks briefly at whether teachers do, in fact, adapt their coursebooks. Most do, of course, and **Sections 3 and 4** respectively examine their reasons (why) and the most frequent forms of adaptation (how). Supplementation is discussed in **Section 5**.

## 2. Whether teachers adapt and supplement their coursebooks

To judge by researchers' estimates of the percentage of classroom time allocated to textbook-use, which vary from study to study (e.g. Richards & Mahoney, 1996: 50–80%; Jazadi, 2003: 67% 'all or most of the time'; Ravelonanahary, 2007: 20%), teachers do not follow their textbooks blindly. While this may be the case, in themselves such estimates tell us nothing about what teachers *are* doing: for the time that they are using the textbook, they may be following it to the letter, or they may be using it but adapting it in the ways described in Chapter Three. Moreover, without information on individual use, such estimates may blur real differences between teachers with more and less experience and those with and without training in textbook use – and, indeed, between native English speaker teachers (NESTs) and non-native English speaker teachers (NNESTs). Teachers' beliefs about or attitudes to their role may also play a part.

There is also the issue of whether we can rely on such statistics. Studies of adaptation and supplementation can be roughly divided into two groups: those which are based on teacher self-report (e.g. Jazadi, 2003; Lee & Bathmaker, 2007) and those which draw on observational or other evidence (e.g. Richards & Mahoney, 1996; Tsui, 2003; Zheng & Davison, 2008). The latter are obviously more reliable, though not without problems as far as data collection and analysis are concerned. A one-off snapshot is also less dependable and less revealing than a series of observations. In Sampson's (2009) study, four teachers were each observed teaching two lessons. In lesson 1, the two inexperienced teachers reportedly used the textbook 94 and 87 per cent of the time, and in lesson 2 both used it 97 per cent of the time. The two more experienced teachers used the book much less and more variably from lesson to lesson, 56 and 62 per cent respectively in lesson 1 and 15 and 40 per cent in lesson 2.

The question of whether adaptation and supplementation actually happen is, of course, only one – and probably the least interesting – aspect of teachers' use of coursebooks. What is of potentially greater interest is how they use the book, *why* they choose to adapt/supplement and, with the expectations engendered by Chapters Two to Four in mind, *when*, *what* and *how* they adapt/supplement. Whether these actions have any effect is, of course, of just as much interest. These are the questions to which we now turn.

## 3. Why teachers adapt and supplement

Various studies have offered insights, general and specific, into why teachers adapt coursebooks and other materials.

Dunford (2004), for example, carried out a questionnaire-based study of 29 NESTs working for the Shane School of English in Japan, a chain of schools which use their own textbooks. One question elicited teachers' views (and evaluation) of the specific coursebooks they were using. Table 6.1 (overleaf) summarizes their responses. Percentages relate to those indicating agreement or strong agreement with each proposition.

In relation to the manageability of the textbook, Dunford (2004: 36) speculates: 'The convenience of the coursebook may be an issue for teachers in terms of their ability to cover material according to the pacing schedule. For instance, they may feel that the volume of coursebook material is too great'. Respondents also offered additional reasons for adapting/supplementing the coursebook. Five referred to the fact that students have individual needs, and one each to the following: variety is necessary; textbooks do not always provide authentic language use; the choice of textbook precedes student

**Table 6.1** Teachers' reasons for adapting and supplementing their coursebooks  $n = 29$

| Rank | Our coursebooks need adapting and supplementing to become more . . . | % |
|---|---|---|
| 1 | involving | 72 |
| 2 | interesting | 71 |
| 3 | challenging | 68 |
| 4 | varied | 57 |
| 5 | manageable | 55 |
| 6 | straightforward | 42 |
| 7 | culturally appropriate | 30 |

(Based on Dunford, 2004: 36)

needs analysis; students expect creativity from their teachers; updating is necessary. These responses may be few in number, but it is possible that the views they express would have also attracted a measure of agreement if they had been included among the multiple-choice options. One teacher, however, questioned the premise underlying the question: 'It shouldn't be necessary to adapt every page of a coursebook. If every section needs to be supplemented and adapted, then it's a defective or unsuitable text . . . Too much adapting and supplementing will reduce the effectiveness of the text, and thus the framework of the course will become tenuous' (teacher cited in Dunford, 2004: 48). The 15 per cent who apparently did not adapt the coursebook did not offer any explanation.

Very similar reasons (e.g. increasing interest, possibilities for involvement, variety, and challenge), seem to have prompted the adaptation and supplementation decisions of the 30 Chinese trainees studied by Yan (2007) during the two-week teaching practice component of a one-year Sino-British teacher education programme held at a university in central China. All teachers used the same set of coursebooks, but since they were teaching different classes, who were at different levels of proficiency or moving at different rates, they were not using exactly the same materials. No further details are provided of the trainees or the course. Observation of teaching did not form part of the study. The main research instrument was a questionnaire for the trainees. Trainees' lesson plans and an interview with some students (mentioned only in passing) were supplementary sources of data. Yan (2007) concludes that the adaptation and supplementation decisions of the trainees in her study were informed by four principles:

1 *The integration of traditional and communicative methods*: while all trainees but one saw the book's focus on language systems as an advantage, and more than a third provided additional language exercises, there was also evidence, according to Yan, that they tried to balance accuracy-oriented and fluency-oriented activities (e.g. by reducing on the one hand the number of grammatical explanations and word-study exercises and the amount of sentence-translation, and on the other incorporating more opportunities for student–student interaction).

2 *Catering for students' needs*: the wish to stimulate students' interest was advanced as one of the reasons for some of the innovations; a number of trainees also attempted to cater for students' 'linguistic and intellectual needs' by adjusting the level of difficulty of exercises.

3 *Integrating listening and speaking skills into lessons based on reading texts*: this stemmed from the recognition by the majority of the trainees that the textbook did not provide listening/speaking practice.

4 *Meeting their own preferences and needs.*

This account includes two points not referred to explicitly by Dunford's respondents: the wish to balance accuracy-oriented and fluency-oriented activities, and supplementation in the form of listening/speaking practice.

Tsobanoglou's (2008) study of 20 teachers, including four school owners, in private language schools in Greece consisted of three components: a questionnaire, interview (seven teachers) and observation (six teachers). Most were qualified to teach English under Greek law by virtue of a pass in the Cambridge ESOL Proficiency examination. Eleven had between two and four years' teaching experience, and the remainder at least seven years' experience. Asked if they followed their textbook, 55 per cent said 'Yes' and 35 per cent 'More or less'. They claimed to omit exercises that appeared to have no clear purpose and exercises which appeared to provide more practice which they judged to be unnecessary – applying what we might see as a relevance principle. A further reason for not using the textbook or for adapting it was the need to stimulate and maintain learners' motivation. One teacher said she would sometimes tell students to keep their books in their bags: '"Today we're not going to use our books" . . . That way she gives them the illusion that . . . they are going to do things that are more amusing. But in reality they are given a proper lesson without realizing it and this is very exciting and motivating for them' (Tsobanoglou, 2008: 41). Another teacher says, 'I can't expect them from the beginning to the end to stay focused just on the book' (p.42). Other reasons mentioned included the need to provide additional help related to specific student difficulties with grammar, vocabulary, listening or examination strategies – that is, supplementation based on an assessment of student need.

Relevance and affective considerations were also mentioned by respondents in Botelho's (2003) questionnaire-based study, which also asked teachers why they felt textbooks need to be supplemented. The majority of the reasons given related to the need to facilitate learning and make it more relevant; to reinforce content; and to keep students' interest (e.g. by providing variety). Explaining why she devises supplementary activities, a teacher cited by Graves (2000: 188) says: 'My main concern was to develop activities that would focus on learners' needs, give some control to the students, allow for students' creativity and innovation to enhance students' sense of competence and self-worth'. Again, although learners' linguistic needs are mentioned, a variety of affective objectives are also specified.

The focus of Gray's (2000) questionnaire-based study of 12 teachers in Barcelona, all NESTs and the majority British, was more restricted. The teachers – nine women and three men ranging in experience from one to 20 years and all working in the private sector – were asked for their reactions to the cultural content in coursebook reading texts and how they responded if they felt 'uncomfortable' with this. All stated that they had experienced some misgivings, citing as reasons 'stereotypical representations, mainly of Britain' and 'irrelevant, outdated and sexist content' (p.276). For instance, Teacher D describes materials in a book he had used:

> Text about pub culture in England, followed by vocab exercises to do with alcoholic drinks, how to order your drink, rounds, etc. (There are dozens of references to drink and pubs throughout the book.)

and why he felt uncomfortable with this:

> Was teaching in Cairo, group included number of women wearing hijab, also 2 young Al Azhar students. Material obviously irrelevant, inappropriate probably offensive to some. Constant references to alcohol seem to imply a culture obsessed with the stuff – didn't feel like having to defend this. (Gray, 2000: 277)

Six of the teachers said that they simply omitted material with which they felt uncomfortable, five said they adapted it (or would do so), and one failed to answer this question. The author does not make this explicit, but we can infer that all the teachers were referring to their teaching of adults and young adults.

The primary reasons for adaptation and supplementation identified in the professional literature (see Chapter Three, Sections 4.3 and 5.1) were to shape the materials to suit the context; to compensate for any intrinsic deficiencies; and to bridge gaps between the materials and learners' needs/wants. All of these reasons are illustrated in the above accounts, but typically as means of maintaining and increasing learners' motivation.

## 4. Adaptation: when, what, how

### 4.1 When?

Teachers in training are required to write lesson plans and it is here that one can expect to see evidence of any intention to diverge from the coursebook script. To judge by their responses to the questionnaires, all 30 trainees in Yan's (2007) study first evaluated the strengths and weaknesses of the textbook. Disadvantages identified were that the textbook focused on reading and writing, while ignoring speaking and listening; it was out-of-date; it did not suit students' needs; it provided little variety of activities; and it was language-based (i.e. not oriented towards skill-development). The trainees then made decisions concerning the need for adaptation and the type of adaptation necessary on the basis of this evaluation. Given the number of deficiencies they had found in the materials, it is not surprising that 'addition' featured as a form of adaptation in all their lesson plans; in contrast, only eight planned to 'delete' and six to 'modify' elements of the original material.

In certain forms, adaptation is just as likely to be spontaneous as to be planned, and in the case of experienced teachers even more likely. For instance, one of the teachers in Tsobanoglou's (2008) study described a change in classroom management:

> The . . . class had a dialogue and it was indicated by the book to divide the class into pairs and ask them to interact. It is difficult to have the whole class interacting at the same time, so I chose a couple each time and I asked the rest of the class to pay attention . . . and actually mark their performance. (Teacher cited by Tsobanoglou, 2008: 43)

Torres's study of teachers' use of an ESP textbook in the Philippines, reported in Hutchinson and Torres (1994), found that:

> . . . teachers and learners do not follow the textbook script. Most often *teachers follow their own scripts* by adapting or changing textbook-based tasks, adding new texts or deleting some, changing the management of the tasks, changing task inputs or expected outputs, and so on. Moreover, what is also clear from the study is that *the teacher's planned task is reshaped and reinterpreted by the interaction of the teacher and learners during the lesson.* (Hutchinson & Torres, 1994: 325, emphasis added)

As the italicized sections illustrate, even a planned adaptation may be adjusted in response to the dynamics of the classroom. Richards (1998b), who compared the interactive decisions made by matched groups of experienced and less experienced teachers, provides further evidence of this. The more experienced group comprised eight teachers with an average of 9.6 years' teaching experience, all with an RSA Certificate in TEFLA and an RSA Diploma (equivalent to the current Cambridge qualifications) in addition to other academic qualifications such as a first degree or a Master's degree. The less experienced group of eight had an average of 1.6 years' experience; one had a professional teaching certificate and the rest an RSA certificate. All were teaching either general English or business writing at the British Council in Hong Kong and using commercial textbooks or materials provided by the British Council. Each teacher was observed twice and provided the observer with a lesson plan and their teaching materials. The lesson plans provided by the experienced teachers tended to be much briefer. No recordings were made, but teachers were interviewed immediately after their lessons and asked to report what major changes they had made from their lesson plans. The types of interactive decision made were then categorized and quantified (see Table 6.2).

**Table 6.2** Interactive decisions made during lessons

|  | Less experienced teachers (n = 8) | Experienced teachers (n = 8) |
|---|---|---|
| *Timing factors* | | |
| Dropped activity because of time | 6 | 3 |
| Added activity to fill out time | 2 | 1 |
| *Affective factors* | | |
| Added activity to liven up class | 2 | 3 |
| Modified activity to increase interest level | 2 | 5 |
| *Pedagogical factors* | | |
| Changed sequence of activities | 1 | 1 |
| Elaborated an activity | 1 | 7 |
| Changed grouping arrangements | 4 | 3 |
| Changed/dropped activity because of difficulty | 1 | 2 |
| Dropped activities that didn't seem necessary | — | 1 |
| Added activities to strengthen lesson | — | 3 |
| *Language focus* | | |
| Modified activities to change language focus | 1 | 3 |
| Added activity to provide more language work | 2 | 6 |

(Richards, 1998b: 115)

What is immediately apparent is that, if we exclude the first category (Timing), where lack of experience probably contributed to poor estimates of the time needed for activities, the experienced teachers made twice as many interactive decisions (a total of 34, as compared to 17), indicating that they were much more flexible. Many of these decisions appear to have involved adding to or developing (elaborating) what had been planned. This flexibility may derive from the possession of a wider repertoire of options or the confidence that comes with experience – knowing how to deal with a problem one has encountered before. We have no way of knowing whether the decisions made by either group were appropriate or effective. What is clear, however, is that the experienced teachers were more responsive to their learners and the evolving situation, and the less experienced were either less aware of the need to modify the materials or their lesson plan, perhaps because more focused on the material than the learners, or less capable of responding to the demands of the situation. Richards summarizes the similarities and differences between the two groups as a set of maxims, or working principles. Maxims used more often by the less experienced, he suggests, include 'cover your lesson plan', whereas those used more often by the more experienced include 'build on students' difficulties' (p.117).

The observational component of Sampson's (2009) study, which was also carried out in Hong Kong and also compared experienced and less experienced teachers, was smaller in scale, but introduced another dimension in that it was designed to investigate the influence on teachers' use of materials of their first language (English vs Cantonese). The teachers in this case were all working in the same university language centre. Four teachers were selected from a larger number who had been involved in other stages of the study and each was observed twice in the course of a week. Two were NESTs, of whom one was inexperienced and the other experienced, and two were native speakers of Cantonese, that is, NNESTs – again, one inexperienced, and one experienced. All four were using the same section of an institutionally produced English language coursebook for students of Business which made use of case studies. The researcher used an observation schedule to collect data during the classes and then conducted post-observation interviews. The differences that emerged are shown below, in Table 6.3. For present purposes, the numbers assigned to the individual teachers have been changed: T1 here is the inexperienced NEST (NEST-I), T2 the inexperienced NNEST, T3 the experienced NEST (NEST-E) and T4 the experienced NNEST. L1/2 = Lesson 1 or Lesson 2.

Again, some of the differences can be clearly seen. For instance, T3 and T4, the more experienced teachers, used less of the coursebook material than the inexperienced teachers; they spent large portions of the second lesson on activities they had devised themselves (and used before); and they took care to build in links to previous lessons. But even apparent similarities may conceal differences. The table shows that in Lesson 1 all four teachers introduced the case study and discussed assessment, but T1 only did so

**Table 6.3** Differences between four teachers working with the same materials

| L1 | T1 NEST-I | T2 NNEST-I | T3 NEST-E | T4 NNEST-E | L2 | T1 NEST-I | T2 NNEST-I | T3 NEST-E | T4 NNEST-E |
|---|---|---|---|---|---|---|---|---|---|
| **Link to previous lesson** | × | × | √ | √ (brief mention of previous case before introducing new case) | **Link to previous lesson** | × | × | √ | √ |
| **Warm up** | × | √ | √ | √ and quiz | **Warm up** | × | √ | √ | √ |
| **Introduction to case (aims, objectives) and assessment** | √ | √ | √ | √ | **Introduction to lesson content** | √ | √ | √ | √ |
| **Group formation** | √ | √ | √ | √ | **Group formation** | √ | √ | √ | √ |
| **Activities omitted** | Some omitted through lack of time | 2 (but carried over to next lesson) | 3 | 3 | **Activities omitted** | × | 1 | 2 | 3 |
| **Activities adapted** | × | × | × | 1 modified to give clearer focus | **Activities adapted** | × | √ | × | × |

| | All groups did all activities | All groups did all activities, but different group reported back each time | Each group did different activity, then new groups formed for within-group sharing | Each group did different activity, then plenary reporting | T checked answers after each activity | Each group worked on the same activities and reported back | Impromptu presentations with immediate T feedback | Each group researched (using laptops), discussed among themselves and then presented on a different topic |
|---|---|---|---|---|---|---|---|---|
| **Class management** | x | x | | | x | | | |
| **Activities reordered** | x | x | 1 change | 1 change | x | ✓ | | |
| **Supplementation using self-designed material** | x | x | x | x | x | x | T-designed activity for second half of the lesson; business-related but not case-related – see above | ✓ T-devised activity for the majority of the lesson – see above |
| **Wrap up** | x | Omitted due to lack of time | ✓ | ✓ | x | ✓ | ✓ | ✓ |
| **Homework** | x | Ss asked to do these on their own after class | 1 activity set as group hwk | 1 activity set as group hwk | x | x | x | x |

(Based on Sampson, 2009: 159–71)

after 25 minutes, when prompted by a student question. Differences were also seen in classroom management. While the inexperienced teachers tended to have all students do each task, the more experienced teachers had students work on different tasks and then pool the feedback. Inexperience also showed in time-management. In Lesson 1, T1 only managed to do a little more than half of what had been planned and T2, who had planned to do less, still had to curtail the final activity and forego the planned wrap-up in Lesson 1; T4, by contrast, simply adjusted the time spent on activities in order to fit in what had been planned.

As we can see from these examples, improvised adaptation frequently manifests itself in the omission or curtailing of exercises or activities for reasons of time-management and in decisions to change classroom management procedures – to use pairwork rather than groupwork, for example, or to modify the planned approach to feedback. We have therefore already begun to look at both what teachers adapt and how they adapt. In the next two sections, we examine these aspects of adaptation in more detail.

## 4.2 What?

On the basis of the professional literature (see Chapter 3, Section 4.4), teachers might be expected to adapt four main aspects of materials: *language* (the language of instructions, explanations, examples, the language in exercises and texts and the language learners are expected to produce); *process* (forms of classroom management or interaction stated explicitly in the instructions for exercises, activities and tasks and also the learning styles involved); *content* (topics, contexts, cultural references); or *level* (linguistic and cognitive demands on the learner) (see Table 6.4). As the table demonstrates, these expectations are confirmed by accounts of teacher practice.

**Table 6.4** Foci of adaptation

| Focus | Study | Specific example |
|---|---|---|
| Language | Ravelonanahary (2007) | Text simplification |
|  | Richards and Mahoney (2006) | Exercise rubrics |
|  | Zacharias (2005) | Examples |
| Process | Tsobanoglou (2008) | Activity procedure |
|  | Richards and Mahoney (1996) | Feedback procedure |
| Content | Gray (2000) | Cultural content |
|  | Zacharias (2005) |  |
| Level | Yan (2007) | Differentiation (exercises) |
|  | Ravelonanahary (2007) | Simplification/complexification (texts/activities) |

## 4.3 How?

### 4.3.1 Selection and omission

Strictly speaking, selection is not a form of adaptation since it implies use without change. It is, however, the result of an evaluative decision. It reflects the fact that the material selected is seen to have value, to be important or useful or interesting or all of these. Logically, moreover, it also entails omission and this is a form of adaptation, as discussed in Chapter Three.

When a coursebook is used as a basic resource in course-planning, selection may involve deciding which units or lessons of the coursebook to use; at the level of lesson planning, selection relates to texts, activities, exercises and possibly to parts of these. The Chinese teacher trainees in Yan's (2007) study chose to omit some of the accuracy-focused material, grammatical explanations and word-study exercises and sentence-translation. In Sampson's (2009) study, the more experienced teachers omitted more exercises at the planning stage than the inexperienced; they also chose to set certain exercises/activities as homework. The less experienced, in contrast, were obliged to omit or curtail exercises simply because they ran out of time (see also the findings of Richards, 1998b, in Table 6.2).

Gray's (2000) study of 12 NESTs' reactions to the cultural content in coursebooks has already been referred to. As part of the study, the teachers were asked for their reactions to a specific text from the *Cambridge English Course*, Book 1 (Swan & Walter, 1994: 52), which includes an extract from a girl's diary describing what she did the previous evening and a dialogue with her father in which she presents a completely different account of events. (This material was modified somewhat in a later edition.) The majority of the teachers felt that it was inappropriate for their classrooms and said they would not use it ('embarrassing'; 'represents a (mercifully) tiny sector of British society'; 'seems to be showing British teenagers to be deceitful/drunken, etc. (and many are) but having it in a book like this condones the behaviour'; 'a very liberal attitude to childrearing – especially of girls – unthinkable in many cultures where girls wouldn't be allowed out unsupervised'). Of the three who said they would use it, 'two saw it as "light-hearted" and "humorous" – no doubt the intention of the authors – and the third thought it might stimulate discussion of stereotypes based on students' own experiences'. Gray makes the point that, faced with what they feel to be inappropriate cultural material, half of the teachers in this small group would just reject ('censor') it out of hand. 'The question is why? Is it easier to censor than to adapt? Or do language teachers always see cultural content as merely incidental, and always secondary to linguistic aims?' (p.278). In the case of this group, he speculates:

> It is possible that, as a consequence of their [Dip TEFLA] training and the context in which they work, they see themselves as technicists rather than educators, as being essentially specialists trained to develop language

skills only. Pennycook (1994) suggests that the commercialization of ELT has had precisely this effect on teachers' perceptions of themselves, and that it serves to perpetuate the notion of language teaching practices as value free. (Gray, 2000: 278)

There are, after all, alternatives to censorship. One (see 4.3.3, below), described by Teacher D, is replacement; another is critical engagement with the material, as exemplified by two of the other teachers. Teacher C recalled: 'I think I followed it up by asking if stereotypes were true reflection (*sic*) of a people/culture', and Teacher E, similarly: 'Told them it was stereotypical/laughed about it – got them to tell me why/their point of view' (p.278).

### 4.3.2 *Adaptation as addition*

Chapter Three differentiated between a number of different forms of what was referred to as adaptation as addition. One of these is the 'exploitation' or ('expansion') of, for instance, a text or topic in a coursebook. The follow-ups just quoted are examples. In addition to allowing the teachers to distance themselves from the material, these also offered an opportunity for learners to express their own views (thus illustrating the principle of personalization). Expansion may also be used to increase local appeal. Writing of coursebook-based lessons that he had observed in Indonesia, Zacharias (2005) notes that instead of simply discussing the dating systems in English-speaking countries as presented in the book, one teacher compared these with those in Indonesia. Another teacher extended pre-speaking activities in a class on asking for forgiveness: 'Before following the activities in the book, she asked the class when and how Indonesians asked for and offered forgiveness' (pp.32–3). As these examples demonstrate, coursebook materials can be developed in either direction (by adding a pre-stage or a post-stage) or both. The individual teachers in Richards and Mahoney (1996) spontaneously adapted the material in a variety of further ways: they clarified rubrics, gave additional examples, expanded on grammar explanations in the textbook, told personal anecdotes and made jokes; and the experienced teachers in Richards (1998b) showed similar flexibility (see Table 6.2).

### 4.3.3 *Adaptation as change*

In Chapter Three, adaptation as change was discussed in relation to procedures and principles. We have already seen some examples of change. The experienced teachers in Sampson's (2009) study *reordered* material, and Teacher D in Gray's (2000) study, who 'dropped the material on alcohol . . . but retained the functional language the text was supposed to teach' (p.277), provides an example of *replacement*: '[I] changed the situation from pub to school cafeteria – found a tape with similar language that didn't mention alcohol' (ibid.). Zacharias (2005) refers to replacement and *simplification* motivated by students' difficulties with the cultural content of global textbooks and their 'rather difficult' language: 'they often needed to modify or even change completely the examples or texts used in the materials' (p.31). He adds: 'I witnessed many instances in which the teachers modified the materials to suit their learners' (ibid.), but unfortunately gives no examples. Ravelonanahary (2007) lists a number of ways in which teachers in Madagascar adapted coursebooks. These seem to have included *localization* (adapting texts to the Malagasy reality – we are not told how), *simplification* (making texts more comprehensible by using simpler vocabulary or including pictures; abridging/summarizing the text; and explaining concepts in Malagasy or French, when necessary); and *complexification* (making activities more challenging). Change can also be more radical, as in information transfer from one text type to another (*conversion*). Some of the Chinese trainees in Yan (2007) 'adapted the text into a play for students to perform, some modified it into a table, some changed dialogues into a roleplay'.

Medgyes (1994) carried out a questionnaire-based study of 325 teachers in 11 countries which indicated that NNESTs use coursebooks but NESTs use a variety of materials. A follow-up observation study in Hungary (Arva & Medgyes, 2000) revealed that while this may be true up to a point, the focus of a teacher's lesson (e.g. a grammar-focused lesson vs a conversation class) may be an important factor. The NNESTs in the study did indeed use textbooks, but drew on up to four books in one lesson, and the NESTs assigned conversation classes 'designed their own material in the form of newspaper cutouts, posters and worksheets. Students were also required to prepare materials for the projects they were going to present' (p.365). The single NEST who was teaching a grammar lesson used a textbook.

Richards and Mahoney (1996) conducted an observation-based study in Hong Kong of seven secondary school teachers (all graduates, average 4.5 years' experience). Findings, based on a single recorded lesson of approximately 40 minutes taught by each teacher, are shown in a table and summarized as follows:

> . . . none of the teachers taught exclusively from the textbook, and none devoted the entire lesson to material from the textbook. Each of the teachers made use of additional materials as part of the lesson, and made a variety of decisions both prior to and during the lesson which subsequently shaped the lesson. These decisions included developing activities as a lead in to the lesson, making links with previous learning, choosing aspects of the unit to use and to omit, following up on

students' questions, giving advice on strategies to use . . . in completing tasks, giving follow-up drills based on students' grammatical and pronunciation errors, and providing vocabulary work. (Richards & Mahoney, 1996: 53)

They add:

> There were clear examples in each case of the teacher making personal, interactive decisions about the use of the textbook or setting [it] aside altogether for sections of the lesson. It seemed that in each case it was the teacher who was in charge of the textbook. (Richards & Mahoney, 1996: 60)

On the basis of the observations and a complementary questionnaire-based survey of 326 teachers, the same authors draw the following conclusions:

> It can . . . be seen that the majority of teachers do not slavishly follow the dictates of the textbook. There was strong evidence to show that teachers chose not to follow the stated order or methodology of the textbooks, or to use all the available tasks, activities and exercises provided in the book. Most teachers made their own decisions about omitting sections of the textbook or modifying or supplementing what was already there. It was also clear that many teachers were involved in making their own materials to supplement the textbook they were using. Many also used textbooks in tandem with other textbooks, using a mosaic of textbooks to meet their teaching needs. There was also clear evidence that many teachers abandoned textbooks altogether for certain lessons when, for example, focusing on a particular topic of interest or using authentic materials. Use of the teacher's book showed that it was being used not as a guide, or as a set of lesson plans but more as a convenience to save time, primarily in the use of the answer key. (Richards & Mahoney, 1996: 59–60)

## 5. Supplementation

Teachers' reasons for supplementing a textbook were discussed in Section 3. Here our focus is mainly on how they supplement. As is the case with adaptation, information comes from both individual studies and large surveys, and is variable in its reliability.

Supplementary materials come from a variety of sources. In Indonesia, teachers are expected to use one of three approved Ministry-produced textbook series. Nevertheless, Jazadi's (2003) survey of 106 school teachers, each representing their schools, found that 74 per cent claimed to use textbooks published by private publishers 'sometimes' and 11 per cent 'most or all of the time', the corresponding figures for 'self-developed materials' being 63 and 13 per cent respectively. Other resources used 'sometimes' included realia (56%), materials from magazines (41%), brochures and pamphlets (37%), newspapers (35%), audio cassettes accompanying coursebooks other than those prescribed (32%) and coursebooks from other countries (25%). All other resources were used only sometimes by 20 per cent or fewer of the respondents. The Malaysian teachers described by Chandran (2003), most of whom used commercial workbooks in preference to national textbooks, 'very rarely' or 'never' designed their own materials, 'as they felt there was no need for such a "daunting and tiring" task' (p.164).

While what is used may depend in part on what is available, the teacher will also be guided by a sense of what is appropriate. In Lee and Bathmaker's (2007) survey of 23 teachers of vocational students in Singaporean secondary schools, the two most frequent forms of supplementation were self-developed materials and past exam papers (used as core materials by two teachers and as supplementary materials by the rest). Hayashi's (2010) study of a Japanese secondary school teacher, which drew on a variety of data sources, includes plans for six consecutive lessons, all of which were observed. Only two of the lessons were based on the coursebook (which was used primarily to practise pronunciation, by repetition after the tape, and translation). In the remaining four lessons, students completed grammar worksheets individually. The teacher then asked for answers/translation and gave explanations when necessary. We might compare this with an approach to coursebook use described in Acklam (1994), in which the teacher was almost certainly teaching young adults in a private language school in the United Kingdom. Acklam's short paper reproduces a two-page lesson on physical description from a coursebook and the teacher's lesson notes for three lessons based on this material. The coursebook materials contained six exercises, plus reading and writing components. An analysis of the planning decisions made by the teacher for the first of the three lessons is shown in Table 6.5.

**Table 6.5** Summary of teacher's planning decisions

| Lesson | Select | Omit | Change | Supplement |
|--------|--------|------|--------|------------|
| One    | Ex. 2  | Ex. 1 | Ex. 3 | • warmer<br>• additional visuals<br>• listening<br>• reading poems<br>• writing poems |

For Lessons 2 and 3, the teacher selected Exercise 4 from the book and adapted Exercises 5 and 6. She replaced the Reading and Writing sections with her own activities, and supplemented the book material with further listening and speaking activities. Her planned lessons thus admirably illustrate the kind of approach advocated in much of the professional literature: she stayed true to the linguistic objectives of the material (i.e. the focus on physical description), using two of the original exercises and adapting four others, but also supplemented the original material by incorporating warm-up activities and additional skills practice.

The trainees in Yan (2007) similarly added warm-up activities and skills practice, as well as 'background information . . . group work and reading comprehension questions'. Ravelonanahary (2007) notes that teachers introduced communicative activities around relevant topics (role play, information gap) and included games, songs and pronunciation activities whenever possible. A recent major survey of 4700 teachers of young learners in 144 countries on all five continents (Garton, Copland & Burns, 2011) indicated that in addition to 'traditional' activities, such as repetition after the teacher, reading aloud, gap-fill exercises and memorization, teachers frequently used games (69.9%) and songs (66.9%). Also mentioned were 'performance and drama activities', including 'children performing actions to songs'; the use of Total Physical Response; and drawing and colouring activities. 'Other interesting and less predictable activities . . . include children carrying out surveys and interviews, giving presentations (from five-minute "show and tell" activities to reports of research projects), art and craft work, dance, activities outside class (from picnics in the playground to sightseeing trips) and Content and Language Integrated Learning (CLIL) work' (p.12). The survey authors also conducted observations of five teachers in different countries. Examples of supplementation involving three of the teachers are described in the following quotation:

> . . . the teacher in Colombia . . . made great effort to enliven the teaching of grammatical items by introducing engaging communicative activities. In particular, he used music and songs, visuals and word puzzles to appeal to the children and maintain their attention. Often an element of play was introduced, as for example, in the UAE where a child was dressed in baseball cap and sunglasses and given a camera in order to play a tourist. In Italy, the teacher had a 'birthday' hat which a child wore on his/her birthday and where the other children offered imaginary presents while repeating a well-rehearsed dialogue. (Garton et al., 2011: 15)

An example of how teachers build supplementation into a textbook-based lesson can be seen in Graves's (2000: 188) description of Simone Machado Camillo, a teacher at a language institute in Brazil. Simone categorizes the supplementary activities as follows:

- *warm up* activity (usually based on previous topics; can therefore be considered as review rather than preview)
- *presentation* activity (based on new topic – preparatory; books closed)
- *practice* activity (after presentation; before or after 'bookwork'; intended for meaningful practice in realistic context)
- *consolidation* activity (after practice; reinforcement or review; usually a game).

Younger learners, in her experience, appeared to enjoy these activities. However, she had found that young adults showed some resistance to non-book-based and less conventional classroom activities. Graves (2000: 191) emphasizes Simone's flexibility:

> Simone's belief in the importance of student participation as a vehicle for learning motivated her to adapt the textbook to provide more opportunities for interaction. She personalized the activities so that they would be more relevant to the students. Each activity challenged the students to think about the meaning of a given statement or response. The activities were structured so that students would interact with each other. In some cases, she bypassed the book activity entirely. Her understanding of what her students needed in order to be able to participate in these activities – feeling at ease, understanding why they were being asked to work in this way – was a key factor in the success of her course.

In addition to two of the more common features of adaptation (modification of classroom management to provide for more interaction, and personalization to increase relevance), Graves again highlights Simone's concern for affective factors ('understanding of what her students needed in order to be able to participate in these activities – feeling at ease, understanding why they were being asked to work in this way').

The Greek teachers in Tsobanoglou (2008) all said that they provided supplementary practice in grammar and vocabulary. Skills supplementation was less uniform, speaking and writing being more commonly supplemented than listening and reading. Twelve of the 20 teachers (60%) stated that they used authentic materials and six that they used other coursebooks, grammar books and supplementary skills books. The school owners interviewed said they subscribed to English language magazines and that these were used in advanced classes for reading practice and as an input to discussion; lower-level classes might use them as a resource for project work. One of the teachers interviewed used completed student projects as examples for other students or as an input to discussion on a specific topic: 'It is better than using a poster as it looks more approachable to the students' eyes due to the fact that it was made by people that were in the same age as them and they had almost the same level of English' (p.45). Other examples of supplementation mentioned included taking students to the computer room to use a popular computer game ('The Sims'), but asking learners to describe to each other the actions of the heroes using Present Simple and Present Continuous; and tense revision based on the fairy story 'Goldilocks and the Three Bears'.

Like Simone, the teachers in Tsobanoglou's study had also reflected on the suitability of supplementary materials for different levels and age groups. Some teachers argued, for example, that students preparing for examinations needed additional practice; and some also believed that advanced level students have a better understanding of the need to go beyond the textbook. An alternative view was that learners at lower levels and young learners respond better to realia (though this need not imply supplementary materials in general). The four most experienced teachers observed (15+ years' experience) stated that they often began a lesson without making use of the books. This was confirmed by the observations.

Many of the questions posed in the course of this chapter (why? what? how?) were explored in Johansson's (2006) small-scale interview-based study of three teachers and six of their students in Swedish upper-secondary schools. One of the teachers, given the pseudonym Alice, only used what Johansson calls 'alternative' materials, that is, materials other than a coursebook – in this case, authentic materials and those Alice had devised herself. Alice explains that her aim is 'above all to create variation, enthusiasm among the students and curiosity, because no lesson is the same and the students appreciate this, they always write this in evaluations . . . tailoring the material to make it suit the group, even if they are heterogeneous, it is possible . . . creating material that is up to date, feels relevant and also to colour the material depending on what [vocational] programme a student has chosen' (Johansson, 2006: 14). The other two teachers, Conrad and Conny, both male, used a combination of coursebook and alternative materials. Conrad makes considerable use of material from the internet, but also uses films as a basis for discussion, song lyrics and newspaper articles. Conny makes less use of the internet, justifying this by saying he wishes to make students aware of other sources of material; he makes more use of novels and their film equivalents and newspaper articles. The three teachers also commented on the relationship between their choice of materials and students' level. Alice felt that beginners need structure and coursebooks provide this. At higher levels:

> As long as the students are motivated and convinced that alternative material can be fun and interesting, it works very well. However, weak and lazy students are more difficult to motivate since they depend on the structure found in coursebooks. They also have trouble understanding

the relevance of alternative materials and that it counts as course material just like coursebooks do. (Johansson, 2006: 13)

Similarly, Conrad felt that weak students may find working with alternative material too difficult. It is often possible, he notes, to simplify instructions; but project work, in which they are expected to exercise independence, may be difficult for them to handle 'since they prefer structure to autonomy' (Johansson, 2006: 16). The experienced Swedish teachers in Fredriksson and Olsson's (2006) study said that the extent to which they use their coursebook would vary according to the nature of the students: with a creative class they might work less with the book, whereas for students with a lower level of proficiency the book would provide more structure and security.

When students are living and studying in an English-speaking country, other factors come into play. The young adults studying in Manchester, United Kingdom, who were interviewed as part of Shawer et al.'s (2008) study, seem to have been strongly in favour of their teachers using authentic materials. The students' comments and observed classroom behaviour (and attendance) provide firm evidence that in this context supplementation using authentic materials had a positive effect on students' motivation, and the converse, that reliance on a textbook and the failure to use such materials had a negative effect on motivation. Softer evidence is also offered in the form of student self-report and observers' impressions for improved language learning.

## 6. Summary and conclusions

Richards and Mahoney's (1996) conclusion to their study of Hong Kong teachers – a study based on a large questionnaire sample and a small observation sample – is that 'Teachers are looking at textbooks critically and they are maintaining a reasonable autonomy from them' (p.60). This might serve as a balanced summary of the studies surveyed in this chapter. It is, however, a generalization, and – like all generalizations – it conceals almost as much as it reveals. Very few studies, for example, give us any insight into whether individual teachers deploy a range of adaptation techniques, nor do we gain any insight into how teachers learn to adapt – is this simply a matter of instinct and personal experience, do they learn through informal means such as exchange with colleagues, or is this an effect of training? In Shawer et al.'s (2008) study, there appears to be no obvious correlation between the teachers' approach to textbooks and their experience, professional training, or the level of students they were teaching. The fact is, of course, that teachers differ just as much as their students, and although institutional and other pressures may in many cases dictate what they do, they use materials in individual ways. Yan's (2007) study of Chinese trainees is illustrative:

> . . . although they all deleted some language exercises, the deleted parts differed. Most of them added some language exercises, but they highlighted different foci. Many of them added warm-up activities at the beginning of the lesson, but their foci were varied: some focused on the vocabulary, and some on the topics. Several trainees modified the text to some extent, but the forms were diversified, either a table, a drama, or a roleplay.

Considerations of space and balance unfortunately prevent discussion of any further examples of adaptation and supplementation (see, however, the detailed descriptions of teachers in Tsui (2003), Zheng & Davison (2008) and Shawer et al. (2008)). The influence of individual characteristics is also well captured in Katz's (1996) analysis of the teaching styles of five writing teachers, four of whom were using the same material.

We now turn to learners' reactions to materials and their teachers.

# CHAPTER SEVEN

# Learner perspectives

> A coursebook is an angry barking dog that frightens me in a language I don't understand.
> 
> (Learner cited in McGrath, 2006: 176)
>
> Our English teacher is terrible, she/he always reads a book to us.
>
> (Hu, 2010: 61)

## 1. Introduction

The suggestion that learners be involved in materials evaluation (Chapter Three) has been heeded in the kinds of coursebook evaluation studies reported in Chapter Five and by teachers such as those studied by Johansson (2006), but Tomlinson (2010b) notes that in his own survey of 12 countries on behalf of a publisher 'not one learner reported having any say in the *selection of their coursebook*' (p.5, emphasis added).

As for the less controversial call that teachers should take learners into account by adapting and supplementing materials, there is some reassuring evidence that supplementation in particular is appreciated by learners themselves. However, much of this evidence is second-hand, in the form of teacher reports on student reactions. For instance, the trainees in Yan's (2007) study made the following comments on learners' responses to adaptation and supplementation of the coursebook:

> It really did work! When the students discussed the topic, most of them could say something related to their own study. When they presented their ideas, every group reported voluntarily.
>
> ... my students felt interested and a lot of fun. They felt they could learn a lot by 'playing' in this way.

> The students seemed to like this kind of activity. They were all involved. They liked to share ideas with each other.
>
> Providing background information helped the students understand the text and made them interested. The students showed great interest in practising the provided exercises in class. (Yan, 2007: 4–5)

These reports reflect the trainees' perceptions of students' responses; we do not know exactly what the students actually thought about the materials and activities or, indeed, how variable their responses were.

A similar point might be made about isolated quotations from individual students. Block (1991) notes that the personal touch in teacher-generated materials is highly appreciated by students: 'When students realize that the teacher has gone outside the course book and prepared something personally, they make remarks such as "Oh, you work hard"' (p.214); and Ramírez Salas (2004: 6) similarly comments: 'I have . . . . received comments like, "You're very creative" or "You really like what you do because you have such beautiful materials"'. While such comments are certainly gratifying, teachers have to resist the temptation to bask in the warm glow of students' appreciation and make the effort to find out how learners in general feel about the materials, and in particular whether they are interesting/fun, and useful – feedback which can be used to inform materials and activity selection and revision. This point applies, in fact, to all the materials teachers use, and not just teacher-made materials.

Section 2 surveys a small number of studies which have attempted to explore learners' perspectives on materials, either as a main focus or incidentally. Section 3 reports on learners' responses to being involved in developing materials or using materials other learners have devised.

## 2. Learners' responses to coursebooks and authentic materials

### 2.1 *Learners and coursebooks*

The Filipino learners in Torres's PhD study saw the textbook as a helpful 'guide' or 'framework' which helped them to learn 'better, faster, clearer (sic), easier (sic), more' (Hutchinson & Torres, 1994: 318), both in class and out of class.

The learners in three of the retrospective evaluation studies reviewed in Chapter Five were, by comparison, less enthusiastic. The Korean university students in Litz's (2005) study of a global textbook were only moderately satisfied (mean of 6 on a scale of 1–10) with the appropriateness of the material for their level, the extent to which it focused on their skills needs, and its relevance. The Ministry-produced textbooks in the studies of Çakıt

(2006) and Al-Yousef (2007) met with more negative reactions, Çakıt's Turkish learners finding the materials lacking in interest and unappealing in appearance, and Al-Yousef's Saudi boys being critical of the supplementary materials and the treatment of phonology.

There is no pattern in the findings of the latter three studies, but this is not surprising. The researchers used different questionnaires and their purpose, after all, was to evaluate the materials rather than discover what learners want from materials. We might infer from the findings that, for example, the kind of school-age Saudi learners studied by Al-Yousef expect the phonological features of English to be introduced and practised systematically or that interest and visual appeal are important criteria for the Turkish learners studied by Çakıt, but these could just be products of the research instruments employed; and we have no way of knowing how significant these points are for the learners concerned, relative to other aspects of the materials.

What we can infer from such studies is that learners are capable of evaluation. They do not always opt for the same point on a scale. They discriminate. Given the opportunity, they can make judgements which may sometimes surprise their teachers. They can, for instance, spot the fake and the irrelevant, as the following quotation illustrates:

> Schon wieder so ein dummes Übungsgespräch [Another stupid practice conversation] (a young German learner referring to tourist–policeman dialogue in an elementary secondary school textbook, cited in Jolly & Bolitho, 2011: 111)

They can also make qualitative judgements about their learning experiences:

> I've been four times in England in different courses: I attended courses in Italy but they were academic courses – I mean – we had a timetable which included writing, speaking, listening exercises and nothing was left to the personal (students' or teachers') imagination. On the other hand this course I have just done comprehend all the basiliar skills [contained all the basic skills] but everything is done with the purpose of making students collaborate with teachers. (Caterina, 2003)

This Italian teenager, who had just completed a summer course in the United Kingdom, has understood that language learning need not be just a dry, cognitive, 'academic' exercise. There can be scope for imaginative exploration and other kinds of student–teacher relationship than that she had previously experienced. She has also come to realize that in certain circumstances students' needs may be better served if a textbook is not used:

> This English course was, for me, a new experience. . . . the choice of having no textbook was really right. When you have a book you are forced to follow it and often you forget what are the real needs of the students. . . . Without any book you can work on any subject that would interest the class, sniffing different books, if it is necessary. (ibid.)

Relevance is a key concern for both teachers and learners. Yakhontova (2001) elicited the written views of Ukrainian doctoral and MA students on the EAP textbook 'Academic Writing for Graduate Students' (Swales & Feak, 1994). Although generally enthusiastic about the non-ethnocentric nature of the book, students professed to being a little surprised that the only reference to Slavic culture was 'one sentence devoted to the Russian language' and 'slightly disappointed about this lacuna' (p.7).

Lack of cultural relevance was just one of the criticisms made by a minority of respondents in Ravelonanahary's (2007) survey of students' attitudes to their coursebooks in Madagascar. These students 'said that the activities in the coursebook were difficult. The texts were often long, difficult and did not relate to their social and cultural environment. The grammatical exercises did not prepare them to take the final examination' (p.172).

As Duarte and Escobar (2008) point out, when learners feel negatively about their coursebook this is likely to affect their motivation. They surmised that their students, who were following a compulsory intensive English course at a Colombian university, might be more motivated if the materials they used had local relevance. With this in mind, they adapted extracts from global coursebooks. As reported by the researchers, students' positive comments referred to the provision of opportunities for free and spontaneous communication, creativity in language use and the localization of the materials through real-life situations and familiar and interesting topics. The following translated comments testify to students' appreciation of the local dimension:

It allows the use of necessary expressions, adapted to our culture.

Local materials motivate language learning. They boost better comprehension of the language in all its areas: grammar, speaking, listening, etc. (Duarte & Escobar, 2008: 71)

## 2.2 Coursebooks and teachers

McGrath (2006) conducted a study in Hong Kong which asked secondary school teachers and their students to supply similes or metaphors to complete the statement: 'A coursebook is . . .'. One of the most powerful negative images produced by the learners was quoted at the beginning of this chapter ('A coursebook is an angry barking dog that frightens me in a language I do not understand'). In fact, the images ranged from the very positive to the very negative, as can be seen in Table 7.1. It will be clear from the positive images that learners respect coursebooks (see the Authority images) and value them both for what they contain and for the benefits they can bestow. In some cases, the book is even anthropomorphized (e.g. 'my mother', 'my friend'; but note also the negative equivalents, for example, 'a devil', 'a professional killer').

**Table 7.1** A thematic classification of learner images for English-language coursebooks

| AUTHORITY | God's messenger | a bible | an elder | time machine | Superman | | a great mind |
|---|---|---|---|---|---|---|---|
| RESOURCE | window to the world | civilization | the sea of wisdom | a key | teacher | | dumb teacher |
| | a bus | a motor | | | | | |
| | dictionary | newspaper | a library | a shrink of English | encyclopaedia | | reference |
| | goldmine | a treasure | knowledge fountains | bottle (of chicken essence) | locker | | super market |
| | glass of water | milk | food | | | | |
| | fruit basket | a beauty | my cup of tea | | | | |
| | tool | money | career | key of exam | the eyes for my future | | climbing ladder |
| SUPPORT | bridge | stepping stone | bricks | a wall | steel bar | | pillow |
| | parents of mine | my mother | the partner of my life | my friend | a helper | | a coach |
| GUIDANCE | guide | compass | map | signpost | | | |
| CONSTRAINT | [like] a wall | a barrier | my school uniform | | | | |
| | glass of water | annoying parent | ugly and terrible girlfriend | | | | |
| | a stone | piece of rock | a [piece of] lead | heavy mass | mountain | | |
| BOREDOM | sleeping pills | bed | toxic, like $CO_2$ | nothing | | | |
| WORTHLESSNESS | rubbish bin | toilet paper | blank paper | | | | |
| SOURCE OF ANXIETY AND FEAR | a tripping stone | nightmares | lions and tigers | toothache | a devil | | professional killer |

McGrath, I. 2006. 'Teachers' and learners' images for coursebooks: implications for teacher development'. *ELT Journal* 60.2: 171–80, by permission of the Oxford University Press.

The negative images capture the sense of a coursebook as something boring (or, worse, 'toxic'), useless, a burden or something that induces fear.

Kesen (2010) used a similar approach to the elicitation of metaphors from 150 adult Turkish learners on a preparatory English course in a university in Cyprus. A total of 57 different metaphors were produced, the most frequently occurring being *foreign country* (18), *puzzle* (12) and *guide* (12). Based in part on learners' explanations, the metaphors were then grouped into 15 categories. In Table 7.2, which combines data from two tables in Kesen's

**Table 7.2** Learner metaphors for coursebooks

| Themes with positive connotations | f | % | Themes with negative connotations | | f | % |
|---|---|---|---|---|---|---|
| Pleasure | 12 | 8 | Fear | Dentist | 4 | 6.6 |
| | | | | Tall building | 1 | |
| | | | | Tiger | 1 | |
| | | | | Dark room | 3 | |
| | | | | Ladder | 1 | |
| Guidance and enlightenment | 22 | 14.6 | Difficulty | Baby | 1 | 10 |
| | | | | Puzzle | 12 | |
| | | | | Sushi | 1 | |
| | | | | Star | 1 | |
| Variety | 14 | 9.3 | Mystery | Planet | 3 | 16 |
| | | | | Foreign country | 18 | |
| | | | | Secret garden | 1 | |
| | | | | Space | 2 | |
| Travel | 10 | 6.6 | Big size | Continent | 3 | 3.3 |
| | | | | Mountain | 2 | |
| Taste | 6 | 4 | Disaster | Flood | 2 | 2 |
| | | | | Hurricane | 1 | |
| Preciousness | 3 | 2 | | | | |
| Attractiveness | 3 | 2 | | | | |
| Reflection | 3 | 2 | | | | |
| Power | 10 | 6.6 | | | | |
| Growth | 8 | 5.3 | | | | |
| **Total** | **93** | | | | **57** | |

(Based on Kesen, 2010)

paper, frequency is indicated by *f* and the themes with negative connotations have been elaborated to show the metaphors used.

Although referring briefly to McGrath's study, Kesen rather surprisingly does not offer any comparison between either the research methodology or the findings of the two studies. Leaving aside such issues as categorization, and the fact that Kesen's study produced quantified results whereas McGrath simply offers examples of his categories, what is evident is that both studies found substantial evidence of negative feelings towards coursebooks. These constitute 61 per cent of the total number of metaphors in Kesen and 44.5 per cent of the examples given by McGrath.

Kesen's informants noted that metaphors such as 'continent' and 'mountain' referred to the quantity of information to be acquired, and 'flood' and 'hurricane' to their feelings of being overwhelmed – 'they got lost and found themselves in failure' (p.114). Metaphors grouped under Difficulty are similarly fairly transparent (the difficulty of reaching a star, eating sushi, bringing up a baby); 'puzzle' captured the common feeling (12 occurrences) that coursebooks were 'confusing' and 'difficult to deal with'. No explanations are offered for the Fear metaphors, but perhaps none are needed. McGrath notes that some images in his sample could not be classified because they represented mixed feelings (e.g. 'A coursebook is [like] white bread which can allay my hunger . . . but is tasteless' and 'A coursebook is a bee hive which has sweet honey and a lot of painful stings'); others (e.g. 'a mouth of a well', 'a child's stick', 'a clumsy clown') were simply impenetrable without an explanation, and none was supplied.

Kesen sees the negative images as an important reason for taking learner attitudes into account when selecting coursebooks. McGrath's conclusion goes further. Pointing out that in his comparison of teacher and learner images the teacher images were predominantly positive, with only one negative category (Constraint), he suggests that learners' negative attitudes might be due either to the selection of an inappropriate coursebook or to the way in which the teacher uses the book.

This distinction between materials and teaching method is clear in Hu's (2010) characterization of Chinese learners' responses to their teachers: '"My English teacher is very good. She/he makes the learning interesting, we like English class very much" and "Our English teacher is terrible, *she/he always reads a book to us*, we dislike her/him"' (p.61, emphasis added). Students expect their teachers to be more than simple transmission agents; they expect them – just as coursebook writers do – to breathe life into the material. Hu comments: 'After hearing the students' comments, some English teachers who are dissatisfied with their performance are trying to improve their teaching skills, but they do not know how . . .' and 'some teachers can't accept unfavourable comments at all, thinking they are wronged, misjudged by their students' (ibid.). One might conclude that both types of teachers would clearly benefit from further training.

Training does not necessarily affect teachers' use of textbooks, however, as is clear from Shawer et al.'s (2008) study of 10 British teachers who were teaching international classes of young adults in colleges in Manchester. Based on 15–22 observations per teacher, individual interviews with teachers and group interviews with students, the researchers assigned teachers to one of three groups. The *curriculum transmitters* (2) followed the textbook, whereas the *curriculum developers* (5) and *curriculum makers* (3) adapted and supplemented their textbooks to varying degrees. Learners commented negatively on the lessons of the two curriculum transmitters, 'Terry' and 'Mary'. One of Terry's students said: 'Terry shouldn't teach everything in the textbook, because some parts are not necessary. He should teach only what's related because, for example, we had a lesson about sports, we didn't even hear their names [have heard of them?] and we were not interested'. Another had already offered some feedback: 'I wrote to him, "if you add some news, topics and materials from outside. If you change, we will feel more interested"'. One of Mary's students said: 'I wish she introduces some simple newspaper stories', and another: 'I think this is the first time for her to teach, because I don't feel I'm learning anything in this class. I'm not interested because it's the same book'. Of the 10 teachers studied, Mary was the best qualified (with an RSA Diploma and an MA TESOL).

## 2.3 Learners and authentic materials

Despite their strongly expressed wish for authentic materials, some of the students in Shawer et al.'s (2008) study seem to have favoured a combination of textbook and authentic materials (e.g. 'mixing is better' – p.18; 'the textbook is essential for knowledge we need to learn, but newspapers and news, for example, help us to acknowledge the English in our environment' – p.19).

Two of the three teachers in upper-secondary schools in Sweden studied by Johansson (2006), Conrad and Conny, used a combination of coursebooks and other (alternative) materials; the third, Alice, only used alternative materials. All three teachers claimed that they encouraged students to evaluate the materials and to make suggestions for materials, and students confirmed that this happened. Conrad, however, pointed out: 'Some students say that they want to decide what to do, but then they won't come round to it because they don't know what they want to do and then it all ends up with me making the decisions for them' (p.17).

The three teachers' approaches to student involvement vary somewhat. Conrad asks his students what they want at the beginning of each semester. Alice administers a questionnaire at the start of each course in which she elicits information from students about their previous learning experiences, how they would like to work now, and what topics would interest them.

She also asks them to complete written evaluations. She adds: 'Every lesson is more or less evaluated, at least orally; the youth of today will tell you if they don't like something and you also observe the atmosphere in the classroom' (pp.14–15). She acknowledges, however, that students may be wary of being critical when this could be taken as a criticism of the teacher: 'Students in the Natural Science programme have more difficulties in giving criticism because they are anxious about their grades and also afraid of getting on the wrong side of teachers . . . Then you have to take the pulse by anonymous written evaluations' (p.15).

The six students interviewed by the researcher (two from each class) were in general very positive about their teachers' use of alternative material, but this did not necessarily mean that they preferred the alternative material to a coursebook. Johansson speculates that students' level may be a factor. The Swedish grading system runs from MVG (Pass with special distinction) through VG (Pass with distinction) and G (Pass) to IVG (Fail). The weaker among the interviewees, as categorized by their teachers, expressed rather more positive views of coursebooks than their classmates, but this was not always the case. Rosa, (a G) student in Conrad's class, prefers coursebooks. Niklas, a G student in Conny's class, sees coursebooks as boring and prefers to use alternative material, but nevertheless 'is convinced that he learns more with coursebooks' (p.21). Natalie, also in Conny's class, but a VG student, commented: 'It's good to follow coursebooks, but then it's always fun to work with something new that's also up to date . . . there are often boring texts in coursebooks, but it's still good to have the vocabulary and grammar that comes with coursebooks' (ibid.).

In addition to the types of material used and the appropriateness of these to students' level, other factors would seem to be involved here, such as the students' need for security and the ways in which teachers use materials. As Adam, an MVG student in Alice's class, observes: 'If we had another teacher who wasn't as ingenious as Alice, I think that coursebooks would probably be better' (p.20).

The following anecdote from Nguyen (2005: 5), a teacher in Vietnam, also shows that students' reactions to the use of supplementary materials are not always predictable, even when the materials have been specially chosen for their local interest:

> . . . my students recently listened to a Voice of America broadcast about the lack of religious freedom in Vietnam. I did not support this premise because Vietnamese people have always enjoyed religious freedom. Nevertheless, this surprising news item provided an interesting cultural topic for discussion, as well as a good lesson on English grammatical structures. After the broadcast I wanted my students to express their views, but one very angry student stood up and told me that the news was untrue and threatened to report the classroom activity to the police. Eventually she calmed down and understood that the intention of the

activity was to raise cultural awareness by looking at another country's perspective, to encourage critical thinking, and to develop English language skills.

Nguyen comments:

> It was unexpected that a student might react in such a way, and the other students seemed to be excited about the broadcast and wanted to share their opinions. Still, it was an unpleasant experience. My intention was to stimulate the students' minds and get them to speak, not to cause distress. However, I mistakenly took for granted that the broadcast would be interesting for all to discuss simply because it was about Vietnam.

He may have also assumed that the very fact that the materials were authentic would be sufficient to make them interesting to students.

One testimony to the use of films comes from the classroom diary of a Japanese university student:

> Now, I think that movies are really useful, interesting, and easy-to-learn tools . . . . In fact, I learned some expressions or words from them, for the English in movies are exactly natural speaking English. I think it's not just me who likes movies as texts, so why don't we use them more if we have extra times? (Gilmore, 2010: 119, citing Gilmore, 2007: 41)

Gilmore comments that this 'supports what many language teachers intuitively believe: learners are highly motivated by authentic materials such as films' (p.117). His paper includes usefully detailed technical guidance on how film discourse can be exploited for learning.

In another Japanese study, Nishigaki (nd) researched the relationship between the level (and type) of listening activity and its perceived effectiveness and enjoyableness. 40 first-year university students (20 English majors and 20 non-English majors) were taught using commercial listening materials ('Listen First' and 'Listen for It') and the film 'The Secret of my Success'. The film was preferred by both groups of students but the level of motivation was higher among the English majors. Nishigaki concludes that this was because the film was linguistically too demanding for the non-English majors and 'overwhelmed' them (p.76; see http://mitizane.ll.chiba-jp/metadb/up/AN10494742/KJ00004297069.pdf).

As Peacock's (1997b) study further demonstrates, the relationship between materials and motivation is quite complex. Peacock conducted a seven-week study of South Korean undergraduates in beginner-level English classes. Over the 20 lessons of the study, the students used authentic materials (poems, TV listings, short articles, advice column from English language magazine, American pop song, magazine advertisements) or 'artificial' materials in alternate lessons as a supplement to their coursebook, their responses being measured by a number of instruments (observation and quantitative measurement of classroom behaviours, self-report questionnaire and pair interviews). From lesson 8, the students' motivation for authentic materials was seen to increase, but overall the correlation between interest and value was weak. Peacock concluded that interest needs to be separated from other aspects of motivation.

As one might expect, one of the key issues for these beginner-level students, as for one group of students in Nishigaki's study, seems to have been the difficulty level of the materials. Table 7.3 presents a selection of students' comments from the pair interviews in Peacock's study. What is noticeable is that difficulty is mentioned in relation to both sets of material and in one case at least this seems to have affected motivation ('less interesting . . . topic is very hard'). Peacock's report does not permit direct comparison between students' comments on the same set of material, but it is evident that the artificial materials also had their attractions.

Krajka's (2001) questionnaire-based survey of 311 Polish 16-year-olds from 10 different schools also investigated learners' attitudes to coursebooks and authentic materials, in this case, web-based materials. The students were using five different UK-produced coursebooks, all published in the period 1996–2000. Almost one-third of the respondents considered the texts and

**Table 7.3** Beginners' comments on artificial and authentic materials

| Artificial materials | Authentic materials |
|---|---|
| language is too easy | very worthwhile . . . but vocabulary was very difficult |
| not different . . . not so good | (interesting . . . because it's different |
| very effective . . . funny | more difficult but useful . . . I like it |
| makes us think about correct expression . . . its very exciting | it was real . . . had meaning to me |
| interesting . . . but a bit too difficult for me | less interesting . . . topic is very hard to us |
| it was all too much (for me) | it's so difficult |

(Based on Peacock, 1997b: 151–2)

recordings in their coursebook to be boring and a similar number found the books a little dated. Krajka argues that the internet can provide a useful supplement for coursebooks – for instance, by offering access to more interesting authentic texts. Asked for their own thoughts about how often they would like to use the internet, most learners gave a guarded response, 77 per cent saying 'sometimes'.

## 2.4 Types of material, activity preferences, topics

When teachers are developing in-house materials, information on the kinds of materials learners like and the types of activities they prefer are important aspects of the needs-wants analysis process.

Fortune's (1992) study of young adults' attitudes to self-access grammar exercises found that the general preference was for the more traditional (deductive) exercises. Learners feel more secure with the familiar. Dat's (2003) attempt to help a Vietnamese teacher increase student participation in his lessons met with mixed reactions from students: for example, '26% wished that the teacher had taught as carefully as he normally did, corrected their mistakes, and trained them in their pronunciation such as reading out loud for everyone to repeat' (p.187). When St Louis, Trias and Pereira (2010) asked pre-university Venezuelan students for their comments on the in-house materials they had developed, most expressed the desire for more grammar-based exercises, while others wanted more grammatical explanations in their L1. Other requests included more opportunities for oral practice and for writing as a form of personal expression.

Spratt (1999) investigated the classroom activity preferences of 997 undergraduates following compulsory English courses in a Hong Kong university. Findings indicated a preference for, for example, small group work over pair work and individual work, for discussion over role-play, and for oral practice activities (e.g. pronunciation, grammar practice) over written exercises (e.g. gap-filling). She makes the point that the study was valuable precisely because it made distinctions of these kinds between what might be thought of as rather similar activities and because there was a relatively poor match (50%) between teachers' beliefs about learners' preferences and learners' actual preferences. At the same time, she is careful to point out that results of this kind are very much context- and student-bound.

Information on learners' wishes and interests can also be helpful for the teacher using a coursebook. For example, Graves (2000) notes: 'My students in Brazil . . . told me they wanted more practice with functional language and less emphasis on grammar, and felt that role plays were an ideal way to practise the functions', and this feedback proved helpful in enabling her to decide which coursebook exercises to give more time to and which to omit or set for homework. Flack (1999) reports on a study in which 50 Polish students aged 16+ were given questionnaires, used as speaking activities, at the beginning and end of their course. The first questionnaire was designed to establish their level of interest in the topics in the coursebook they would be using. The second questionnaire asked how interesting they had found the texts related to these topics. The majority of the topics were found to be more interesting than the texts, the lowest scores being given for 'anglo-specific' texts. Overall, this approach was useful, Flack notes, because it enabled him to identify topics of most interest to his students and texts of little interest. His conclusions are that where a topic and its associated text were felt to be uninteresting, both should be replaced; where a text was considered interesting but the topic boring, the text should be retained and more intensively exploited and where a topic was of interest but the text not, the text should be replaced. Other conclusions could be drawn, of course – that, for example, it may be preferable to start from potentially interesting texts, or that a relatively dull text, if considered important for its linguistic content or carrier content, can be exploited in interesting ways.

For the teacher who simply wishes to know what topics or activity types are likely to interest a particular class, a few questions may suffice. In the following interview with eight Turkish children the teacher gains a great deal of potentially useful information. The children, who are aged five to six, have been learning English for between two and four years; several are bilingual.

| | |
|---|---|
| **Teacher:** | Why do you like learning English? |
| **Artun:** | Because I go to the Chicago and in the Chicago many many speak English. I goed to Dinosaur museum and dinosaur man speak English me. |
| **Arda:** | I watch Fox Kids and BBC Prime. I can see all the films in English. Jordan (Arda's friend) doesn't speak English. Sometimes I stay at his house. We play the Batman, pirates, everything in English. |
| **Aykun:** | I like come this school. I like make lesson, nice pictures. I like do the puzzles in English. Many many nice things English class. |
| **Teacher:** | What activities do you like to do in the English classroom? |
| **Haruka:** | I like the circle time. I like listen to story and look pictures. Especially, I like play the puppets my friends. |
| **Melisa:** | I like the school play. I like doing shows with my friends and making the masks. The girls are the good people and the boys are the bad people, but Artun and Aykun can sometimes be good people even though they are boys. |
| **Artun:** | I like singing the songs and dancing the songs. I sing very very good. |
| **Teacher:** | What is your favourite word in English? |
| **Bora:** | I like 'bottom'. 'Bottom' you move your mouth a lot. When we say 'bottom' my friends laugh. My friends say 'bottom' is a bad word, but I not think 'bottom' is bad! |

| | |
|---|---|
| Yasemin: | My favourite word is 'lovely' because it's lovely. I also like horse and sweetheart. My mummy calls me sweetheart and I call my horse sweetheart. Will you call me 'sweetheart'? |
| Melodi: | My favourite word is 'horse' because I like horse riding. I like all horses. |
| Teacher: | Are there any words you don't like in English? |
| Evren: | I don't like 'thief' because thief is a bad man. My daddy says they put thieves in prison. If you don't work hard in school or you don't listen to your mommy, you can become a thief. (*Humanising English Teaching*, 2001: 1–2) |

No one seems to have reacted to Melisa's comment about the boys and the teacher's response to Yasemin's request is not recorded, but Evren's stern warning about the need to work hard in school no doubt ensured that the children worked hard for the rest of that lesson at least.

What learners say they are interested in may not match, of course, their response to specific materials. Saraceni (2003), who criticizes the materials in (low-level) coursebooks on the grounds that they are 'trivial', 'undermine the learners' and 'do not motivate them' (p.79), elicited from her UK university students the topics they found controversial. These included the death penalty, abortion, genetic engineering, politics, racism, television. However, when she tried out a range of discussion topics in class, those which proved most provocative related to family, relationships, emotions and inner self. She comments: 'These are universally appealing but, at the same time, culturally different and very subjective and therefore they provoke different reactions' (ibid.). She also acknowledges that some students prefer the safe topics.

## 3. Learners' responses to working with learner-generated materials

The point was made in earlier chapters that one of the logical developments from learner-centred teaching is the concept of learner-generated materials – that is, the use for teaching purposes of materials produced by learners. Such materials and related activities range along a spectrum the breadth of which is determined by the readiness of the teacher to share responsibility with learners. For instance, at the low-risk end of the spectrum a teacher might present learners with examples of errors that occurred in their written work or a spoken task and ask them to correct these; towards the other end of the spectrum, learners might be tasked with devising teaching materials to teach other learners.

A common theme in the accounts of such activities (see McGrath, 2002 for review) is that they were very popular with learners, but what tends to be missing – as noted at the beginning of this chapter – is any systematic attempt to evaluate the experience from the learners' perspective.

Kanchana (1991) reports on the use in a Thai university of projects which required 27 students to produce materials with which to teach their classmates. In Kanchana's positive evaluation, reference is made to the value of the teamwork involved and the use of 'real and authentic language' (p.38) at the task-design stage (students were encouraged to use English, but permitted to use Thai). However, translated student feedback also testifies to students' own perceptions of the value of the activity. Several of these comments focus on the affective dimension (e.g. 'relaxed', 'entertaining', 'enjoyable); others touch on the linguistic value ('knowledge', 'vocabulary', 'listening') (p.39). It is not clear whether students who had previously been uninterested in English had been converted, but one student at least said, 'I used to think that English was difficult but now I think I can cope with it', and another said firmly, 'Group projects should be continued' (ibid.).

It might be assumed that the use of learner-generated materials for teaching purposes is only feasible if students are relatively mature (i.e. older teenagers and adults) and have a fairly high level of language proficiency. Positive reports from primary school teachers in Singapore, all of whom were following a part-time in-service course, are therefore revealing and encouraging. One teacher notes: 'I . . . went through with them the aim of this experiment and how they will be the "designers and co-authors" of this learner-generated material for future learners. All were smiling and grinning with excitement' (Rayhan M. Rashad, 2011); and another teacher comments: 'the pupils found it . . . thrilling to see their own creations being used in place of the textbook or teacher produced work. . . . A high level of pupil involvement was observed and I must admit I got the best feedback ever' (Dhilshaadh Balajee, 2011). High levels of motivation were mentioned frequently. In one class, pairs wrote poems; 'some pairs were even motivated to write a second poem. . . . There was also one particular student who wrote a separate poem at home, and presented it to me next day. I promptly put it up on the notice board for everyone to share and learn'. Other effects were also observed: 'As the group reads their writing aloud, it is clear how deep a sense of accomplishment they experience from their smiles and their chuckles. The other groups are then asked to say three best things (appreciation) that they see in their friends' work. The positive affirmations make the recipients glow with pride' (Anusuya Ramasamy, 2011).

Some teachers conducted rather more formal evaluations. In one class, the teacher asked pupils how they felt about creating their own worksheet based on their own text. 'Most said that they experienced a sense of ownership over their self-created worksheet as it was unique, "the one and only", and exclusively theirs'. Some felt like teachers and found the experience fun. They were 'excited' to find out whether their partner would be able to answer the questions they had set.

Pupils in several classes also suggested ways in which the activities could be improved, by allowing more time, working in groups rather than pairs, using a computer lab, and some pupils who discovered that their partners were able to answer most of the questions in their worksheets 'concluded that it was because of the clues given' and asked if they could have a similar activity but 'without having to give the clues'.

In these Singapore studies (see McGrath (forthcoming) for further discussion), teachers experimented with very different forms of learner-generated material. One particular form which has received some attention in the literature is the transcription by students of their presentation, say, followed by self-correction (see, for example, Lynch, 2001, 2007). In an elaborated version of this, Stillwell, Curabba, Alexander, Kidd, Kim, Stone and Wyle (2010) used a series of activities with 20 students in a freshman English programme at a Japanese university which started with an audio-recorded poster presentation and then included pair work on self and peer transcription, self and peer correction, teacher correction and a second attempt at the spoken presentation. A quantitative summary of students' responses to a post task questionnaire is shown in Table 7.4 (1 = not at all useful, 5 = very useful).

The authors add that although in many cases the second presentation was very different from the first some students made use of the corrections. In such cases, teacher corrections were rather more likely to be reused than students' self-corrections, but accuracy of reuse was roughly similar at

**Table 7.4** Students' ratings of the usefulness of each stage of the activity (in percentage)

|  | 1 | 2 | 3 | 4 | 5 |
|---|---|---|---|---|---|
| Transcribing what I said | — | — | 4 | 52 | 44 |
| Transcribing what my partner said | — | 8 | 48 | 28 | 16 |
| Correcting my own mistakes | — | — | 4 | 12 | 84 |
| Correcting my partner's mistakes | — | 4 | 32 | 32 | 32 |
| Getting teacher corrections | — | — | — | 8 | 92 |
| Trying the speaking activity a second time | — | — | 12 | 24 | 64 |

Stillwell, C., Curabba, B., Alexander, K., Kidd, A., Kim, E., Stone, P. and Wyle, C. 2010. 'Students transcribing tasks: noticing fluency, accuracy, and complexity'. *ELT Journal* 64.4: 445–55, by permission of the Oxford University Press.

55 per cent. The preference for teacher corrections, which is also reflected in the above table, was explained by the fact that the teacher was a native speaker of English. No comment is made by the authors on the relatively lower ratings given to the stages when students worked on their partner's text, or on the spread of ratings on the final item.

The learner responses described above may have been predominantly positive, but little warning signs can also be discerned in the lower rating of the students in the Stillwell et al. study to the activities involving their partner. Learners, it would seem, do not always respond positively to opportunities for learning through peer evaluation. Sengupta (1998) designed an activity for a class of 15- to 16-year-old girls in a Hong Kong secondary school in which, following teacher input, students first evaluated their own work, then gave feedback to a partner and finally revised their own work. The work of 12 students (six pairs) was chosen for analysis and six girls agreed to be interviewed about the activity. The analysis revealed that none of the revisions made appeared to be a direct response to peer feedback, a finding illuminated by the subsequent interviews. The students were apparently preoccupied with accuracy, were conscious that this would be a key criterion of assessment in the national examination, and felt that their teacher (a native speaker) was the only person who could make an authoritative judgement on this:

> **Student 1:** I think it was useless. . . . I want to know from the teacher how to make this composition better . . . to get more . . . to get good HKCE pass. . . .
>
> **Student 2:** It is her work . . . job. (Sengupta, 1998: 23)

They were also embarrassed to have their peers read their work and treated the evaluation exercise in a desultory fashion:

> **Student:** I do not like my neighbour to read my composition. I have many mistakes. I am not . . . I do not like . . . my class friend will laugh. . . . So I read quickly and write something on – in – the sheet.
>
> **Interviewer:** What do you mean by 'something'?
>
> **Student:** Something. I mean, a comment or something. I fill it – ah – just fill it. (pp.22–3)

Sengupta concludes:

> The traditional roles of the teacher and learner in the school curriculum seem so deep-rooted that the only possible interpretation

of knowledge appears to be that it is transmitted from the teacher to the student, and not constructed by the classroom community. Unless these perceptions regarding teachers' roles are addressed, it is probable that little value will be attached to peer evaluation, and collaborative and autonomous learning by secondary school ESL students may not become a reality. (p.25)

There seem to be implications here for both learner education ('training') and teacher education. However, one is also left wondering whether the reactions of the Hong Kong learners is a result of their educational conditioning and whether earlier experience with learner-generated materials might have made a difference.

## 4. Summary and conclusions

As the studies described in this chapter illustrate, learners can provide feedback on materials, activities, teaching practices and leisure interests which is helpful in informing materials development and teacher decision-making. While much of this information will be of most direct relevance to the teachers concerned, it could also be of value to other teachers working with learners with similar characteristics. At present, however, learners' perspectives seem to be very under-represented in the literature. This suggests that teachers either do not attempt to obtain learner feedback systematically or do not report what they discover. The implications of this and other points emerging from our discussion so far are considered in the next chapter.

# CHAPTER EIGHT

# Contextual influences and individual factors

> Teachers ... are traditionally expected to impart knowledge to their students and most classes are teacher-fronted and controlled. The predominant teaching style is expository. Even where textbooks are supposedly communicative in orientation, teachers will often read out dialogues and other texts, ask the students to repeat them and then translate the dialogue or text.
>
> (Hayes, 2008: 60)
>
> When I'm spending [many hours] a week which I'm not being paid for, am I dedicated or am I an idiot?
>
> (Teacher quoted in Crookes & Arakaki, 1999: 4)

## 1. Introduction

What we have seen in Chapters Five to Seven is that there appears to be a gap between expectations of how teachers will interact with materials and draw on input from learners and what typically happens. To judge by the available descriptive literature – which can only partly represent reality, of course – experienced teachers improvise in the way they use materials, but *planned* teacher adaptation is often limited to omitting certain exercises or activities and modifying procedures, and teacher supplementation to adding warm-up activities and the use of photocopied or downloaded exercises; textbook selection tends to be a largely intuitive process; and the potential contribution of learners is rarely exploited.

Some of the reasons for this state of affairs suggested by Bell and Gower (2011) and cited in Chapter Two are: 'lack of teacher preparation time, the excesses of ministry or institution power, the demands of examinations, or the lack of professional training' (p.138). On a more general level, Sampson (2009), writing about a university language centre where an institutionally prepared coursebook was being used, distinguishes between institutional and personal constraints. In addition to a reported lack of time for materials preparation, institutional constraints included pressure towards standardization. Personal constraints highlighted are lack of experience in evaluating and adapting materials, lack of confidence in developing original materials; and what Sampson calls a 'self-limiting' tendency, 'the idea . . . that the coursebook is the authority in terms of methodology and content as it was written by someone with experience and knowledge' (p.202). In their discussion of the factors which influenced the practices of three Chinese secondary school teachers, Zheng and Davison (2008) highlight three 'complex forces' which might be more broadly applicable in state school contexts. These are:

- *external forces*: the intended curriculum, the intended method, and the national assessment system
- *internal forces*: teachers' own learning and teaching experiences, their conceptions of teaching and learning, their professional education, their life stories, and their meta-cognitive thinking processes
- *situated forces*: expectations of school authorities and parents, students' aptitudes and attitudes, school culture, resources, and collegial interaction (based on Zheng & Davison, 2008: 172–3).

In this chapter, we examine these forces and factors and their consequences in a little more detail. **Section 2** considers why teachers may not use materials in the way they are expected to; **Section 3** why textbook selection and materials evaluation more generally is not as systematic as it might be; and **Section 4** why teachers do not normally involve learners in materials development and evaluation.

## 2. Why do teachers not use coursebooks in the way they're expected to?

In some settings, and especially when the textbook in question is the official, Ministry-produced book or an in-house coursebook for a large institution, teachers may be expected to follow the textbook faithfully in the interests of standardization. In contrast, the writers of global textbooks, who realize that their books will not be wholly appropriate for all contexts, typically encourage teachers to adapt the materials. Based on the evidence surveyed in Chapter Six, it would seem that teachers do not always conform to either of these expectations: they may deviate from a book when expected to follow it and follow a book carefully when expected to adapt it.

The tendency to follow global materials slavishly seems to be a characteristic of the inexperienced teacher, especially one with limited linguistic proficiency and little or no training. As a Thai teacher recalls, 'When I start my career in the school, the head of the department gave me the book before I went to class. I don't know what the curriculum was and I don't care. I follow the book and I think the book is the curriculum' ('Arunee', cited in Hayes, 2008: 63). Through experience, teachers develop an instinct for what will work well and less well and the confidence to do things differently. Professional training and the opportunity to work with more experienced colleagues who are willing to share ideas also make a difference (Tsui, 2003). We might therefore expect that in most cases, over time, teachers would begin to make increasingly independent pedagogic decisions –that is, adapting the way in which they use the materials.

From his perspective as a writer, Maley (1995) agrees that teachers should adapt materials, but is concerned by what he calls 'sabotage':

> . . . whoever uses my materials will interpret them differently. And even the same teacher will not use them identically on two different occasions. . . . this does not worry me overmuch. Teachers know their own classes far better than I, who have not met them ever could. They have a feeling for what is right at what moment in their class. . . . What I want to try to avoid is having my materials completely sabotaged, either because the teacher does not understand them or does not sympathise with them. In the latter case, it is not unknown for teachers to subvert the materials they have had foisted upon them. (p.224)

An example of the kind of sabotage he is referring to is provided by Hayes (2008: 60), describing teachers in Thai schools: 'Even where textbooks are supposedly communicative in orientation, teachers will often read out dialogues and other texts, ask the students to repeat them and then translate the dialogue or text into Thai'. Maley has identified two possible reasons for this very radical form of adaptation: the teachers do not understand what they are supposed to do (lack of training) or they are unsympathetic to it (i.e. opposed to the communicative approach in principle or on the grounds that it is unsuited to their learners' needs). Lee and Bathmaker (2007), in a study of Singaporean teachers working with students in secondary vocational schools, note that the teachers typically omitted activities designed to teach learning strategies and higher order interpretative skills because they were doubtful these would benefit students judged to be of 'low ability' (p.365).

Table 8.1, offers an analysis of how and why teachers' practices differ from what is expected.

**Table 8.1** Why teachers do not conform to expectations

| Expectation of T role | Non-conforming T behaviour | Reasons for T behaviour |
|---|---|---|
| T will follow the coursebook | T uses the coursebook very little, if at all<br>T adapts (by omitting or changing) | Lack of fit between coursebook and learner needs<br>Opposed to approach |
| T will use material **critically**, omitting what is inappropriate | T works through everything | Faith in materials<br>Lack of confidence (inexperience)<br>Lack of training<br>Lack of time<br>Lack of motivation<br>Lack of systemic freedom |
| T will adapt material **creatively** | T omits items, but makes no further changes to original material | Lack of confidence<br>Lack of training<br>Lack of time<br>Lack of motivation<br>Lack of systemic freedom |
| T will **supplement** coursebook to meet Ls' needs | T may use occasional photocopied exercises, but uses no other additional material | Logistical constraints<br>Lack of confidence<br>Lack of training<br>Lack of time<br>Lack of motivation<br>Lack of systemic freedom |

Under the third column (Reasons) we can see a number of recurring themes. These have been arranged in the same order merely for reasons of neatness; their relative importance will differ according to the nature of the teacher's role, the context and a teacher's professional and personal characteristics. Let us consider each of these themes in a little more detail.

## 2.1 *Logistical constraints*

Many teachers struggle because of factors beyond their control. These include lack of even basic resources. There are contexts where there are insufficient textbooks for the number of learners (Chavez, 2006; Ravelonanahary, 2007) or the recordings which are an integral part of a coursebook package cannot be used because either the hardware to play them is not available or a reliable electricity supply cannot be guaranteed. Even when hardware is available, it may have to be shared. A Colombian teacher notes: 'In my school, we have a single tape recorder for the whole school. Sometimes, I find myself reserving the tape recorder two weeks in advance because the music teacher, the French teacher and the physical education teacher would also like to use it at the same time' (González, 2000, cited in González Moncada, 2006: 8). Al-Yousef (2007), writing of the situation in Saudi Arabia when a new course was introduced, notes that there was a delay in supplying components such as visual aids and audio cassettes to some schools and that there were insufficient copies of the Teacher's Manual. In the developing world, supplementary resources may also be scarce or non-existent (St George 2001, cited in Farooqui 2008). Although access to the resources of the Internet has increased enormously in recent years, there are still many institutions around the world where even facilities for reproduction are lacking and dedicated teachers feel obliged to use photocopying shops and pay for the copies themselves (Yan, 2007).

Classroom furniture which constrains easy student and teacher movement can also militate against certain types of classroom activity, such as group work and pair work. Farooqui (2008: 203) describes a classroom in Bangladesh:

> Students sit in rows with desks facing the blackboard on long wooden benches which line up and are bolted to the floor. There is hardly any space for the teachers to move around and see what the students are doing. Since the classes are very large . . . if a teacher asks students to get involved in pair work, students who are around the teacher do those, others do not. They talk to each other and it creates noise.

The average number of students in the classes observed as part of Farooqui's study was 70–80, and teacher shortages sometimes meant that classes had to be combined. Faced with such large numbers, the teachers felt that they had no choice but to revert to traditional lecturing techniques. However, this was also ineffective since students sitting towards the back of the class could not hear and may not have been able to see what the teacher wrote on the board.

## 2.2 *Lack of fit*

Such constraints as those discussed above may have the effect of preventing teachers from using the coursebook in the way the writer(s) intended. However, teachers may choose not to use a book, or to make little use of it, if they feel that it is largely unsuitable for their students. A study of materials use by 58 English teachers in Peninsular Malaysia (Fauziah Hassan & Nita Fauzee Selamat, 2002), indicated that teachers used workbooks more than the textbook. Reasons given by the teachers included the following:

> . . . the textbook is very rigid, and some of the passages there are very difficult.

> I hardly use the textbook because I feel it is not appropriate . . . it does not challenge the learners' thinking skills.
>
> I cannot use the textbooks because they are so outdated . . . so irrelevant, so unauthentic.
>
> . . . they do not match the syllabus.

The issues mentioned in these quotations and related issues such as the lack of fit between the coursebook and the national examination, recur in other studies (see, for example, Wang, 2005; Lee & Bathmaker, 2007; Zheng & Davison, 2008; Tomlinson, 2010b). In some situations, economic or political factors may play a role. In Madagascar, according to Ravelonanahary (2007), such textbooks as are available were designed for other contexts (the *Go for English* series, for example, was originally designed for West Africa) and match neither the curriculum nor the needs of the learners. However, lack of fit is probably most common when one or more elements in the system have changed but others have not. The Malaysian textbooks referred to above seem not to have changed despite the changes around them (the syllabus, and teachers' views of what they want from materials). In Farooqui's (2008) study of 26 Bangladeshi teachers from a variety of settings the teachers approved of the content of the new textbook; however, some felt the lack of a literature component and there were also doubts about its suitability for students in rural areas, who – as is the case in many countries – had a lower proficiency level than students in urban areas. Moreover, many of the teachers were sceptical about whether all the activities included could be taught as described in the teacher's guide. Farooqui (2008: 206) concludes: 'The study indicates a disjunction between policy-level curriculum rhetoric and pedagogical reality'.

Similarly motivated, but more strongly voiced feelings were expressed by the teachers in Arikan's (2004) study of nine Ankara-based teachers' experiences of in-service programmes, which revealed a profound dissatisfaction with the failure of teacher educators to take participants' concerns into account. As one participant put it during an interview:

> Here we go again. There is always this mentality. We always have the English language teaching methodology coming from another galaxy. What about us? What about a method that works in our classrooms? In Turkey? In Ankara? (Arikan, 2004: 46)

– and, the teacher might have said, a method that works in the villages of Anatolia, far from urban centres such as Ankara or Istanbul.

One of the most obvious forms of lack of fit is that between a coursebook and an examination. Referring to the situation in Taiwanese junior high schools, a teacher observes: 'It is a paradox that the new textbooks do not correspond with the Basic Competence Test. Now the textbooks tend to emphasize the communication, the dialogue, but the focus of the test is still on reading and writing' (Teacher 2, cited in Wang, 2005: 77). Farooqui's (2008) study found that listening and speaking activities in the coursebook were neglected because these skills were not tested in the final examination.

Smotrova (2009) describes the difficulties experienced by Ukrainian teachers during the transition from one syllabus/approach to another:

> As the new syllabus was phased in [from 2004], teachers had to teach using different syllabi for different age groups of students: an older one based on grammar-translation principles, with students as passive recipients of linguistic information, and the new one based on communicative principles, with students as active and creative learners. Given that most primary and secondary school teachers were trained in grammar translation and have not travelled abroad, implementing the new syllabus has proved difficult. One outcome is that repetition and memorization are still widely used in EFL teaching. At the same time, some teachers have reportedly been able to integrate grammar-translation's form focus with communicative elements, yielding an approach which better matches most teachers' strengths. (Tarnopolsky, 1996)

One might interpret this to mean that the teachers who have been able to achieve an integration of grammar translation and the communicative approach are adapting the materials, as the literature advocates. The designers of the new syllabus and the textbook writers tasked with realizing it would probably take a different view. To judge from the middle part of the quotation, a lack of training in how to do things differently and perhaps a lack of conviction in the new approach seem to have resulted in the teachers continuing to teach largely as they had always done, a common scenario.

A number of papers have also dealt with the difficulty of using the Communicative Approach in Asia (see, for example, Burnaby and Sun (1989) on China and Li (1998) on Korea). In one recent paper, Ning Liu (2009) cites Hinkel (1999: 15–16):

> . . . the western teachers usually use the textbooks as a resource that they exploit selectively, attempting to involve the students in active discussion; while Chinese students usually regard textbooks as teachers and authorities, expecting the teacher to expound the book. They learn through attentive listening while accepting the knowledge from the textbook uncritically.

Learners' expectations of what and how they will be taught can thus be a further obstacle to the introduction of novelty in materials or method. Chowdhury (2003) says, apparently in reference to Bangladesh: 'the home culture and the EFL classroom/textbook culture are very often at odds and the values and teaching methods presented in class are alien and therefore often unappreciated'. The point is relevant more generally. Teachers who are themselves not fully persuaded of the value of the new element or confident in how to implement it may decide to take the easier route and give the learners what they want.

## 2.3 Lack of systemic freedom

Teachers' freedom as far as the use of materials is concerned is externally constrained by one or more forces. For state sector institutions where educational systems are highly centralized, policy as determined by the Ministry of Education is reflected in an official textbook, and in all systems national examinations will be key factors. In some contexts, parents may also be influential: a book has been paid for and it should be used.

Institutions exert their own forms of pressure. University language centres operating compulsory English courses for large numbers of students may produce their own materials and, for obvious reasons, try to ensure that these are used in more or less the same way by all instructors (Sampson, 2009). In the private sector, similarly, a chain of schools may have produced its own coursebooks and even prescribe the method to be used.

Hayes (2009) shows the impact of peer pressure on a Thai teacher whose first teaching post was in the school where she had been a learner herself:

> . . . the first time that I came here my teacher, my old teacher, show me how to teach English and I realise that they taught the old way – just only show them [students] how to pronounce, how to read and then have them do by themselves, just teacher centred.
>
> So just read and translate into Thai?
>
> Yeah, and a lot of worksheets – have them do and after tell them the correct answers. Hayes (2009: 91)

When the teacher tried to do things differently, in a more student-centred way, she encountered opposition, not from students but from her colleagues, who were particularly unhappy about the noise level in her class:

> The first year I want to retire. I told my mother I didn't want to teach here, I didn't want to be a teacher, because I can't do anything that I want to. Every time when I teach [senior teachers said] 'Sudarat's class again'.
>
> Because they were noisy?
>
> Yes, [they] scold my students when I stood in the front of the class. I went to the bathroom and I cry and I cry a lot. (ibid.)

*Implications — PDC*

There is a happy ending to this story. 'Sudarat' (not the teacher's real name) stuck to her guns and went on to become a teacher trainer. Sudarat's is not an isolated case. One of the Swedish teachers interviewed by Johannson (2006), who preferred to use alternative materials rather than coursebooks, reported that in her former school she had also been criticized by her former colleagues 'both directly and behind her back' (p.15). Johansson, who had observed this teacher in her new school and knew how popular she was with students, speculates: 'One explanation could be that the other teachers had difficulties accepting her popularity among the students' (ibid.).

The pressure to conform typically has a pragmatic dimension, however. Referring to Hong Kong secondary schools, Law (1995: 113) points out: '. . . the lower form teachers were expected to follow the textbooks more strictly to ensure uniformity and coverage. Tests and examinations were also largely based on what had been taught in the textbooks'.

In her case study of 'Mrs Tanaka', a Japanese teacher teaching lower-secondary classes in a private language school, Hayashi (2010) identified what she terms 'horizontal' and 'vertical' constraints within the 'micro culture' of the school and teachers teaching the same subject. The horizontal constraint is described in the first set of quotations below and the vertical constraint in the final quotation:

> 'One constraint requires her to be conscious of conformity and keep "in step" with the teachers in the same year' (p.130) . . . 'She is not allowed to modify any part of the lesson plans or add an original activity into the lessons' (p.320). 'She needs to adhere to an inflexible schedule.' (p.130)

> 'Another pressure comes from the teachers in the affiliated [upper] secondary section. . . .. As the school is a comprehensive institution, the teachers in the lower secondary section are considered to be key determiners and take almost all the responsibility for the students' basic achievement.' (p.130)

Since the school has a good academic reputation and parental expectations are that their children will ultimately gain entrance to universities, the vertical pressure on the teacher is considerable: 'The school aims at a higher success ratio for the university entrance examinations and stresses English as one of the major subjects for the examinations. She is expected to understand and pursue this school goal' (p.321).

The importance attached to examination success and the pressure on teachers from all sides are also reflected in these comments by Malaysian teachers:

> If the results go down, you know you'll be called up and the principal will say, 'OK, look at all the other subjects, why is English the lowest?' . . . so teachers would tend to focus on this . . . I don't blame them.

In the eyes of the learners, yes, of course they'll say, so and so was the one who taught me English . . . but if they get a C or a B, they may say I'm not a good teacher . . . at the end of the day, he's also basing his evaluation on the grade he gets. (Fauziah Hassan & Nita Fauzee Selamat, 2002: 7) *CB use, standardization*

One teacher who dissented from the prevailing view of teachers in this study still conceded that she had to conform at a certain point: 'I'm not much of an examination-oriented person as I'm more for educating learners . . . trying to help them . . . understand what they are learning', but 'perhaps in the second semester, I'll be examination-orientated because that is more practical' (pp.7–8).

The kinds of pressure referred to above will be familiar to many teachers. In the quotation below another Japanese teacher acknowledges the effects that horizontal peer constraints, examination-orientation and the instrumentally motivated (test-focused) students that it breeds can have on a teacher. In his closing sentence particularly, we sense the real frustration that this kind of situation can engender.

> I would like to select, adapt and supplement materials more consciously so that I can help my students learn English more efficiently. The problem is that I am supposed to teach the same content as the other teachers do. One educational year has more than 100 students, and a few teachers teach them using the same coursebook. If I want to do something different from the coursebook, I have to let my colleagues know what I want to do. If they decide to use what I do for their class, it is fine. However, if they decide not to, I cannot use this material for testing because that would be unfair for students who take other teachers' lessons. All the students are supposed to take the same test in the middle and at the end of the term. Students often do not want to study what they will not be tested about. With various constraints, it is so easy to flow along with what I am supposed to do. However, I do not want to keep producing students who study English for more than 6 years and cannot do anything in English. (Matsumara, 2010)

As the reference here to students' exam fixation implies, student pressure to follow the book can also be perceived as a constraint, but pressure can come from parents too. Writing of private schools in Greece, Tsobanoglou (2008) notes: 'parents . . . believe that their children will only learn English if they complete all the tasks in the book, read all the texts and do all the exercises' (p.41).

Institutional, student and parental pressure are likely to combine when university entry is at issue. As Crookes (2009) points out: 'in those countries where . . . "scores on tests of English proficiency" . . . are used as a major entry criterion to higher education providers . . . teachers of English are under enormous pressure to teach to the test' (p.201). He adds that similar pressure 'to deliver' may also be felt when students need a communicative command of English for specific forms of employment.

## 2.4 Lack of time

Time is an issue for teachers for a number of reasons. They may feel, for instance, that there are insufficient hours for English ('Mrs Tanaka', the teacher in Hayashi's (2010) study referred to above, whose students are privileged in having more hours of English per week than would be normal in a state school, still says: 'I have little time. I want to have more than five lessons in a week and want to do more'.). As a consequence, they may feel that they can do little more than teach to the syllabus or book, regardless of learners' needs. This is especially the case when examinations are involved.

This kind of exam-dominated teaching may also mean that, when students are preparing for an internationally recognized exam which can be taken at any time and using a book in preparation for this, 'getting through the book' becomes the primary objective and certain activities are either skipped or dealt with only superficially.

Hsiao (2010) describes the situation in Taiwan among teachers and students preparing for the Test of English for International Communication (TOEIC):

> Time pressure is . . . a common problem for teachers in exam preparatory programs in Taiwan because most learners are eager to achieve their goals in as short a period of time as possible. Therefore, the program is scheduled as intensively as possible: for instance, a 350-page textbook has to be fully covered in only 24 hours of instruction. Obviously the teaching load is way above average, but most students are under the impression that speedy learning is best, particularly in an exam-orientated course.

His observation of a number of classes indicated how this 'speedy learning' is achieved:

> . . . course coordinators are forced to speed up the learning and teaching pace and consequently omission of in-class drills and some exercises becomes inevitable. In the classroom observation, some printed exercises were assigned as homework and the rest were left out; but even so, the homework sections were barely reviewed in the following session.

Even when teaching is not dominated by exams, other non-teaching tasks may intrude. Farooqui (2008), for instance, points out that classes in

Bangladesh are typically 30–40 minutes long and tasks such as checking attendance and collecting the previous day's homework can take 10–15 minutes of this. It is therefore easy to understand why teachers choose not to do activities which they accept as desirable but see as non-essential. One teacher interviewed by Farooqui commented:

> ELTIP [The English Language Teaching Improvement Project] taught us to do warm-up activities which are mostly speaking activities in first three minutes of the class but in reality we have to call the roll first, then have to collect the homework. In today's class, as you saw, I had to distribute the report card of the first term final exam. After doing all these, I was left with 15 minutes to teach those students. We should have done those warm up activities if we did not have to do those works. (Farooqui, 2008: 202)

The time teachers need to think about adaptation, find supplementary materials or design their own materials can also be a problem, especially when they have a heavy administrative load or need to do a second job to make ends meet. In Law's (1995) study of 101 secondary school teachers in Hong Kong, a context in which teachers are expected to take on extra-curricular activities, 77.3 per cent said that they relied on a textbook because they did not have time or resources to do anything else. In Nicaragua, the low salaries of state school teachers obliged several of the teachers studied by Chavez (2006) to work two or three shifts a day (see also Arva & Medgyes, 2000 on teachers in Hungary). Similar pressures can apply even in contexts where it might be assumed that teachers are much more privileged. Crookes and Arakaki (1999) carried out a three-month study of 20 ESL teachers working on an intensive ESL programme in the United States of America, many of whom had MA degrees in ESL. All were on 10-week contracts without any form of longer-term security; as a result, many were holding down two or three jobs and reportedly working an average of 50 hours per week. The minority of teachers without formal training tended to rely on 'conventional sources like dictionaries, textbooks (without modifying them), workbooks, and teachers' handbooks' (p.3). Among the majority of trained teachers 'a proven repertoire of teaching ideas and a cautiously pragmatic attitude was common' (p.4). Explanations for this pragmatism were predictable: the need to prioritize ('I want a quality personal life. And I don't want my work life to take over'); to survive, even ('I'm trying to avoid the hospital') and resentment at working conditions, the feeling that if you do more than is strictly necessary you are allowing yourself to be exploited ('When I'm spending [many hours] a week which I'm not being paid for, am I dedicated or am I an idiot?') (ibid.).

## 2.5 Lack of training

Even when the time is available, teachers may not feel able to rise to the challenge of creating their own materials:

> Even if I have enough time for material writing, I do not think I can write good communicative materials. First, I have never been taught how to do it. Secondly, there are few authentic English materials around me. That means I have to create everything. That's beyond me. (teacher cited in Li, 1998: 689)

This teacher was alluding to a period (the mid-1990s) in Korea in which teachers were being encouraged to use Communicative Language Teaching (CLT) but no help was available from colleagues or administrators and the curriculum and materials to support this had not yet been published. It is generally acknowledged that at times of curriculum change teachers need practical support and that suitable teaching materials and especially a Teacher's Book can be extremely helpful in making concrete what is expected (Hutchinson & Torres, 1994). In order to be able to use the materials in the way expected or to make adjustments if the recommended approach does not work, however, teachers must have access to the Teacher's Book (which must contain suggestions on using the material flexibly) and have the necessary training or background understanding to feel confident about implementing ideas with which their students may be unfamiliar. Erdoğan (nd), reporting on the reactions of two Turkish secondary-school teachers to the Learning Diary section of a coursebook based on principles of learner training, notes that both decided to omit this because learners seemed reluctant to speak about their diaries when asked. Invited to suggest improvements to the book, the teachers did not suggest omitting the Learning Diary section but instead 'requested more guidance in the Teacher's Book, including:

- better explanation of learner training theory
- examples of practical problems that are likely to occur
- possible solutions to these problems
- a bibliography for further reading about learner training' (p.2).

As Erdoğan points out, 'simply promoting learner training via teaching materials is not enough to prepare teachers psychologically to cope with unexpected problems' (ibid.).

Graves (2003), who together with a colleague conducted an online research project with teachers from four countries, concluded that coursebook activities were unsuccessful not because they were boring or too complicated but because learners had not been properly prepared:

> Preparing the learners means two things. First it means orienting them to the content and purpose of the activity, that is, making sure they know *what* the activity is about and *why* they are doing it. Second, it means making sure they understand the steps of the activity, *how* to do it. However, simply telling the learners the *what*, *how*, and *why* of an activity doesn't prepare them. They need to demonstrate either verbally or in action that they have understood. (Graves, 2003: 231, original emphases)

This is good advice, but the best follows: 'Preparing the learner means preparing yourself' (ibid.) – and Graves suggests the sorts of question teachers might ask themselves in order to prepare clear explanations and anticipate problems.

The importance of training is explicitly highlighted in Al-Yousef's discussion of factors which impeded the effective implementation of the new communicatively oriented national textbook in Saudi Arabia: 'teachers were not provided with any training on the Communicative Language Teaching (CLT) techniques . . . [or] . . . informed of the overall objectives of this new curriculum; thus most teachers follow the traditional approach to teaching, which emphasize the use of translation, writing, and reading rather than speaking' (p.55). He concludes: 'There is an urgent need for training that addresses both linguistic competence and methodology' (ibid.).

For some teachers in some contexts, lack of training means lack of alternatives: they simply follow the book. Ravelonanahary (2007) summarizes the responses of a minority of the teachers she surveyed in Madagascar as follows: 'We have no choice since this is the only book existing at school and we find it perfect. We follow the content and methods because we have no training in using it effectively. . . .. We find it difficult to select materials from the various activities, exercises or situations given in the textbook' (p.171).

## 2.6 Lack of confidence

Where contextual constraints are strong, a focus in training on language proficiency development, methods and materials, though important, may not be enough. Akbulut (2007) assessed the impact of training on 13 novice teachers who had completed a 4-year undergraduate degree in TEFL at Boğazici University, Turkey, which had included 'two comprehensive materials development courses given in successive semesters' (p.6). As a result of this training, '85% of the participants (11/13) felt competent in materials evaluation and preparation', yet when they found themselves in schools '55% of them (7/13) stated that they generally followed the textbook or the materials that were assigned by the institution' (p.9). One reason for this seems to have been the requirement to prepare for common exams. However, the situation was apparently more complex than this: 'a few of the teachers claimed that their teaching was almost always textbook-based . . . because they did not feel confident enough to move beyond the textbook' (ibid.). In part, this may have been because they felt obliged to work with the book and found this difficult: 'They claimed that they spent much time in trying to make their students understand the instructions and the material via using L1 instructions and translations of the lexical structures provided in the books' (ibid.). The novice teachers' own conclusion, as represented by the researcher, is interesting: they felt unable to apply what they had learned during their undergraduate course 'either because of the strict curriculum or lack of proper facilities' (ibid.). An outsider might question this analysis: while curriculum/exams and facilities can undoubtedly limit teachers' freedom, the lack of confidence that the novice teachers also referred to is certainly an influential factor. One might therefore wonder whether one of the aims of teacher education in materials evaluation and design – indeed, any teacher education programme – should not be to prepare teachers for the kinds of constraints they are likely to encounter and equip them to deal with these.

Though increased confidence may come with experience (and 63% of the teachers in Law's (1995) study of 101 Hong Kong secondary school teachers believed that they would be less dependent on textbooks if they had more experience), other factors also contribute to confidence. One of these is the teacher's perceptions of their own language proficiency, and another the nature of the teacher's professional education. Almost 40 per cent of the teachers in Law's study acknowledged that they did not have the expertise or knowledge to design their own materials. We are told that approximately a quarter of the respondents did not hold a professional qualification. If the training received by the remaining teachers included a component on materials adaptation and development, then it was clearly not sufficient.

## 2.7 *Lack of motivation*

This applies to those teachers who have come to see teaching as simply a way of making a living and their responsibility as being to teach the book. They do not need to prepare for lessons because they begin again where they left off. The reality is often more complex, of course, as Crookes and Arakaki (1999) discovered. Teachers' motivation can be affected by pressures such as lack of systemic freedom, lack of time and logistical constraints, as well as lack of opportunities for professional development (training). As Chavez (2006: 33) comments: 'It is certainly very difficult to be motivated if the resources are limited, the contextual conditions are not adequate, the work is extreme, and the salary is too low'. In the Nicaraguan situation described by Chavez, the books that were being used had been published 20 years earlier and were not suitable for the context; there were not enough books for learners; and there were not enough Teacher's Books. In these situations, we may feel sympathy for the teachers (and blame whatever bodies are responsible on their behalf), but we need to remember that if lack of teacher motivation means that learners are deprived of the opportunity to learn it is the learners who suffer.

### 2.8 Faith in materials

One further reason why teachers may not adapt and supplement a coursebook is that they do not see any reason to do so. After all, as Ramírez Salas (2004: 3) puts it, 'everything they need is already in a textbook elaborated by people who really know'. The textbook is, in effect, a 'holy book', to be followed religiously. This attitude is most likely to be found in contexts where one or more of the factors already discussed also apply – for example, where teachers are untrained or inexperienced. It can also be reinforced when teachers are given little freedom.

## 3. Why do teachers not use systematic approaches to textbook selection and subsequent evaluation?

As we have seen in Chapters One and Three, much hangs on textbook selection. If a suitable textbook is chosen, both teachers and learners feel better supported, and less adaptation and supplementation is needed. Yet when a decision needs to be made as to the choice of a textbook those most affected (teachers and students) are often not involved. The decision is made for them by the Ministry, an administrator or a head of department (Chapter Five). Unfortunately, even when teachers have the freedom to make the choice, either collectively or individually, they seem not to approach this in a systematic way (Chapter Five). One of the strongest recommendations in the professional literature is that a checklist be used (Chapter Three). This would encourage detailed examination of the materials under consideration and allow for easy comparison of both materials packages and teacher-evaluator judgements of these. Careful thought is needed, however, as to the design of checklists in terms of what they demand of teachers and how they are used (Chapter Five).

Some of the reasons why teachers do not follow this professional advice, such as lack of time, lack of training and lack of confidence, have been referred to in Chapter Five and are identical or similar to those discussed above in relation to adaptation and supplementation.

Although lack of time is a factor frequently mentioned by teachers themselves, this is arguably less important than two other lacks: lack of training (and the related lack of awareness of the professional literature) and lack of confidence (see, for example, Law, 1995; Wang, 2005 and Sampson, 2009). Peacock's (1997a) speculations that teachers may be 'unaware of the existence of checklists' or 'cannot obtain them, do not want to make the effort of using them or are put off by their length and apparently complicated nature' (p.1) all point to the necessity for teacher education in materials evaluation.

If textbook evaluation does not form part of teacher training (initial or in-service) and if teachers do not attend conferences or subscribe to teachers' magazines or professional journals in which this subject is discussed, it is hardly surprising if they are not aware of the advice that is available (though papers on the topic of materials evaluation are now easily accessible on the internet). As a consequence, when they are in a position to make a decision about textbook choice they simply rely on their individual or collective instinct. Moreover, experienced teachers who feel they have a good understanding of the needs of the kinds of learners they teach will often feel quite confident that they can make the right choice. They may also reject suggestions that they should approach textbook selection in a different, more systematic way on the grounds that this would be too time-consuming, implying that they also feel it to be unnecessary (see, for example, Fredriksson & Olsson, 2006). Faced with this wall of confidence, a new but very inexperienced junior teacher is unlikely even to offer an opinion. As a relatively inexperienced Japanese teacher confided, 'When I and my co-workers chose coursebooks, I just said "Yes" to their selection. I was the youngest, and they were more experienced and knew students' needs more' (Matsumara, 2010). In such circumstances, even those who happened to have some knowledge of the procedures suggested in the professional literature might well think it best to keep such knowledge to themselves.

Although the focus of much of the materials evaluation literature has been on predictive evaluation, the argument for careful evaluation also extends to in-use and retrospective evaluation (Chapter Three). Many teachers will evaluate coursebooks and other materials at the point when they are planning schemes of work and individual lessons, principally in order to determine what to use/omit. However, inexperienced teachers are likely to be less comfortable adapting materials in the course of a lesson than their more experienced colleagues (Sampson, 2009), and there is little evidence of organized in-use evaluation. Ellis (1998) has speculated that after using a book day after day teachers know all they need to about it or that they see the task as just too daunting, and McGrath (2002) has suggested that in-use and post-use evaluation do not happen because time has not been allocated for this. What teachers themselves tend to say is that they do carry out both forms of evaluation but in a much more impressionistic, less formal way than is suggested in the literature (see, for example, Law 1995).

## 4. Why do teachers not involve learners in materials evaluation and development?

We have heard a great deal in recent years about the shift to learner-centred classrooms and some of the evaluation research discussed in Chapters Five and Seven did indeed elicit learners' views. However, there is no evidence of learners' views being sought as an input to the coursebook selection process, and relatively few accounts of their being involved in materials development.

Explanations may again be similar to those offered above. Lack of training, for example, might account for a lack of awareness of the contributions that learners could make, particularly in relation to learner-generated materials, which have still not had the attention they deserve. The perceived pressure to get through the book (lack of systemic freedom) also militates against openness to learner inputs. Asked if he ever encouraged pupils to bring materials to class, a Chinese teacher in a senior middle school said: 'I will ask my students to find something interesting, to bring to the class and we will stick it to the board, for example, for students to refer to after class if they have interest'. The same teacher added: 'the textbook is very much important in my educational setting. We didn't talk about students, just about teachers. We have competition pressure. . . . All of us want to follow the textbook first, because the content of the exam will be selected from the textbook, and exams we cannot decide by ourselves, but by the school or the coordinator of our team'.

## 5. Summary and conclusions

Comparison of Chapters Five to Seven with Chapters Two to Four revealed some gaps between 'practice' (what actually happens) and 'theory' (as recommended by textbook writers, in the professional literature and on teacher education courses). The focus of this chapter has been on explanations. As we have seen, various contextual constraints ('situated' and 'external' in Zheng & Davison's terms) limit opportunities for teacher autonomy, and individual factors such as time, inexperience and, related to this, lack of confidence, also play a part. Because there is no single, simple explanation for the gaps, they cannot be bridged by a single solution. In Part Three, we will consider how teachers and those interacting with them directly and indirectly might respond to this challenge.

# PART THREE
# Implications

# CHAPTER NINE

# Implications for teachers, managers, ministries, publishers and coursebook writers, and research

> . . . although teachers are aware that language textbooks contain pedagogically useful materials designed to help learners adopt a broader orientation to language learning and use, their use of textbooks was often replaced by test format worksheets.
>
> (Lee & Bathmaker, 2007: 368)
>
> Despite the good work of journals and international and local teachers' associations, ELT is still profoundly isolationist. In sequestered educational pockets the world over there are enthusiasts busily re-inventing the wheel for themselves. There comes a point at which the diversity inherent in ELT teacher-training and educational practice becomes nothing less than a confusion which impedes professional development. *Nowhere is this clearer than in the inchoate state of affairs surrounding the development and evaluation of textbooks.*
>
> (Sheldon, 1987b: 5, emphasis added)

# 1. Introduction

One of the most obvious implications of Part Two of this book is that the case for teacher education in materials evaluation and design can be argued not only on theoretical grounds but is also a practical necessity. This has been recognized in some quarters, but not all: materials evaluation and design is not a core component of pre-service curricula, and on postgraduate programmes usually figures only as an elective or as a small part of a broader module.

More generally, Chapters Five to Eight have revealed a gap between what (many) teachers do and the expectations of the professional community, as reflected in the views expressed in Chapters Two to Four. To point to such a gap seems to imply that teachers are failing to live up to their responsibility, that their practice is deficient relative to the theory. However, another possibility is that the theory is deficient because it fails to take into account the reality experienced by teachers. The studies referred to in Chapter Eight demonstrate very clearly that many teachers are asked to work with tools (books) which are inappropriate or inadequate in work environments which militate against the kind of critical, creative teaching advocated in Part One.

In **Section 2**, below, we consider what teachers themselves can do to improve the situation. We then discuss the implications for those who, in one way or another, influence the published materials that teachers work with and how they work with them. **Section 3** is addressed to managers – such as Heads of Department – in institutions, **Section 4** to Ministries of Education, and **Section 5** to publishers and coursebook writers. **Section 6** makes recommendations for further research. Teacher education is the focus of Chapter Ten.

# 2. Implications for teachers

## 2.1 Introduction

As Tomlinson (2011e) points out, 'many teachers who come to conferences and workshops are *untypically* knowledgeable, enthusiastic and discerning' (p.296, emphasis added) and this applies equally to those who subscribe to magazines and journals for teachers and read books about teaching. Although there is an opportunity dimension to this (some have opportunities to attend conferences, the money to buy journals or access to libraries and others do not), motivation – the enthusiasm of which Tomlinson writes – is also a factor. The teachers who probably need to read this section most are those who would not read it of their own accord. It is therefore addressed primarily to the self-directed minority, in the hope that they will act as change agents within their own professional communities.

## 2.2 Towards more learner-centred teaching

One of the strongest reasons for teachers to adapt and supplement textbooks is that voiced by students in Chapter Seven. Many students accept that a textbook has value but they do not want teachers simply to work their way through the book. They want the teacher to breathe life into the book; and they want some variety in the form of supplementary materials which have intrinsic interest and relevance. This means that materials selection and materials use have to take learners' interests and preferences into account, ideally directly rather than on the basis of assumptions or predictions.

Some teachers may be reluctant to spend class time in seeking information or feedback from learners. An excellent source of ideas for supplementary language practice activities which will also reveal learners' attitudes to their coursebooks is Davis, Garside and Rinvolucri (1998). This contains activities which variously encourage language learners to preview, analyse, evaluate, comment on, teach from their coursebooks – and even imagine what the authors of the coursebook are like and interview 'them' (or the empty chair which represents them). The teacher using such materials would learn a great deal about students' beliefs and attitudes and, indeed, about their often underrated capacities for judgement. Within the language proficiency component of a pre-service teacher education course for non-native speakers of English, activities of this kind could have particular appeal. Learners might also enjoy and benefit from being asked to find or create materials that can replace or supplement part of a coursebook lesson. The responses of learners quoted in Chapter Seven suggest that this is at least worth trying.

## 2.3 The value of collaboration

Any solitary enterprise is difficult and teachers working alone to develop materials can feel lonely. By working in a wholehearted way with others, they can become aware of common problems, exchange ideas for overcoming them, work together to produce materials, then pilot and evaluate them. What probably seemed a time-consuming, laborious, even impossible task for the individual becomes manageable, interesting, and satisfying when one works as a group; and the more seriously one takes this process, the better the results. As Yan (2007) points out: 'Joint team efforts may provide teachers with opportunities to share experience and expertise, to exchange various skills, talents and points of view'; moreover, 'with a supportive team culture established, the institutional understanding and support is more likely to occur' (ibid.). This last point is also important: a group may well be able to negotiate changes within an institution that would have been impossible for an individual.

Where encouragement and facilitating structures are not provided by the institution (e.g. time set aside for meetings, a place to meet, resources), teachers may feel the need to set up a self-help teacher development (TD) group (see, for example, Head & Taylor, 1997 for ideas). Even where an institution has a staff development programme, a TD group can be a good idea. Staff development programmes, especially in large organizations, are not always responsive to the subject-specific needs and concerns of classroom teachers. In one of the three teaching contexts studied by Johansson (2006), the four English teachers met regularly for what they called 'ideas seminars' in which they would 'discuss new ideas, show each other material and exchange material with each other' (p.15).

## 2.4 *Professionalism*

Underlying everything that has been said here is a notion of the teacher as professional. This implies a sense of responsibility towards those with whom one is working (learners, in the first instance), but also a self-directed determination to develop one's own expertise. If support for professional development is not provided by the employer, then it falls to teachers themselves to acquire the necessary expertise through their own efforts, by accessing the experience of others (through reading, attending conferences and talking to colleagues, for instance) and by experimentation and self-evaluation, with input from students and colleagues. A professional teacher can be expected to exercise autonomy (McGrath, 2000). This is much easier, of course, in an encouraging and supportive environment.

# 3. Implications for institutional managers

'Managers' here refers to those within institutions who have responsibility for decisions which impact on teacher freedoms. In most institutions, this will be someone in the role of head of department or director of studies, but it may also be a head teacher or an administrator. Managerial roles may also be distributed among senior staff.

## 3.1 Materials selection, evaluation and resource development

The situation described in Chapter Five has certain clear implications as far as materials (and particularly coursebook) selection is concerned. In some contexts, teachers feel disenfranchised, and resentful and frustrated as a consequence: they are expected to teach with a book, but do not have any say in the selection of that book. The voting system adopted in some institutions may have its disadvantages, but it is at least an acknowledgement of teachers' right to be involved in a decision that affects them.

In addition to wanting a voice in the selection of materials, teachers call for principles/criteria which can make the selection process more systematic. As we have seen in Chapter Three, a great many ready-made instruments are available, but if the decision is taken to use one of these, then collective customization is advised. The alternative is to start from a basic set of criteria which can be elaborated in ways which are relevant and meaningful to those who will use them, but which can also be easily revised in the light of experience. Both approaches would offer an opportunity for teacher development and should ensure an even greater feeling of ownership.

Systematic predictive coursebook evaluation can also identify gaps in the materials selected which can only be filled by resource development, and collaborative work to create these resources will be of practical benefit to all. It will also raise critical awareness, provide a further opportunity for teachers to learn from each other and develop teachers' confidence in their ability to adapt and design materials.

Chapter Eight posed the question 'Why don't teachers do what they're supposed to?' Some of the answers lie in factors which are outside teachers' control (such as the fit between prescribed materials and examinations – see Section 4), but others are very much in the hands of managers. Apart from the manager's willingness to share responsibility for decision-making concerning materials selection with teachers, these would include creating time for meetings in which materials in use could be discussed and ideas for adaptation and supplementation exchanged; providing the kind of in-house training and ongoing support that would give teachers the confidence to use the materials critically and creatively; and setting up systems for the sharing of the resources that are developed. A good manager would also want to take care that coursebooks and other materials that are purchased are also evaluated at the end of a period of use to ensure that the procedure by which they were selected is as reliable as it could be (see Chapter Three).

## 3.2 Teacher autonomy

Institutional policies which constrain teacher freedoms may be well-intentioned, but are not necessarily in the best interests of learners (many of whom, as we have seen, are bored by an undiluted diet of textbook) or teachers, whose professional development is stunted if they cannot experiment. A constant theme in these suggestions is therefore the shift from a bureaucratic structure in which a single individual directs the separate activities of other individuals to a more democratic structure in which the same individual has responsibility for coordinating the collaborative activity of others or may even delegate some responsibility to working groups. The latter structure not only makes fuller use of the human resources within the teaching force, it also encourages collegiality and professionalization.

Commenting on teacher freedom from the perspectives of both a teacher and a manager, Twine (2010: 51) concludes:

> Learners and teachers need to feel they belong to a body in which things are done in a certain, effective and professional way. This can only be achieved through a degree of conformity and managers may have to set limits. . . . Lesson planning, recording and acting upon individual student needs meaningfully, and selecting or inventing learning activities within the classroom, are where freedoms for teachers should lie.

This implies not only a level of understanding on the part of teachers as to what is expected of them and the limits of their autonomy, it also assumes a level of trust in teacher professionalism on the part of managers. Where either of these conditions is lacking, some form of positive action on the part of the manager may be necessary. Tsui's (2003) study describes Marina, a panel chair in Hong Kong:

> Marina worked hard to keep up the tradition of modifying and adapting textbooks. This was not easy because this practice had been questioned by some colleagues who thought that it would be simpler just to follow the textbook. Marina had to insist on being critical about textbooks and improving them. If they gave up this practice, the English panel [department] would stagnate, she felt. To set an example, she adapted the materials and shared them with colleagues. (p.97)

As this quotation illustrates, the cultural converse of a lack of systemic freedom need not be total freedom and individualism: it may instead be a climate in which the desirability of certain goals are agreed, but teachers use their own preferred means to reach these – and support and stimulate each other by sharing ideas and materials. Where adaptation is the norm and there are models available, the inexperienced will gain the confidence to adapt; where website-sharing is the norm, the inexperienced can contribute on an equal basis; and, when necessary, the manager may have to lead from the front.

## 4. Implications for ministries of education

### 4.1 Integration of teaching syllabus, textbook and examination

Teachers frequently complain of a lack of fit between the materials they are expected to use and the examination for which students are preparing. What makes matters worse, is that they often have no say in which materials are to be used. The response of Singaporean teachers in vocational schools, described by Lee and Bathmaker (2007), is typical: 'although teachers are aware that language textbooks contain pedagogically useful materials designed to help learners adopt a broader orientation to language learning and use, their use of textbooks was often replaced by test format worksheets' (p.368).

For an outsider, possible solutions to the problem of incoherence in centralized systems are easily described, if perhaps harder to implement. Syllabus development, textbook production and examinations need to be part of an integrated operation. It helps if they are housed in the same building, but regular coordination meetings should be a *sine qua non*. Teacher interests are best catered for if there is teacher (and, if appropriate, inspector) representation on committees.

### 4.2 Research-informed, realistic, contextually sensitive syllabuses

There is another kind of disjunction that is just as important, and that is the variation in teaching situations within a country (often characterized as the urban–rural divide). In such cases, official/institutional goals and syllabuses often seem to be out of step with classroom realities and, if this is the case, are meaningless. Context-specific research is needed which takes in the whole spectrum of teaching situations, teachers and learners that constitute the system. Goals derived from that research can then be formulated which are realistic in terms of their minimum expectations; teaching syllabuses established which are appropriate (and perhaps flexible) in terms of their content; and, forms of assessment devised which reflect the objectives, content and emphases of these syllabuses, but above all permit learners to show what they know and can do.

## 4.3 Materials

The starting-point for writers of national textbooks may be a syllabus, a national examination framework, and current theories of language learning and language teaching, but in order to produce materials which will facilitate teaching and learning writers also need to consider what is known about effective practices and constraints in the context, that is, the research mentioned above. As successful textbook writing projects have demonstrated (see, for example, Popovici & Bolitho, 2003 on the Romanian textbook writing project, and Tomlinson, 2011b: 24–5 and Lund, 2010 on the Namibian project directed by Brian Tomlinson), individual writers need not have prior textbook writing experience, but they must have access to professional expertise. Regular meetings between the writing team and Ministry are also desirable.

Piloting during the writing process is highly desirable, but regular review/evaluation of the materials also needs to follow the full-scale introduction of the book. Feedback should be elicited from inspectors/supervisors (if appropriate), teachers, and learners and used to inform revisions so that those who have contributed know they have been listened to. From a longer-term perspective, evaluation should also consider learning outcomes, as measured by examination results but also performance in subsequent levels of the educational system (e.g. the transition from primary to secondary, lower secondary to upper secondary, secondary to tertiary). Ministries also need to remember that when there are insufficient materials for learners, when teachers do not have access to a Teacher's Book, or when components of a new course are not supplied, a teacher's task is made much more difficult.

In contexts where a Ministry requires that textbooks be approved, approval processes must be explicit and criteria transparent. Committees should include elected teacher representatives. Where institutions have a choice of textbook, either from an approved list or a free choice, guidelines should be provided on selection (and ongoing evaluation) processes. Advice on course planning which recognizes that schools and learners differ is also desirable.

## 4.4 Teacher education

If, within a particular educational system, pre-service and in-service programmes are part of the same vision and the latter can build on the former, it should be possible to plan an approach to materials evaluation and design that differentiates between the likely needs of future teachers (in the first instance, for teaching practice) and practising teachers. However, the reality is that there is not always a materials component in pre-service programmes, and even when there is, the objectives and content of this component might differ markedly from one institution to another. The following quotation comes from a book published some 25 years ago:

Despite the good work of journals and international and local teachers' associations, ELT is still profoundly isolationist. In sequestered educational pockets the world over there are enthusiasts busily re-inventing the wheel for themselves. There comes a point at which the diversity inherent in ELT teacher-training and educational practice becomes nothing less than a confusion which impedes professional development. *Nowhere is this clearer than in the inchoate state of affairs surrounding the development and evaluation of textbooks.* (Sheldon 1987b: 5, emphasis added)

Although there has been progress, evidenced in the number of courses dealing with the topic of materials evaluation and development and writing about this, Sheldon's basic point still holds good: there is as yet no agreement as to the objectives and, therefore, content of such courses (see Chapters Three and Four).

At the same time, it needs to be recognized that teachers' level of linguistic confidence (related to their language proficiency or their knowledge about the language) will influence the extent to which they are able to critique and adapt the language content of the materials. Support for teachers who are not English-trained or who lack confidence because their language proficiency is weak must therefore go hand in hand with any attempt to change the way they use textbooks.

# 5. Implications for publishers and textbook writers

## 5.1 Design

The criticisms made of visual design in both student and teacher materials (see Chapter Three) suggest that much could be done to improve clarity, coherence, variety and general visual appeal.

## 5.2 Meeting the demand for relevance

The point has been made in earlier chapters that hard-pressed teachers need materials that require little preparation. At the same time, they want materials that are relevant to their learners. National coursebooks and privately published local coursebooks are often seen as inferior to global coursebooks because they are less attractive or less interesting, but global coursebooks are criticized for their lack of relevance. International publishers have responded to these needs and wants in a number of ways. These include multi-component courses, the provision of photocopiable and customizable materials, such as tests, and the development of local versions of global courses.

Multi-component courses are expensive for publishers to produce and therefore expensive to buy; to be fully exploitable, they require certain technological resources to be available; and the 'mix-and-match' (or 'pick and mix') approach is demanding in terms of teacher planning time. Tomlinson et al. (2001: 98) note: 'A number of publishers have told us that they only publish multiple-component courses because their rivals do, and that they would be happy to jettison many of the money-losing components (such as videos and resource packs) and to return to the days when a course consisted of a student's book, a cassette, and a teacher's book'.

From a publisher's point of view, the local version represents an extra expense, and has to be justified in financial terms. Tomlinson (2010b), who seems to be thinking primarily about the relevance of texts, suggests that publishers might provide more material online so that it can be modified more easily by teachers themselves. Masuhara et al. (2008: 298) are therefore adopting a different perspective when they criticize the trend towards photocopiable and customizable materials on pedagogic grounds (the materials 'favour teaching and testing explicit and discrete knowledge' rather than 'nurturing skills' or providing 'interactive face-to-face feedback'). While there may be some force in this criticism, it has to be recognized that there is a place in language learning for discrete knowledge, provided this is balanced by opportunities for other kinds of learning and practice; and that interactive feedback need not be face-to-face – indeed, many learners like the instant neutral feedback provided by a computer. There are important differences, however, between photocopiable and customizable materials. From a pedagogic perspective, photocopiable materials lend themselves to unthinking use, and yet are just as likely to need adaptation as any general-purpose material. As far as logistics are concerned, both require a photocopier, while customizable materials need a computer and printer. These facilities are still not available in institutions universally.

## 5.3 *Further steps*

Publishers and writers could take a number of further steps which might be both simpler and more cost-effective.

- **The provision in Teacher's Books** (whether accompanying global or local courses) **of ideas for adaptation** (and especially personalization and localization) **and additional activities.** More specifically, Teacher's Books can include lesson plans which show how the material could be adapted for different lesson lengths; illustrate how materials can be adapted to cater for different learner needs and different levels of proficiency; and provide additional photocopiable materials (Bell & Gower, 2011).

- **The provision in Students' Books of engaging texts.**
  A textbook was initially, of course, a book which contained written texts and, as we have seen, teachers are concerned that texts – and they seem to be thinking primarily of reading texts – should be interesting to their learners. One of the findings of Tomlinson et al.'s (2001) survey of adult courses was that: 'The reading texts which are provided are usually too short and bland to provide anything to think or talk about. The listening texts also tend to be fairly mundane interviews, or monologues about hobbies, jobs, journeys, customs, routines, etc. Many of them are quite realistic (and even interesting) but responding to them calls for very little cognitive or affective engagement' (p.299). Masuhara et al.'s (2008) review of eight further adult courses found that these were dominated by listening and speaking activities.

- Teachers and learners also need **materials that offer scope for differentiation**, different levels of challenge and options to suit learners' activity preferences – in short, choice. Tomlinson's (2008b) suggestions include the provision of different versions of the same text with generic questions.

- **Activities which invite learners to draw comparisons** (e.g. between their own culture or experience and that depicted) would be one way in which global courses could attempt to reduce the sense of alienation felt by some learners. If the topics, situations, images and underlying values presented are too far removed from learners' experience, there will still be a problem, of course.

- The coursebooks examined by Tomlinson et al. (2001) looked very European, 'despite what seems to be a token attempt to include a few photographs of other continents and cultures' (p.89). Masuhara et al. (2008) note in their review that 'Almost all the photos we see in the current courses seem to be things British or western . . ., possibly biased towards young, healthy and smiling faces', although some books 'offer some variety of figures from different ethnic groups and different age ranges' (p.303). The same point applies to cultural values (see Chapter Three). **Learners need to feel that the material is relevant to their worlds, their lives.** Teachers can try to localize and personalize, but this is only a partial solution to the problem of identification, and teachers would need to do less if publishers did more.

## 5.4 The courage to be different

Suggestions have been made over the years that the kind of dynamic, creative interaction between teacher and learners and among learners that stimulates motivation and leads to real learning can best be facilitated by the provision of core resources that can be used flexibly (see, for example, Brumfit, 1979; Allwright, 1981; Sheldon, 1988; Maley, 2011). One of the problems with this proposal is that it makes assumptions on the one hand about teacher expertise and proficiency and on the other about the willingness of students (and, if relevant, their parents and administrators) to accept the fact that 'the course' that one group of students follow will be very different from that experienced by another, and that opportunities for students of previewing and reviewing lesson material will be greatly reduced. In contexts where teachers are capable and learners open, this is nevertheless an exciting possibility; but for it to be more than a possibility, a publisher must be willing to take a financial risk.

There is also the not insignificant issue of determining what ought to constitute the core.

One of the criticisms made of coursebooks is that they fail to reflect the findings of applied linguistics research (see Chapter Three). In response, Richards (2006: 23) makes this point: 'the success of teaching materials is not dependent upon the extent to which they are informed by research . . . research-based teaching materials have sometimes been spectacular failures in the marketplace because they failed to consider the role of situational constraints'. The argument for situational research was made in Section 4, above. The problem for materials developers (textbook writers and publishers) is, of course, to decide which other research is relevant.

In Chapter One, brief reference was made to English as a lingua franca (ELF). The potential implications of this movement are wider and perhaps much more momentous than has yet been realized. As outlined by Ur (2009), these include:

- A change in the concept of what 'English' is: an internationally comprehensible variety of the language rather than a single 'native' model.

- A change in the goal of English teaching: to produce fully competent English-knowing bilinguals rather than imitation native speakers.

- A change in the cultural background to English courses: 'home' and 'international' culture predominate.

- A change in materials and test design, relating to both content and language.

- A change in the image of the English teacher: 'native-speakerness' less important than linguistic competence, teaching competence, intercultural competence.

The logic of the fourth bullet point is inescapable. Will this encourage a publisher to dare to be different?

# 6. Implications for research

## 6.1 The need for further research

Earlier chapters of this book have revealed that teachers may not be doing (especially in relation to materials evaluation) what coursebook writers and others expect them to. It would be helpful to know why: is it that the theory fails to take account of practical reality or that practitioners are unaware of the theory? We have also seen that descriptions of adaptation procedures and principles in the professional literature are somewhat confusing and discussion of supplementation very limited. Further research into teachers' practices in both these areas would appear to be necessary to establish a firmer theoretical foundation for descriptions of desirable teacher practices.

Research agendas have, of course, been suggested by a number of previous writers on materials (e.g. Byrd, 1995b; McGrath, 2002, chapter 10; Tomlinson, 2003c: 455–6; 2011d; Harwood, 2010b; Masuhara, 2011). The purpose of this section is not to summarize those proposals but rather to draw implications from the evidence presented in earlier chapters. It would be surprising, of course, if there were not some overlap.

## 6.2 Suggested research foci

### 6.2.1 The institution

All systems can benefit from a fresh scrutiny from time to time, and the following suggestions might be used by an institutional manager, for instance, as a form of quality assurance check. They might also be used as part of a study for comparing perspectives (and any overlap with the questions in Sections 6.2.2 and 6.2.3 is therefore deliberate).

- What stages are involved in course planning? How are these justified?

- How are materials selected? What is the process and what criteria are used? What evidence is there that this process works optimally?

- If a coursebook is used, are teachers expected to adapt and supplement the book? If so, what evidence is there that they do so? Is practical guidance available? For example, are they made aware of suitable sources of supplementary material?

- If decisions concerning material selection and evaluation are delegated to teachers, what forms of guidance, support and monitoring are in place?

- Is there a formal system for sharing and storing supplementary materials or materials which teachers have written themselves?
- Are coursebook materials evaluated during use and after use? If so, how is the information used?

## 6.2.2 The teacher perspective

The following questions could be explored by a lone teacher, a group of teachers or an in-service teacher working with a teacher educator. There is a particular need for observation-based studies, preferably with a longitudinal dimension to provide an evidential basis for descriptions of effective practices to be used in teacher education. These might also serve other purposes, both institutional and personal-professional. The answers to several questions would be of particular interest to coursebook writers.

- How is planning for courses organized – what steps are involved? Do teachers feel the planning process works well?
- What do teachers see as the role of materials (and specifically a coursebook, if one is used)?
- How are materials selected (process and criteria)? What is the role of teachers in the selection process? Do they feel the selection process works well?
- What do teachers see as their role vis-à-vis materials and learners?
- Do teachers feel they have enough knowledge of what materials are available (including online materials)? Do they have easy access to enough material?
- Where teachers are using one or more coursebooks, what do they think of these? What do they like/dislike? What do they want from coursebooks?
- Where teachers are using a single coursebook, are they free to adapt it in any way they wish (e.g. by omitting or making changes to exercises or activities)? If they have this freedom, do they use it? Are they free to supplement the coursebook? If so, do they?
- At the lesson-planning stage, what influences teachers' specific decisions to adapt coursebook or other materials (e.g. which exercises to omit/adapt and, in the case of adaptation, how to do this)? What influences specific supplementation decisions (e.g. whether to borrow from an existing source, look for authentic materials, write original materials)?
- What influences further materials-related decisions during a lesson?

- Do teachers share materials? Do they work together to develop materials?
- Do teachers advise learners on how to use and access materials out of class?
- Do teachers evaluate materials while using them? If so, what kinds of record do they keep of this process, and how is this record used subsequently?
- Do teachers involve learners in materials evaluation, selection or creation? If so, how? If not, why not?
- Do teachers evaluate materials at the end of a period of use? If so, in what ways and how is this information used?
- Do teachers agree that they should possess the necessary knowledge and skills to plan courses, select, adapt, supplement, write and evaluate materials? What training have they received in these areas, and what effect has this had on their practices? What training and ongoing support is available in the workplace? What do they see as their continuing needs?

## 6.2.3 The learner perspective

We know far too little about learners' perspective on materials, on the roles of the teacher, or on their own roles. Answers to the following questions would provide useful input for individual teachers and, more widely, for coursebook writers and teacher educators.

- Where a coursebook is being used, what do learners see as the purpose of the book? What do they like and dislike about the coursebook they are using? What do they want from coursebooks and materials, more generally?
- What do they see as their own role in relation to materials? If they have a coursebook, how do they use it outside class? Do they tend to pay attention only to those parts emphasized by the teacher (or those parts relevant to an external exam, if these are different)? What do they do with handouts after a class?
- What do learners see as the role of the teacher in relation to the coursebook?
- What do they feel about the teacher's use of the coursebook? Do they feel s/he uses it too much/not enough? Are they aware of any adaptations made by the teacher? If so, what do they feel about these?

- What do learners feel about any non-coursebook materials provided by the teacher and the relative interest and value of these?
- Have they been asked by their teacher for their opinions about the materials they are using (coursebooks and/or other materials), their interests or their preferred classroom activities? Do they feel their interests, preferences and opinions should be considered?
- Do learners feel they should have a role in deciding which materials to use (e.g. choosing a coursebook, selecting texts)? Do they feel it would be a good idea for the teacher to ask them to bring useful materials to class or even create them?
- How do they react when asked to use materials selected or created by other learners or when given the opportunity to create such materials?

### 6.2.4 Teacher education

There seems little doubt that much of what has been written about materials, their selection and their use has not been read by classroom teachers. Crookes and Arakaki (1999) conclude their small-scale study of teachers in the United States with the tongue-in-cheek suggestion to teacher educators that 'those privileged to be in positions in which they can investigate the extent to which they have grounds for optimism concerning the uptake of their work among the population it is presumably intended to benefit' might find it enlightening to undertake such research (p.8).

If it is indeed the case that classroom teachers, for the most part, do not read the professional literature, this strengthens the argument that materials evaluation and materials development should be a core component of pre-service and in-service undergraduate and postgraduate programmes. The next and final chapter of this book offers a set of choices for the teacher educator, methodological building 'blocks' and 'threads' (Woodward, 2001) which can be discarded, cut and shaped, arranged and added to in whatever way seems to suit the needs of particular participants in a specific context. It is essential, however, that the decisions that are taken (objectives, content, processes and evaluation) and the effects of these should also be a focus of research, and that the findings of this research are disseminated as widely as possible. The 'inchoate state of affairs', characterized by diversity, isolationism and wheel-reinvention, of which Sheldon (1987b: 5) complained has gone on long enough.

# CHAPTER TEN

# Implications for teacher educators:

# A practice-based proposal

> One of the major problems with the current approach to English language teacher education in the UAE is that it relies heavily on the lecturing approach. A second problem is the lack of contact between the university faculty and teachers in the schools. In fact, university lecturers have very little, if any, contact with what is happening in secondary and elementary schools.
>
> (Guefrachi & Troudi, 2000: 189)
>
> An in-service training course or programme is likely to be most useful if it grows directly out of the experiences, assumptions and perceived problems of the trainees.
>
> (Breen et al., 1989: 134)

## 1. Introduction

There are very few published accounts of the success or otherwise of teacher education in materials evaluation and design (but see Breen et al., 1989; McGrath, 2000; González Moncada, 2006; Akbulut, 2007). It is therefore difficult to know whether gaps between practice and theory are a result of lack of training, ineffective training, or the interaction between either of these and contextual and individual factors. Where courses (or course components) do not at present exist, an obvious first step would be to put these in place; and a second step would be to ensure that courses are appropriately targeted and as effective as possible.

With the latter consideration in mind, this chapter focuses on method in teacher education, and specifically the means by which teachers, pre-service and in-service, can be helped to develop the awareness, knowledge, skills and attitudes to fulfil the roles identified in previous chapters. These are represented in Table 10.1, in the form of a set of basic building 'blocks'. From left to right, there is a gradual shift in focus from materials evaluation to materials design (although evaluation continues to be important in design-focused activities). Not all blocks would be equally relevant in all contexts, and on pre-service courses coursebook selection would logically follow work on lesson planning.

**Table 10.1** Course building blocks

| coursebook-based teaching | | | | | |
|---|---|---|---|---|---|
| coursebook evaluation | | lesson planning | | | materials writing |
| selection | in-course/ post-course | analysis | adaptation | supplementation | |

MATERIALS EVALUATION ⟶ MATERIALS DESIGN

There is, of course, a substantial literature on teacher education and, since the 1990s, a growing body of book-length publications on language teacher education (e.g. Richards & Nunan, 1990; Wallace, 1991; Roberts, 1998) and even trainer training (e.g. McGrath, 1997; Malderez & Wedell, 2007; Wright & Bolitho, 2007). Method, in the sense of how to conduct courses for language teachers, is a central theme of Woodward (1991), and Woodward's (1992) 'Ways of Training' is an invaluable source of practical ideas. Much of what holds good for language teacher education in general – as represented by these volumes – has relevance for teacher education in materials evaluation and design. Our concern here, however, will be with process options (procedures, activities and tasks) with this particular focus. These options include tutor input and assigned readings, but the overall emphasis of the chapter is on activities which illustrate theory in practice.

The selection and organization of the building blocks and decisions on process options represent only part of a course design. Something else is needed to bind course components together. This coherence can be provided through the kinds of recurrent activities, or threads, shown in Table 10.2. The threads encourage the continuous reconsideration of professional responsibilities and roles which is essential if teachers are to exploit the full potential of materials for language learning. From a broader perspective, they also stimulate the development of criticality and creativity, thereby contributing to teachers' personal growth and capacity for professional autonomy.

Section 2 draws on the teacher education literature to consider the process options that might be used to develop teacher awareness and competence

# IMPLICATIONS FOR TEACHER EDUCATORS

**Table 10.2** Course threads

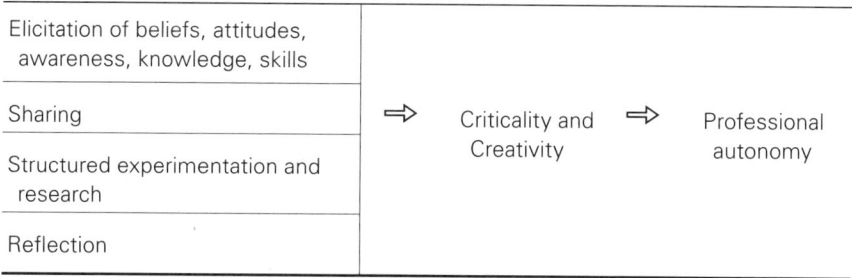

in each of the blocks shown in Table 10.1; and **Section 3** discusses the threads. In both sections, the examples are intended simply to illustrate types of activity. It is assumed that teacher educators will substitute their own content and experiment with procedures.

## 2. Blocks

### 2.1 Coursebook selection

Two basic approaches have been suggested as ways of encouraging and facilitating systematic textbook evaluation for selection purposes. One of these is to start from an existing evaluation checklist. Tanner and Green (1998), for instance, provide their own 'evaluation chart'. Trainees use this to evaluate a coursebook, and then evaluate the chart itself.

For more experienced teachers, a different approach might be more appropriate. Cunningsworth (1979) recommends the following procedure, in which participants are first helped to develop and organize their own criteria for evaluation before the teacher educator presents a checklist:

1  Participants, in small groups, discuss their own criteria for deciding the usefulness of a coursebook.
2  Groups share their conclusions. The teacher educator organizes these under headings such as Language, Methodology, and Psychological Factors, and suggests any additions.
3  The teacher educator presents his/her own set of criteria in the form of a checklist (which conveniently makes use of the same headings). These criteria are then compared with those suggested by participants and either accepted or modified.
4  Participants, again in small groups, are asked to use the agreed criteria to evaluate a coursebook and then to report back to the class. Each group is given a different book and the supporting materials and directed to look at the book as a whole but examine a (specified) typical unit in depth.

A further advantage of the kind of workshop approach suggested by Cunningsworth (1979), exemplified in Guefrachi and Troudi (2000), and made explicit in the final stage of Tanner and Green (1998), is that it allows or even encourages participants to look critically at the criteria/checklist with which they have been working. Richards (1998a) reproduces the criteria which one group of teachers produced under the headings that he supplied (Teacher factors, Learner factors and Task factors). Teacher educators wishing to replicate this particular activity could use these criteria (and categories) as an initial input for discussion or for comparative purposes after a group has generated its own criteria. McGrath (2002) contains a number of tasks which encourage course participants to critique existing checklists (extracts from which are reproduced in an appendix) and develop their own.

On longer courses and especially those which include a historical treatment of methods, Cunningsworth suggests that participants can also be asked to evaluate materials produced at different points in time. This can raise awareness of how 'TEFL thinking has developed and is still developing, and gives access to practical examples of methods and approaches which otherwise they may only hear about in lectures on language teaching theory' (1979: 32).

Harmer (2001: 9) proposes a more wide-ranging approach to coursebooks consisting of a series of four stages. Although he has pre-service courses in mind, there seems no reason why, with minor adaptations, this should not work well on in-service courses too. In Stage 1, trainees are asked: 'How would you write a coursebook, if obliged to do so?' Discussion, Harmer suggests, would touch on issues such as:

> . . . theories and beliefs about language learning, on (types of) syllabus, on topic (including looking at culture and the cultural realities of possible users), on balance (fair representation of different genders and ethnicities), on how authentic the language used should be, and on other issues such as price, design, length and components. . . . Imagining what they would have to think about brings a number of critical issues into play, providing a comprehensive theoretical framework to the training course. (ibid.)

This prepares the ground for Stage 2 and a second question: 'How would you choose a coursebook, if you were in a position to do so?' To answer this question, trainees might be referred to published checklists or alternatively be asked to choose an aspect of textbook design and write statements expressing their own beliefs.

> Thus the trainees concentrating on layout and design might write that 'The page should look clean and uncluttered/The illustrations should be attractive and appropriate', etc. These statements of belief can then form the basis of a new checklist with which to measure a series of books. The point is that in being forced to think about what they believe in (in order

to produce statements), trainees will have to reflect on everything they know and feel about language learning. (ibid.)

Breen et al. (1989) argue that 'an in-service training course or programme is likely to be most useful if it grows directly out of the experiences, assumptions and perceived problems of the trainees' (p.134). This is all the more important when 'lecturers have very little, if any, contact with what is happening in secondary and elementary schools' (Guefrachi & Troudi, 2000: 189), and is just as relevant to pre-service courses. The kinds of activity described above provide an introduction to procedures for systematic coursebook selection and draw on participants' experience. What seems to be missing, however, is the opportunity for participants to talk about their attitudes to and experiences with coursebooks and, in the case of in-service teachers, the selection procedures with which they are familiar. Coursebook use and selection first need to be *problematized*.

## 2.2 In-course and post-course materials evaluation

A variety of practical suggestions for in-course and post-course materials evaluation which could form the basis for discussion tasks can be found in McGrath (2002, chapter 9) and Masuhara (2011).

## 2.3 Materials analysis

Materials analysis activities vary principally according to their scope, their focus, and the approach suggested or implied.

At the macro level, such activities focus on a coursebook, and potentially the various elements of which it is composed. Graves (2000, chapter 9) suggests a number of questions:

- What is the content? (what aspects of language, learning or social context have the authors chosen to focus on? – for example, skills, learning strategies, North American culture)
- How are the materials organized (e.g. according to topics, grammatical features . . .?)
- On what basis are the materials sequenced?
- What is the content of a unit?
- What are the objectives (intended learning outcomes)?
- How will the material help the learner to achieve the objectives?

Specific foci suggested by Richards (1998) include:

- cultural content (the treatment of, for instance, gender, ethnic minorities, the elderly)
- linguistic content (comparison of how a particular linguistic form is presented in a coursebook with, say, the description of the same form in a reference grammar, or instances of its use in corpus data)
- pedagogical content (how particular objectives are realized through tasks). An example based on reading skills is given.

On academic courses, all of these would be suitable research topics. Littlejohn (2011) and Ellis (2011) include examples of task analysis.

McGrath (2002, chapter 5) includes analytically oriented tasks focussing on the objectives, language and format of coursebook exercises. Scrivener (2005) contains examples of tasks which combine analysis with consideration of pedagogical implications. In one task, participants are asked to consider the pros and cons of a number of different ways in which learners might carry out an activity – for example, individually in writing, as pair work discussion (Task 15, p.42). The task thus provides ideas as well as encouraging reflection. A more extended task (Task 17, pp.47–9) incorporates analysis of the objectives of a coursebook activity and the steps involved in using it. A series of tasks in Wright (1987) invite reflection on the roles of materials and teacher (Tasks 40–3).

## 2.4 Materials adaptation

Structured activities focussing on adaptation tend to have two main purposes: to raise awareness of generic forms of adaptation, and to develop the capacity for criticality and creativity through consideration of specific examples.

Tanner and Green (1998) set two useful tasks which illustrate these differences. In the first, participants think of ways of adapting a coursebook, compare those with the actions recommended (remove, add, change, replace) and reflect on the amount of work each would involve – an important consideration. In the second, participants evaluate the adaptations made to part of a coursebook unit, then suggest ideas for alternative adaptations. McGrath (2002, chapter 5), writing for teachers with some experience, asks participants to reflect on their reasons for adapting published materials and the kinds of adaptation they normally make (Task 4.5, p.67). Other tasks encourage experimentation with various forms of adaptation and an opportunity to compare decisions with those offered.

Training activities frequently simulate lesson-planning procedures. For example, the final stage of Harmer's proposed approach is to present trainees with a particular coursebook and ask: 'If you were using this book, would you use this bit of it?' Harmer states:

> For every lesson or extract in the book, they will have to decide whether or not it should be used. . . . If the decision is not to use it, they must say if they would just omit it, or whether they would replace it with something

better. If they do want to use the extract, they will have to say whether or not they will change it in any way and, if so, how. (Harmer, 2001: 9)

There is undoubted value for novice teachers in repeated exercises of this kind, though most teacher educators (and trainees) would probably balk at evaluating 'every lesson . . . in the book'. The same basic procedure can, of course, be used with extracts from a variety of books or the procedure can be varied. In order to make the kinds of decisions required, however, course participants would need some basic contextual information (e.g. on the learners, on course objectives and on lesson length) or first determine this themselves.

A good deal more scaffolding is provided by an activity in Brown (2007). This reproduces a two-page lesson spread containing eight exercises. Brown classifies each of the exercises by type/purpose (e.g. warm-up, question-answer (display), information-exchange), sets a fairly general context, and then poses a set of prompts to encourage reflection on how the exercises might be operationalized or adapted/supplemented. Examples include:

- Is Exercise 1 really the best way to begin the lesson? . . .

- Exercise 7 looks like it needs some background setting and some directions for what students should do *while* they read – what they should look for in the article as they are reading. Maybe I should follow this with some oral whole-class questions to serve as a comprehension check (rather than Exercise 8)?

- Instead of Exercise 8, I think I will consider a 'mixer' in which I get students to line themselves up according to how much they like some of the foods listed in Exercise 1. That might wrap up this lesson with a focus on the message that sweet foods aren't all that healthy. (Brown, 2007: 191)

A task such as this is not only a good example of the kind of questioning that ought to form part of coursebook-based lesson planning but also strikes a balance between suggesting the kinds of answers that might extend the teachers' own pedagogic repertoires and encouraging them to give their own answers. Rather than being provided with a classification of the exercises, as in this case, teachers might be asked to do the classification themselves (Brown provides a useful taxonomy).

McGrath (2002, pp.85–9), in a task intended for more experienced teachers, turns this procedure around by asking participants first to create their own lesson plans based on a two-page coursebook lesson reproduced in Acklam (1994), and then compare their decisions (to select, reject, adapt and supplement) with those of the teacher whose lesson notes are featured in Acklam's article. On a course where participants are using the same teaching materials, teachers' comparison of their own existing lesson plans would provide a more relevant stimulus for discussion and reflection.

Other examples are typically variations on these procedures: that is, participants are given a coursebook extract with adaptations and asked to comment or suggest their own adaptations and then compare these with those supplied. Graves (2003) contains three types of data (a teacher's notes on lesson material, a description of a lesson, and a lesson transcript) illustrating adaptation and supplementation. Readers are invited to think about why the various decisions indicated were made, and Graves gives her own commentary. Hughes (2006), in a very short, practical article on worksheets, invites criticism and adaptation of the first version of a worksheet, then provides an improved version. He also offers a number of further ideas for consideration. This article lends itself very well to a split presentation: participants first critique and adapt version 1; they then compare their adapted exercises with Hughes's version 2 (which is not presented as the last word), and finally discuss his further suggestions. The examples in Graves could be exploited in a similar way – by getting participants to consider first whether the adaptations were really necessary, for instance, or what alternative forms of adaptation might have been used – and Graves's commentary could be withheld until participants have expressed their own views.

Tomlinson (2003c: 451), with in-service courses in mind, advocates a systematic approach, in which participants are taken through the following process:

- profiling a class
- analysing a set of materials
- evaluating the materials
- subtracting sections of the materials
- reducing sections of the materials
- replacing sections of the materials
- expanding sections of the materials
- modifying sections of the materials
- adding sections of materials.

He claims that having been through this process 'a couple of times', participants can usually apply the approach quickly and without too much conscious thought. The next step, ideally, would be that participants have an opportunity to apply the approach to the materials they normally use, thereby creating a bridge between the course and teachers' own contexts.

What is missing from Tomlinson's framework, however, is any reference to the principles that would guide adaptation. Graves (2000) suggests that participants think of a class and an activity in a textbook with which they are familiar and respond to one of a number of questions: for example, 'How would you adapt it to make it more challenging/more personal/to integrate the four skills?' Challenge, or differentiation by level, and personalization were just two of the principles discussed in Chapter 3. Awareness-raising which highlights these and other principles is desirable.

## 2.5 Supplementation

Lesson-planning logically involves consideration of supplementation as well as adaptation (Acklam, 1994). For inexperienced teachers, who are unfamiliar with the range of resources available, sourcing suitable materials can be a problem. Morley (1993) describes a 'book fair', in which trainees are given an evaluation questionnaire and choose in pairs/threes a book to review (coursebook, skills book or language practice book) from those on display. Reports are typed up and comments and suggestions invited; final versions of the reports are circulated at the end of the course. The activity thus provides experience of both evaluation and collaboration as well as reviews of materials with which participants may be unfamiliar. Where easy access to the internet is available, both inexperienced and more experienced teachers can be asked to review online websites as sources of texts, worksheets or games, say.

## 2.6 Materials writing

In a course primarily designed to equip participants to develop materials, experience of writing has to be the central component, as Tomlinson (2003c) argues: the skills involved 'cannot be gained from instruction; they can only be developed gradually, as a result of quality, hands-on experience' (p.452).

Graves (2000, chapter 10) suggests a small-scale materials development task based on text input (four short, authentic housing advertisements are offered as an example). Subsequent reflection on their approach to the task serves to raise participants' awareness of what they consider to be important – their beliefs, in effect. Fifteen design considerations suggested by course participants in response to this task are reproduced.

Writing need not be the starting-point, of course. For Tomlinson (2003c), the demonstration of 'innovative' materials can 'stimulate curiosity, provide the participants with potentially engaging experiences as "learners" and provide concrete illustrations of novel procedures for the participants to reflect on and discuss' (p.449). Such demonstrations are structured in a specific way, by asking participants to switch from the role of learner (experiencing the lesson) to teacher (group analysis of the stages of the lesson, and then the objectives and principles underlying each stage) and then, still in groups, to profile a group of learners for whom the lesson might be intended and the potential effectiveness of the materials used for these learners. During a final plenary discussion in which the groups give their evaluations, the teacher educator might mention any intentions or principles that had gone unnoticed. There might be several such demonstrations, depending on the length of the course.

Participants are also likely to benefit from reading accounts of the working principles and procedures of other writers. Research on expertise has identified qualitative differences between language learning tasks designed by teachers with different levels of specialist experience. Writing about such tasks, Samuda (2005: 232) concludes:

> By focusing on the working practices of expert and non-expert designers, this body of work highlights a number of issues of potential relevance not only to professionals engaged in task design, but also to teachers working with tasks, teacher educators preparing teachers to work with tasks and researchers studying task performance.

Graves (2000, chapter 10) offers insights, in the form of materials and the teacher-writers' reflections on these, into why materials have been developed in the way they have. Further useful sources for a much wider range of writing purposes include the collections edited by Byrd (1995a), Hidalgo et al. (1995), Alexander (2007), Harwood (2010a) and Tomlinson and Masuhara (2010), and papers in Tomlinson (1998a, 2003a and 2011a).

Richards (1998a) suggests an interesting alternative which parallels an activity discussed above under Adaptation: to give course participants a set of goals and an input text taken from published materials (again, we might also want to supply a teaching context/learner profile) and have them develop exploitation materials based on the text. These are then compared with the decisions taken by the professional writer. The participants' products will not necessarily be inferior.

The issue of individual versus small-group writing is considered by Kennedy and Pinter (2007), who describe an MA module in the United Kingdom in which 15 international students, in self-selected groups, designed a syllabus, teaching materials and a teacher's guide for use in their own contexts. Although factors such as time-management and interpersonal relationships affected the smooth functioning of some groups, including one containing students of the same nationality, the comments of one student at least suggest that this was a more beneficial experience than writing alone: 'It was important having others look at your materials. You can't see all the weaknesses for yourself easily' (Susie, interview) (p.212), and 'I would never have thought I could write materials. As a teacher I taught the materials. Now I can see that this is something every teacher can do, and in a way already does, because we do change our materials intuitively as we teach' (Susie, reflection) (p.213). The authors note, 'not all the comments were so upbeat' (ibid.), but saw broader value in the group work in relation to the theoretical aims of the course: 'Some teachers became aware of their own lack of understanding of principles in course design' (p.212) and would then make a self-directed effort to research these further.

# 3. Threads

## 3.1 Introduction

Tomlinson (2003c) argues that to be effective, experience in writing needs to be organized in a particular way and meet certain criteria. It needs to:

- *respect the participants 'as individuals'* and the knowledge, awareness and skills that they bring with them
- *be 'staged and sequenced* so that awareness and skills gained are immediately made use of to facilitate the gaining of further awareness and skills'
- *encourage 'experimentation and risk taking while providing safety and security'*
- *be monitored sensitively and supportively* by tutors who have earned credibility as materials developers themselves
- *allow for sharing of products* so that all participants gain from the pooled resources
- *provide opportunities for 'reflection and modification'*
- *'be stimulating and enjoyable* for the participants'. (Based on Tomlinson, 2003c: 452, emphases added)

Alongside such important considerations as fun and sensitive monitoring and support by appropriately experienced tutors, there is reference here to the kinds of thread identified in the introduction to this chapter: the importance of drawing on participants' existing awareness, knowledge and skills; the need for experimentation; opportunities for sharing and reflection; and progressive capacity building.

## 3.2 Elicitation of beliefs, attitudes, awareness, knowledge, skills

We can perhaps assume that a course in materials evaluation and design will lead to gradual gains in participants' awareness, knowledge and skill and that their beliefs and attitudes will be influenced as a result of this process. The problem with this assumption is that unless we make an effort to discover what participants' starting points are we have no way of knowing how or even whether they have changed.

One of the most obvious ways of getting course participants to articulate their beliefs is a questionnaire. Wright (1987) contains a short questionnaire on teachers' beliefs about materials (first part of Task 40 on pp.76–7) which is suitable for teachers with some experience.

An alternative is to present participants with a list of statements with which they agree or disagree. However, a variation on this which is potentially more engaging and valuable is 'statement modification' (Woodward, 1992; Tomlinson, 2003c). Participants are first asked to agree or disagree individually with a set of categorized statements, rewriting any with which they disagree in a form that expresses their own beliefs. Group discussion is followed by plenary discussion, the purpose 'not being to reach agreement but to explore the issues . . . . An example of a statement under "Texts" would be "Low-level learners should only be given short texts to read and listen to"' (Tomlinson, 2003c: 450). Finally, participants are asked to write individual responses to each statement. Woodward (1992: 159–60) provides a full-length example (relating to dictionary use) of basically the same activity. She comments: 'Reacting to other people's statements by changing them in detail, in part or completely, according to your own opinions, makes you feel powerful. A statement, once modified, can be modified again. Opinions seem to be less rigid once you have crossed out or rephrased words on a page' (p.160). The plenary stage of this activity allows the teacher educator not only to get a sense of individual attitudes and beliefs but also to contribute his/her own ideas to the discussion, if this seems desirable. This would therefore be a very suitable activity for the first session of a course. Tomlinson (2003c) suggests that participants look at their statements again at the end of the course and consider whether their views have changed. Reflective journals (see Section 3.5) can also yield insights, for participants and tutors, into changes in awareness or attitude and what has prompted these.

For beginner teachers, an understanding of, for example, how experienced teachers use a textbook and what they feel about this might be both enlightening and interesting. One possibility would be to play a recording of a teacher talking about textbooks or invite a teacher to attend a training session and answer trainees' questions. Tanner and Green (1998) suggest that trainees carry out their own interviews of two teachers about the coursebooks they use.

Beginner teachers are also likely to benefit from demonstrations of how lesson plans are transformed in the course of a lesson. This can be demonstrated by comparison of lessons plans and videorecorded lessons or lesson transcripts. Recordings of teachers explaining the reasons for the changes would be a valuable complement.

## 3.3 Experimentation and research

Practically focused courses should lead to products: materials (redesigned or original) and evaluation checklists, perhaps. Logically, these should be trialled, ideally in participants' own contexts. On international Masters courses this may only be possible at the dissertation stage, when willing colleagues in participants' own countries may be persuaded to use the materials and give feedback. Checklists can, of course, be initially trialled on peers.

Systematically organized experimentation and evaluation of this kind, though not without logistical difficulties, serves broader purposes than simply discovering how well a product works in that it leads to learning both through the process and about the process. This is clearly the intention underlying tasks in Wright (1987) which involve observation of materials in use (Tasks, 62, 68, 69) and tasks which involve obtaining learner feedback on materials (Tasks 65, 66, 69). McGrath (2006) outlines a procedure in which teachers first experience the research process as participants by supplying and categorizing their own images (metaphors and similes) for coursebooks, then collect and analyse the same kind of data from their students, and compare the two sets of data. One of the experienced teachers who went through this process commented that it was the first time she had really listened to her students' voices.

Research was a key thread running through the Leeds University BA in Educational Studies (TESOL) programme conducted over a nine-year period (1999–2008) for Diploma holders in Oman (Al-Sinani, Al-Senaidi and Etherton, 2009). The approach evolved over time, as these examples of tasks illustrate:

- Early cohorts were asked to design a communicative task to develop students' listening and speaking skills, discuss the theoretical background and criteria for determining effectiveness; later cohorts to teach and evaluate the task, analyse pupils' performance and propose changes.

- For the 'Stories in Language Learning' module, participants in early cohorts were given the task of adapting or design their own 'Big Book' story (for use with young children); those in later cohorts were asked to evaluate the effectiveness of different approaches to the use of Big Books (e.g. story-telling, shared reading, use of powerpoint, or acting out stories).

Al-Sinani et al.'s report is noteworthy for its self-critical tone: the recognition that the approach to assessment of earlier cohorts was unduly constrained by traditional views. Over time, there was a shift in concrete terms from what might be characterized as 'proposal + rationale' (which may be all that is feasible in off-site courses limited by time and logistics) to experimentation/trialling, evaluation and reflection:

> the programme could have started building students' knowledge of and skills in teacher research from the very first assignment, by encouraging teachers to investigate their own learners and their own classrooms. This could have been done through, for example, asking them to carry out case study research with one or more students . . . through simple observation and interview. It could have been done through guided and supported action research, with students implementing a change in their classroom to further explore ideas learnt in the module, and investigating the effect

of that change through analysis of observation, documentary and even conference evidence. (Al-Sinani et al., 2009: 103)

As the tutors involved in the Leeds-Oman project realized, classroom-based tasks on *in situ* courses afford rich opportunities for learning about research, about one's learners, and about one's own capacities.

## 3.4 Sharing

Discussion tasks and practical tasks provide opportunities for participants to share experiences and ideas. On a more formal level, participants may be asked to make individual or group presentations of their research or products. Gebhard (1993) describes a 'materials/media fair' in which course participants organize and invite guests to an event at which their project materials are displayed (materials may include videos, computer activities and games as well as print materials). 'Sooner or later, the guests focus on a popular display, the food table' (p.57).

The notion of sharing might also involve dissemination beyond the course. On the University of Luton MA in L2 Materials Development described by Tomlinson (2003c) participants were expected to present at both internal and external conferences, support being offered through tutorials and a mini-course in 'Making Oral Presentations'. Participants might also be asked to prepare a submission to a journal (see, for example, Woodward, 1992: 83–4). For first-time writers, publication in journals such as *English Teaching Professional*, *Modern English Teaching*, the *RELC Journal* and *English Teaching Forum* is a reasonable objective, and if participants have already read articles from sources such as these during the course they will have some insight into what is required. In some contexts, presentation at a local conference followed by publication in the Proceedings might seem a more achievable first step.

## 3.5 Reflection

Reflection, as Tomlinson (2003c: 453–4) emphasizes, should be a key feature of courses, with participants being 'encouraged to reflect on their views, theories and materials during all phases . . ., outside the course and after the course'. At the beginning of a course, for example, 'they are asked to think about and to articulate their beliefs about language learning and the role that materials should play in it'; they reflect 'when they are evaluating, adapting or producing materials, and at the end of the course when they are evaluating their own and other participants' materials'. Although Tomlinson is here thinking primarily of courses focusing on materials development, his insistence on the importance of reflection has general relevance.

On the assumption that writing encourages deeper reflection than is possible during a class discussion, many teacher educators ask participants to keep journals/diaries/learning logs in which they reflect on course inputs and experiences. On part-time courses or pre-service courses with a practicum component, reflection on the use of materials can also be prompted by recording of lessons and observation, including peer observation (Wright, 1987; Richards & Lockhart, 1994). Careful scaffolding and monitoring is needed, however, to ensure that journals are reflective rather than simply descriptive (see, for example, Jarvis, 1992; Richards & Ho, 1998). Where facilities permit, shared web logs (blogs) are an alternative to the individual journal. Kiss (2007) reports on the use of an online blog during a two-week residential in-service course for teachers in the Philippines. As the following extract from the end of the first week illustrates, teachers had been faced with challenges to both their current practices and what they had learned previously, but were very positive about the experience:

> Looking back yesterday's activity, I could say that I was given the chance to grow up (being one of the youngest of the group). I have to act maturely so we can accomplished the task given. Growing up does not necessarily mean we have to leave all the things we learned in college but it entails utilizing what we learned and join them together to make a better material; a material not for ourselves but for our students. Growing up would also mean sharpening our skills for us just to be independent and critical in dealing with material designing. (Kriscentti Exzur Barcelona, 17 January 2007)

Continuing contact and post-course reflection can be stimulated using a shared blog.

## *3.6 Progression*

One of the course design principles listed by Tomlinson (2003c) is that of staging and sequencing (see Section 3.1). This principle is demonstrated in the following graded sequence of tasks from a course/block focusing on writing materials:

**1** participants decide on the 'voice' they wish to adopt in addressing learners (e.g. 'formal, authoritative' or 'informal, chatty')
**2** writing instructions
**3** writing questions
**4** giving explanations
**5** giving examples
**6** selecting texts
**7** writing texts

**8** exploiting texts
**9** using illustrations
**10** layout and design
**11** writing teachers' notes
**12** writing units of materials. (Tomlinson, 2003c: 451)

The same principle underlies the progression of tasks illustrated in Table 10.1, which shows how criticality can be systematically developed throughout a course:

### Table 10.1: Tasks to encourage criticality

**1 Criticality of the ideas and products of peers (other course participants)**

Tasks:
- Giving feedback during a discussion
- Critique (oral or written) of materials produced by peers (e.g. worksheets, choice of texts, design of tasks, textbook selection checklist).

    NB strict protocol: acknowledge strengths first, then make suggestion

**2 Self-criticality**

Tasks:
- Written reflection on own attitudes to textbook and use of this
- Self-evaluation of own materials in response to criteria provided
- Response to feedback from classmates and peers

**3 Criticality of academic authority**

Tasks:
- Critique (oral or written) of published materials, including websites, and recommendations for adaptation or supplementation
- Written critique of the ideas of published authors (including, if relevant, those of the tutor)

**4 Criticality of systems and attitudes within the teaching context**

Tasks:
- Reflection on procedures used in own teaching context (e.g. criteria and process used to choose textbook and to evaluate

> its effectiveness; expectations in relation to how textbook will be used; opportunities for sharing ideas and materials)
> 
> - Reflection on relationship between examination, syllabus and teaching materials. (McGrath, 2009)

As will be evident from the above tasks, 'criticality' here refers to the ability to recognize both strengths and weaknesses. It should be easier for most participants to be critical of the ideas and products of their peers (point 1), for example, than to be critical of academic authority (point 3), as represented by published authors, especially if, as may sometimes happen, one of those authors is their own tutor. However, there need to be ground rules: for instance, that positive comments should precede suggestions for improvement.

To be critical in the ways referred to above – especially in relation to points 3 and 4 – requires confidence, but that confidence develops as a result of awareness that there are criteria on which we can base judgements, and also through encouragement. The same point applies to creativity. 'Everyone is capable of creativity in varying degrees' (Maley, 2003: 184). This can easily be demonstrated, even when a course does not lead to original materials writing. For some teachers, it is a revelation to realize that things do not have to be like this, that there are other possibilities.

## 4. Summary and conclusion

In the previous chapter we looked at the implications for a variety of groups of gaps between teachers' practices on the one hand and theory relating to the desirable behaviours of teachers on the other. The general conclusion was that there needs to be a rapprochement of the groups involved. Publishers and textbook writers, Ministries and institutional managers all need to be aware of the tools and other forms of support that teachers need if they are to fulfil the roles assigned to them, and endeavour to make their task easier; and teachers themselves need to know what is expected of them, and respond willingly to what they may see as new responsibilities. Teacher education has a vital part to play in shaping teachers' attitudes and developing their abilities, and a carefully designed, contextually sensitive and practice-based approach to teacher education in materials evaluation and design, based on the suggestions in this chapter, could make a real difference.

# REFERENCES

Acklam, R. 1994. 'The role of the coursebook'. *Practical English Teaching* 14.3: 12–14.
Adrian-Vallance, D. and Edge, J. 1994. *Right Track*. Harlow, Essex: Longman.
Akbulut, Y. 2007. Exploration of the beliefs of novice language teachers at the first year of their teaching endeavours. Retrieved 13 February 2010 from www.sosyalbil.selcuk.edu.tr/sos_mak/makaleler/YAVUZ%20AKBULUT/AKBULUT,%20YAVUZ2.pdf
Alamri, A. 2008. 'An evaluation of the sixth Grade English language textbook for Saudi Boys'. Unpublished MA in Applied Linguistics dissertation, College of Arts, King Saud University, Saudi Arabia. Retrieved 26 April 2010 from http://repository.ksu.edu.sa/jspui/handle/123456789/8806/
Alexander, O. (ed.) 2007. *New Approaches to Materials Development for Language Learning*. Proceedings of the 2005 joint BALEAP/SATEFL conference. Bern: Peter Lang.
Allwright, D. 1981. 'What do we want teaching materials for?' *ELT Journal* 36.1: 5–18.
Allwright, R. 1979. 'Abdication and responsibility in language teaching'. *Studies in Second Language Acquisition* 2.1: 105–21.
Alptekin, C. and Alptekin, M. 1984. 'The question of culture: EFL teaching in non-English- speaking countries'. *ELT Journal* 38.1: 14–20.
Al-Sinani, S., Al-Senaidi, F. and Etherton, S. 2009. 'Developing teachers as researchers: The BA Educational Studies (TESOL) programme'. In J. Atkins, M. Lamb and M. Wedell (eds) *International Collaboration for Educational Change: The BA Project* (pp.95–104). Muscat: Ministry of Education, Sultanate of Oman. Retrieved 05 March 2011 from www.moe.gov.om/Portal/sitebuilder/Sites/EPS/Arabic/IPS/Importa/tesol/4/contents.pdf
Altan, M. 1995. 'Culture in EFL contexts – classroom and coursebooks'. *Modern English Teacher* 4.2: 58–60.
Al-Yousef, H. 2007. 'An evaluation of the third grade intermediate English coursebook in Saudi Arabia'. Unpublished MA in Applied Linguistics dissertation, King Saud University, Saudi Arabia. Retrieved 21 April 2010 from ksu.edu.sa/
Amrani, F. 2011. 'The process of evaluation: A publisher's view'. In B. Tomlinson (ed.) 2011a: 267–95.
Angouri, J. 2010. 'Using textbook and real-life data to teach turn taking in business meetings'. In N. Harwood (ed.) 2010a: 373–94.
Ansary, H. and Babaii, E. 2002. 'Universal characteristics of EFL/ESL textbooks: a step towards systematic textbook evaluation'. *The Internet TESL Journal* 8.2. Retrieved 17 September 2010 from http://iteslj.org/Articles/Ansary/-Textbooks/
Appel, J. 1995. *Diary of a Language Teacher*. Oxford: Heinemann.
Arikan, A. 2004. 'Professional development programs and English language instructors: A critical- postmodern study'. *Hacettepe Üniversitesi Eğitim Fakültesi Dergisi* 27 (40–9). Retrieved 13 September 2010 from www.efdergi.hacettepe.edu.tr/200427ARDA%20ARIKAN.pdf
— 2005. 'Age, gender and social class in ELT coursebooks: A critical study'. *Hacettepe Universitesi Egitim Fakultesi Dergisi* 28: 29–38. Retrieved 28 August 2011 from www.eric.ed.gov/PDFS/ED494162.pdf
Arva, V. and Medgyes, P. 2000. 'Native and non-native teachers in the classroom'. *System* 28.3: 355–72.

# REFERENCES

Bahumaid, S. 2008. 'TEFL materials evaluation: A teacher's perspective'. *Poznan Studies in Contemporary Linguistics* 44.4: 423–32. Retrieved 08 November 2010 from http://versita.metapress.com/content/93h1466444p1274n/fulltext.pdf

Balajee, D. 2011. B.Ed. coursework, National Institute of Education, Singapore.

Barbieri, F. and Eckhardt, S. 2007. 'Applying corpus-based findings to form-focused instruction: The case of reported speech'. *Language Teaching Research* 11.3: 319–46.

Bardovi-Harlig, K., Hartford, B., Mahan-Taylor, R., Morgan, M. and Reynolds, D. 1991. 'Developing pragmatic awareness: Closing the conversation'. *ELT Journal* 45.1: 4–15.

Bell, J. and Gower, R. 2011. 'Writing course materials for the world: A great compromise'. In B. Tomlinson (ed.) 2011a (135–50) [revised version of paper with same title in Tomlinson, B. (ed.) 1998a: 116–29].

Berardo, S. 2006. 'The use of authentic material in the teaching of reading'. *The Reading Matrix* 6.2: 60–8.

Block, D. 1991. 'Some thoughts on DIY materials design'. *ELT Journal* 45.3: 211–17.

Bolitho, R. 1990. 'An eternal triangle? Roles for teacher, learners and teaching materials in a communicative approach'. In S. Anivan (ed.) *Language Teaching Methodology for the Nineties* (pp.22–30). Singapore: SEAMEO Regional Language Centre.

Botelho, M. 2003. 'Multiple intelligence theory in English language teaching: An analysis of current textbooks, materials and teachers' perceptions'. Unpublished MA dissertation, Ohio University. Retrieved 12 April 2010 from http://etd.ohiolink.edu/view.cgi?acc_num=ohiou1079466683

Boxer, D. and Pickering, L. 1995. 'Problems in the presentation of speech acts in ELT materials: The case of complaints'. *ELT Journal* 49.1: 44–58.

Breen, M. and Candlin, C. 1987. 'Which materials? A consumer's and designer's guide'. In L. Sheldon (ed.) 1987a: 13–28.

Breen, M., Candlin, C., Dam, L. and Gabrielsen, G. 1989. 'The evolution of a teacher training course'. In R. K. Johnson (ed.) : 111–35.

Breen, M. and Littlejohn, A. 2000. *Classroom Decision-Making: Negotiation and Process Syllabuses in Practice*. Cambridge: Cambridge University Press.

British Council. 1975. *English for Academic Study with special reference to Science and Technology: Problems and Perspectives*. ETIC Occasional Paper. English Teaching Information Centre, British Council.

— 1978. *English for Specific Purposes*. ELT Documents 101. English Teaching Information Centre, British Council.

— 1980. *Projects in Materials Design*. ELT Documents Special. London: The British Council.

Bromseth, B. and Wigdahl, L. 2006. *New Flight 8*. Textbook, Teacher's Book and Workbook. Oslo: Cappelen.

Brown, H. 2007 (3rd edn). *Teaching by Principles*. New York: Pearson.

Bruder, M. 1978. 'Evaluation of foreign language textbooks: a simplified procedure'. In H. Madsen and J. Bowen (eds). *Adaptation in Language Teaching* (Appendix 2) (pp.209–17). Rowley, MA: Newbury House.

Brumfit, C. 1979. Seven last slogans. *Modern English Teacher* 7.1: 30–1.

Brumfit, C. and Rossner, R. 1982. 'The "decision pyramid" and teacher training for ELT'. *ELT Journal* 36.4: 226–31.

Burnaby, B. and Sun, Y. 1989. 'Chinese teachers' views of Western language teaching'. *TESOL Quarterly* 23.2: 219–38.

Byrd, P. (ed.) 1995a. *Materials Writer's Guide*. Boston: Heinle and Heinle.

— 1995b. 'Writing and publishing textbooks'. In P. Byrd (ed.) 1995a: 3–9.

— 2001. 'Textbooks: Evaluation for selection and analysis for implementation'. In M. Celce-Murcia (ed.) (3rd edn) *Teaching English as a Second or Foreign Language* (pp.415–27). Boston: Heinle & Heinle [Appendix A reproduces the checklist in Daoud & Celce Murcia (1979) and Appendix B a checklist designed by Byrd & Celce-Murcia].

Çakıt, I. 2006. 'Evaluation of the EFL textbook 'New Bridge to Success 3' from the perspectives of teachers and students'. Unpublished MSc thesis, Middle East Technical University, Ankara, Turkey. Retrieved 27 April 2010 from http://etd.lib.metu.edu.tr/upload/12607694/index.pdf

Campbell, C. and Kryszewska, H. 1992. *Learner-based Teaching*. Oxford: Oxford University Press.

Canagarajah, A. 1993. 'American textbooks and Tamil students: Discerning ideological tension in the ESL classroom'. *Language, Culture and Curriculum* 6.2: 143–56.

— 1999. *Resisting Linguistic Imperialism in English Teaching*. Oxford: Oxford University Press.

Candlin, C., Bhatia, V. and Jensen, C. 2002. 'Developing legal writing materials for English second language learners: Problems and perspectives'. *English for Specific Purposes* 21.4: 299–320.

Canniveng, C. and Martinez, M. 2003. 'Materials development and teacher training'. In B. Tomlinson (ed.) 2003a: 479–89.

Carroll, M. and Head, E. 2003. 'Institutional pressures and learner autonomy'. In A. Barfield and M. Nix (eds) *Autonomy You Ask!* (pp.69–84). Tokyo: Learner Development Special Interest Group, Japanese Association of Language Teachers.

Caterina. 2003. 'A student-centred language course'. *Humanising Language Teaching* 5.2: 1.

Chambers, F. 1997. 'Seeking consensus in coursebook evaluation'. *ELT Journal* 51.1: 29–35.

Chan, C. 2009. 'Forging a link between research and pedagogy: A holistic framework for evaluating business English materials'. *English for Specific Purposes* 28.2: 125–36.

Chandran, S. 2003. 'Where are the ELT textbooks?' In W. Renandya (ed.): 161–9.

Chavez, E. 2006. 'In-service teachers' beliefs, perceptions and knowledge in the Nicaraguan EFL context'. *Encuentro* 16: 27–39. Retrieved 24 February 2011 from www.encuentrojournal.org/textos/16.4.pdf

Chowdhury, R. 2003. 'International TESOL training and EFL contexts: The cultural disillusionment factor'. *Australian Journal of Education* 47.3. Retrieved 10 September 2010 from www.questia.com/PM.qst?a=o&d=5008899023

Clarke, D. 1989. 'Materials adaptation: Why leave it all to the teacher?' *ELT Journal* 43.2: 133–41.

Coleman, H. 1985. 'Evaluating teachers' guides: Do teachers' guides guide teachers?' In C. Alderson (ed.) *Evaluation*. Lancaster Practical Papers in English Language Education Vol.6 (pp.83–96). Oxford: Pergamon.

Cowie, A. and Heaton, J. (eds) 1977. *English for Academic Purposes*. Centre for Applied Language Studies, University of Reading: BAAL/SELMOUS.

Crawford, J. 2002. 'The role of materials in the language classroom: Finding the balance'. In J. Richards and W. Renandya (eds) *Methodology in Language Teaching: An Anthology of Current Practice* (pp.80–91). Cambridge: Cambridge University Press.

Crookes, G. 2009. *Values, Philosophies, and Beliefs in TESOL: Making a Statement*. Cambridge: Cambridge University Press.

Crookes, G. and Arakaki, L. 1999. 'Teaching idea sources and work conditions in an ESL program'. *TESOL Journal* 9.1: 15–19. Retrieved 17 February 2011 from www2.hawaii.edu/~crookes/CandA.html/

Cullen, R. and Kuo, I.-C. 2007. 'Spoken grammar and ELT course materials. A missing link?' *TESOL Quarterly* 41.2: 361–86.

Cunningsworth, A. 1979. 'Evaluating course materials'. In S. Holden (ed.) *Teacher Training* (pp.31–3). Oxford: Modern English Publications.

— 1984. *Evaluating and Selecting ELT Materials*. London: Heinemann.

— 1995. *Choosing Your Coursebook*. Oxford: Heinemann.

Cunningsworth, A. and Kusel, P. 1991. 'Evaluating teachers' guides'. *ELT Journal* 45.2: 128–39.

Daoud, A.-M. and Celce-Murcia, M. 1979. 'Selecting and evaluating a textbook'. In M. Celce-Murcia and L. McIntosh (eds) *Teaching English as a Second or Foreign Language* (pp.302–7). Rowley, MA: Newbury House.

Darian, S. 2001. 'Adapting authentic materials for language teaching'. *English Teaching Forum Online* 39.2. Retrieved 03 May 2010 from http://eca.state.gov/forum/vols/vol39/no2/p2.htm

Dat, B. 2003. 'Localising ELT materials in Vietnam: A case study'. In W. Renandya (ed.): 170–91.

Davis, P., Garside, B. and Rinvolucri, M. 1998. *Ways of Doing*. Cambridge: Cambridge University Press.

Deller, S. 1990. *Lessons from the Learner*. Harlow, Essex: Longman.

Dendrinos, B. 1992. *The EFL Textbook and Ideology*. Athens: N.C. Grivas.

Dickinson, L. 1987. *Self-instruction in Language Learning*. Cambridge: Cambridge University Press.

Donovan, P. 1998. 'Piloting: A publisher's view'. In B. Tomlinson (ed.) 1998a: 149–89.

Duarte, S. and Escobar, L. 2008. 'Using adapted material and its impact on university students' motivation'. *PROFILE* 9 (online): 63–87. Retrieved 19April 2010 from www.scielo.org.co/pdf/prf/n9/n9a05.pdf

Dubin, F. and Olshtain. E. 1986. *Course Design. Developing Programmes and Materials for Language Learning*. Cambridge: Cambridge University Press.

Dudley-Evans, T. and St John, M. 1998. *Developments in English for Specific Purposes*. Cambridge: Cambridge University Press.

Dunford, N. 2004. 'How do teachers interpret the need for the adaptation and supplementation of coursebooks, with specific reference to data collected by questionnaire from Shane English Schools Japan?' Unpublished MA dissertation, University of Nottingham.

Edge, J. and Wharton, S. 1998. 'Autonomy and development: Living in the materials world'. In B. Tomlinson (ed.) 1998a: 295–310.

Edwards, T. 2010. Review of Meddings, L. and Thornbury, S. 2009. *Teaching Unplugged: Dogme in English Language Teaching*. Peaslake, Surrey: Delta Publishing.

Ellis, M. and Ellis, P. 1987. 'Learning by design: Some design criteria for EFL coursebooks'. In L. Sheldon (ed.) 1987a: 90–9.

Ellis, R. 1997. 'The empirical evaluation of language teaching materials'. *ELT Journal* 51.1: 36–42.

— 2010. 'Second language acquisition research and language teaching'. In Harwood, N. (ed.) 2010a: 33–57.

— 2011. 'Macro- and micro-evaluations of task-based teaching'. In B. Tomlinson (ed.) 2011a: 212–35.

Erdoğan, S. nd. Learner training via course books, and teacher autonomy: A case of need. Retrieved 30 January 2007 from http://lc.ust.hk/~ailasc/newsletters/onlinepaper/sultan.htm

Ewer, J. and Boys, O. 1981. 'The EST textbook situation – an enquiry'. *The ESP Journal* 1.2: 87–105.

Farooqui, S. 2008. 'Teachers' perceptions of textbook and teacher's guide: A study in secondary education in Bangladesh'. *The Journal of Asia TEFL* 5.4: 191–210.

Farrell, T. (ed.) 2008. *Novice Language Teachers: Insights and Perspectives for the First Year*. London: Equinox.

Fauziah Hassan and Nita Fauzee Selamat 2002. 'Why aren't students proficient in ESL: The teachers' perspective'. *The English Teacher* XXVIII, June 2002. Retrieved 21 May 2010 from www.melta.org.my/ET/2002/wp10.htm

Fenner, A. and Newby, D. 2000. *Approaches to Materials Design in European Textbooks: Implementing Principles of Authenticity, Learner Autonomy, Cultural Awareness*. Graz/Strasbourg: European Centre for Modern Languages.

Flack, R. 1999. 'Coursebook deficiency disorder'. *Modern English Teacher* 8.1: 60–1.

Fortune, A. 1992. 'Self-study grammar practice: Learners' views and preferences'. *ELT Journal* 46.2: 160–71.

Fredriksson, C. and Olsson, R. *English Textbook Evaluation: An Investigation into the Criteria for Selecting English Textbooks*. Malmo, Sweden: Malmo University. Retrieved 08 March 2010 from http://dspace.mah.se/handle/2043/2842

Freebairn, I. 2000. 'The coursebook – future continuous or past?' *English Teaching Professional* 15: 3–5.

Freeman, D. and Cornwell, S. (eds) 1991. *New Ways in Teacher Education*. Alexandria, VA: TESOL.

Gardner, H. 1983. *Frames of Mind: The Theory of Multiple Intelligences*. New York: Basic Books.

— 1999. *Intelligence Reframed: Multiple Intelligences for the 21st Century*. New York: Basic Books.

Garinger, D. 2002. *Textbook Selection for the ESL Classroom*. Report No. EDO-FL-02–10. US Department of Education, Office of Educational Research and Improvement, National Library of Education. ERIC Document Reproduction Service No. ED-99-Co-0008.

Garton, S., Copland, F. and Burns, A. 2011. *Investigating Global Practices in Teaching English to Young Learners*. ELT Research Papers 11–01. London: British Council/ Aston University.

Gearing, K. 1999. 'Helping less-experienced teachers of English to evaluate teachers' guides'. *ELT Journal* 53.2: 122–7.

Gebhard, J. 1993. 'The materials/media fair'. In D. Freeman and S. Cornwell (eds) 1993: 56–9.

— 1996/2006 (2nd edn). *Teaching English as a Foreign or Second Language*. Ann Arbor: University of Michigan Press.

Gilmore, A. 2007. 'Authentic materials and authenticity in foreign language learning'. *Language Teaching* 40.2: 97–118.

— 2010. 'Exploiting film discourse in the foreign language classroom'. In F. Mishan and A. Chambers (eds): 109–48.

Gomes de Matos, F. 2000. 'Teachers as textbook evaluators: An interdisciplinary checklist'. *IATEFL Issues* 157. Retrieved 20 June 08 from www.iatefl.org/content/newsletter/157.php

González Moncada, A. 2006. 'On materials use training in EFL teacher education: Some reflections'. *Profile* [online] 7: 101–16. Retrieved 03 November 2010 from http://redalyc.uaemex.mx/redalyc/pdf/1692/169213802008.pdf

Grant, N. 1987. *Making the Most of Your Textbook*. Harlow, Essex: Longman.

Graves, K. (ed.) 1996. *Teachers as Course Developers*. Cambridge: Cambridge University Press.

— 2000. *Designing Language Courses*. Boston: Heinle and Heinle.

— 2003. 'Coursebooks'. In D. Nunan (ed.) *Practical English Language Teaching* (pp.225–46). New York: McGraw Hill.

Gray, J. 2000. 'The ELT coursebook as cultural artefact: How teachers censor and adapt'. *ELT Journal* 54.3: 274–83.

— 2002. 'The global coursebook in English Language Teaching'. In D. Block and D. Cameron (eds) *Globalization and Language Teaching* (pp.151–67). London: Routledge.

Greenall, S. 2011. 'New Standard English – the first ten years . . .' In Ken Wilson's blog. Retrieved 11 May 2011 from www.kenwilsonelt.wordpress.com/2011/03/02 [edited and updated version of article first published in *The Author*, autumn 2007].

Guefrachi, H. and Troudi, S. 2000. 'Enhancing English language teaching in the United Arab Emirates'. In K. E. Johnson (ed.) *Teacher Education* (pp.189–204). Case Studies in TESOL Practice Series. Alexandria, VA: TESOL.

Hadfield, J. and Hadfield, C. 2003a. 'Hidden resources in the language classroom: Teaching with (next to) nothing'. *Modern English Teacher* 12.1: 5–10.

— 2003b. 'Hidden resources in the language classroom: Teaching with nothing'. *Modern English Teacher* 12.2: 31–7.

Haig, E. 2006. 'How green are your textbooks? Applying an ecological critical awareness pedagogy in the language classroom'. In S. Mayer and G. Wilson (eds) *Ecodidactic Perspectives on English Language, Literatures and Cultures* (pp.23–44). Trier: Wissenschaftlicher Verlag.

Haines, S. and Stewart, B. 2000. *Landmark*. Oxford: Oxford University Press.

Harmer, J. 1991. *The Practice of English Language Teaching*. Harlow, Essex: Longman.
— 2001. 'Coursebooks: A human, cultural and linguistic disaster'. *Modern English Teacher* 10.3: 5–10.
— 2007. *The Practice of English Teaching* (4th edn) Harlow, Essex: Longman.
Harwood, N. 2005. 'What do we want EAP teaching materials for?' *Journal of English for Academic Purposes* 4.2: 149–61.
Harwood, N. (ed.) 2010a. *English Language Teaching Materials: Theory and Practice*. Cambridge: Cambridge University Press.
Harwood, N. 2010b. 'Issues in materials development and design'. In N. Harwood (ed.) 2010a: 3–30.
Hayashi, C. 2010. 'A teacher's perceptions of students' transformational creativity in a secondary language classroom in Japan: A case study of professional development'. Unpublished PhD thesis, University of Nottingham.
Haycraft, J. 1978. *An Introduction to English Language Teaching*. Harlow, Essex: Longman.
Hayes, D. 2008. 'Occupational socialization in the first year of teaching: Perspectives from Thailand'. In T. Farrell (ed.): 57–72.
— 2009. 'Learning language, learning teaching: Episodes from the life of a teacher of English in Thailand'. *RELC Journal* 40.1: 83–101.
Head, K. and Taylor, P. (eds) 1997. *Readings in Teacher Development*. Oxford: Heinemann.
Helgesen, M. n.d. 'Adapting and supplementing textbooks to include language planning'. *Selected Papers from the Twelfth International Symposium on English Teaching and Learning* (pp.56–64). Retrieved 07 October 11from www.mgu.ac.jp/~ic/helgesen/adapting_-_LP_ETA_.PDF
Henrichsen, L. 1983. 'Teacher preparation needs in TESOL: The results of an international survey'. *RELC Journal* 14.1: 18–45.
Hidalgo, A., Hall, D. and Jacobs, C. 1995. *Getting Started: Materials Writers on Materials Writing*. Singapore: SEAMEO Regional English Language Centre.
Holden, S. (ed.) 1977. *English for Specific Purposes*. Oxford: Modern English Publications.
Holliday, A. 1994. *Appropriate Methodology and Social Context*. Cambridge: Cambridge University Press.
Holmes, J. 1988. 'Doubt and certainty in ESL textbooks'. *Applied Linguistics* 9.1: 21–44.
Horsley, M. 2007. 'Textbooks, teaching and learning materials and teacher education'. In M. Horsley and J. McCall (eds): 249–60.
Horsley, M. and McCall, J. (eds) 2007. *Peace, Democratization and Educational Media*. Papers from the Ninth International Conference on Textbooks and Educational Media. September, 2007, Tonsberg, Norway. Retrieved 15 July 2010 from www.iartem.no/documents/9thIARTEMConferenceVolume.pdf
Howard, J. and Major, J. 2004. 'Guidelines for designing effective English language teaching materials'. *Proceedings of the 9th conference of the Pan-Pacific Association of Applied Linguistics* (pp.101–9). Retrieved 11 September 2010 from www.paaljapan.org/resources/proceedings/PAAL9/pdf/Howard.pdf
Howatt, A. with Widdowson, H. 2004. *A History of English Language Teaching* (2nd edn). Oxford: Oxford University Press.
Hsiao, J. 2010. 'Suggestions for using "A Very Practical Guide to the New TOEIC"'. Coursework assignment, MA TESOL module in Materials Evaluation and Design, University of Nottingham (Malaysia).
Hu, Z. 2010. 'EFL teacher development: A reflective model'. *Modern English Teacher* 19.2: 60–3.
Huang, S-e. 2010. *Ideal and Reality in Coursebook Selection*. Paper presented at IATEFL Conference, Harrogate, April, 2010.
Hubbard, R., Jones, H., Thornton, B. and Wheeler, R. 1983. *A Training Course for TEFL*. Oxford: Oxford University Press.
Hughes, J. 2006. 'Over to you . . . designing an exercise'. *English Teaching Professional* 43: 8–9.

*Humanising English Teaching.* 2001. Turkish voices. *Humanising English Teaching* 3.2: 1–2.
Hutchinson, T. and Torres, E. 1994. 'The textbook as agent of change'. *ELT Journal* 48.4: 315–27.
Hutchinson, T. and Waters, A. 1987. *English for Specific Purposes: A Learning-Centred Approach.* Cambridge: Cambridge University Press.
Hyland, K. 1994. 'Hedging in academic writing and EAP textbooks'. *English for Specific Purposes* 13.3: 239–56.
Inal, B. 2006. 'Coursebook selection process and some of the most important criteria to be taken into consideration in foreign language teaching'. *Journal of Arts and Sciences* 5: 19–29 (Cankaya University, Turkey). Retrieved 19 April 2010 from http://jas.cankaya.edu.tr/gecmis/yayinlar/jas5/03-bulent.pdf/
Ioannou-Georgiou, S. 2002. 'Selecting software for language classes'. *Modern English Teacher* 11.3: 63–8.
Islam, C. and Mares, C. 2003. 'Adapting classroom materials'. In B. Tomlinson (ed.) 2003a: 86–100.
Jarvis, J. 1992. 'Using diaries for teacher reflection on in-service courses'. *ELT Journal* 46.2: 132–43.
Jazadi, I. 2003. 'Mandated English teaching materials and their implications to teaching and learning: The case of Indonesia'. In W. Renandya (ed.) 2003: 142–60.
Jiang, X. 2006. 'Suggestions: What should ESL students know?' *System* 34.1: 36–54.
Johansson, T. 2006. Teaching material in the EFL classroom: Teachers' and students' perspectives. Växjö University, Sweden. Retrieved 20 September 2010 from lnu.diva-portal.org/smash/get/diva2:207078/FULLTEXT01
Johnson, K. (ed.) 1977. *SELMOUS Occasional Papers No.1.* Centre for Applied Language Studies, University of Reading.
— 2003. *Designing Language Teaching Tasks.* Basingstoke: Palgrave Macmillan.
Johnson, K., Kim, M., Liu, Y.-F., Nava, A., Perkins, D., Smith, A.-M., Soler-Canela, O. and Lu, W. 2008. 'A step forward: investigating expertise in materials evaluation'. *ELT Journal* 62.2: 157–63.
Johnson, R. K. (ed.) 1989. *The Second Language Curriculum.* Cambridge: Cambridge University Press.
Jolly, D. and Bolitho, R. 2011. 'A framework for materials writing'. In B. Tomlinson (ed.) 2011a: 107–34 [revised version of paper with same title in Tomlinson, B. (ed.) 1998a: 90–115].
Jones, K. 1997. 'Beyond "listen and repeat": Pronunciation teaching materials and theories of second language acquisition'. *System* 25.1: 103–12.
Jordan, R. (ed.) 1983. *Case Studies in ELT.* Glasgow: Collins.
Kanchana, P. 1991. 'Cooperative learning in a humanistic English class'. *Cross Currents* 18.1: 37–40. Retrieved 14 July 2008 from http://pioneer.chula.ac.th/~pkanchan/html/coop.htm
Karamoozian, F. and Riazi, A. (nd) Development of a new checklist for evaluating reading comprehension textbooks. Retrieved 24 September 2011 from www.esp-world.info/Development_of_a_New_Checklist.doc/
Katz, A. 1996. 'Teaching style: a way to understand instruction in language classrooms'. In Bailey, K. and Nunan, D. (eds) *Voices from the Language Classroom* (pp.57–87). Cambridge: Cambridge University Press.
Kayapinar, U. 2009. 'Coursebook evaluation by English teachers'. *Inonu University Journal of the Faculty of Education* 10.1: 69–78. Retrieved 21 April 2010 from http://web.inonu.edu.tr/~efdergi/101/69–78.pdf
Kennedy, J. and Pinter, A. 2007. 'Developing teacher autonomy through teamwork'. In A. Barfield and S. Brown (eds) *Reconstructing Autonomy in Language Education* (pp.209–21). Houndmills, Basingstoke: Palgrave Macmillan.
Kesen, A. 2010. 'Turkish EFL learners' metaphors with respect to English language coursebooks'. *Novitas ROYAL* (Research on Youth and Language) 4.1: 108–18. Retrieved 09 November 2010 from www.novitasroyal.org/Vol_4_1/kesen.pdf

Kiss, T. 2007. Unpublished report on British Council summer school in the Philippines on the use of authentic materials in English language teaching.

Kivistö, A. 2005. 'Accents of English as a lingua franca: a study of Finnish textbooks'. Unpublished MA thesis. University of Tampere, Finland.

Kopperoinen, A. 2011. 'Accents of English as a lingua franca: A study of Finnish textbooks'. *International Journal of Applied Linguistics* 21.1: 71–93.

Krajka, J. 2001. 'Online lessons – using the Internet to help the coursebook'. In K. Cameron (ed.) *CALL and the Challenge of Change: Research and Practice*. Exeter: Elm Bank Publications.

Lackman, K. 2010. 'The student as input'. *English Teaching Professional* 67: 28–31.

Lamie, J. 1999. 'Prescriptions and cures: Adapting and supplementing'. *Modern English Teacher* 8.3: 49–53.

Law, W.-H. 1995. 'Teachers' evaluation of English Textbooks: An investigation of teachers' ideas and current practices and their implications for developing textbook evaluation criteria'. Unpublished M.Ed dissertation, University of Hong Kong. Retrieved 30 April 10 from http://sunzi.lib.hku.hk/hkuto/view/B3195785/ft.pdf/

Lee, R. and Bathmaker, A.-M. 2007. 'The use of English textbooks for teaching English to 'vocational' students in Singapore secondary schools'. *RELC Journal* 38.3: 350–74.

Li, D. 1998. '"It's always more difficult than you plan and imagine": Teachers' perceived difficulties in introducing the communicative approach in South Korea'. *TESOL Quarterly* 32.4: 677–703.

Liao, K.-M. 2009. 'Using a checklist to evaluate Taiwanese junior high school textbooks'. Unpublished MA TESOL dissertation, University of Nottingham, UK.

Littlejohn, A. 1983. 'Increasing learner involvement in course management'. *TESOL Quarterly* 17.4: 595–608.

— 2011. 'The analysis of language teaching materials: Inside the Trojan Horse'. In B. Tomlinson (ed.) 2011a: 179–211 [revised version of paper with same title in Tomlinson, B. (ed.) 1998a: 190–216].

Littlejohn, A. and Windeatt, S. 1989. 'Beyond language learning: Perspectives on materials design'. In R. K. Johnson (ed.): 155–75.

Litz, D. 2005. 'Textbook Evaluation and ELT Management: A South Korean Case Study'. *Asian EFL Journal* (online). Retrieved 02 April 2011 from www.asian-efl-journal.com/Litz_thesis.pdf

Loewenberg-Ball, D. and Cohen, D. 1996. 'Reform by the book: What is – or might be – the role of curriculum materials in teacher learning and instructional reform?' *Educational Researcher* 25.9: 6–8, 14. Retrieved 23 May 2010 from www.compassproject.net/Sadhana/teaching/readings/ballcohen1996.pdf

Low, G. 1989. 'Appropriate design: The internal organisation of course units'. In R. K. Johnson (ed.): 136–54.

Lund, R. 2010. 'Teaching a world language for local contexts: The case of Namibian textbooks for the teaching of English'. *IARTEM e-Journal* 3.1: 57–71. Retrieved 09 October 2011 from www.biriwa.com/iartem/ejournal/volume3.1/Lund/_paper_IARTEM_eJournal_Vol3_No1.pdf

Lund, R. and Zoughby, K. 2007. 'English language textbooks in Norway and Palestine'. In M. Horsley and J. McCall (eds): 203–11.

Lynch, T. 1996. 'Influences on course revision'. In M. Hewings and T. Dudley-Evans (eds) *Course Evaluation and Design in EAP* (pp.26–35). Hemel Hempstead, Herts: Prentice Hall.

— 2007. 'Learning from the transcripts of a communication task'. *ELT Journal* 61.4: 311–20.

Mackay, R. and Mountford, A. (eds) 1978. *English for Specific Purposes*. London: Longman.

Madsen, H. and Bowen, J. 1978. *Adaptation in Language Teaching*. Rowley, MA: Newbury House.

Malderez, A. and Wedell, M. 2007. *Teaching Teachers: Processes and Practices*. London: Continuum.

Maley, A. 1994. *Short and Sweet 1*. London: Penguin Books.
— 1995. 'Materials writing and tacit knowledge'. In Hidalgo, Hall and Jacobs (eds): 220–39.
— 2001. Interview with *ELT News*. Retrieved 18 February 2010 from www.eltnews.com/features/interviews/2001/06/interview_with_alan_maley.html/
— 2003. 'Creative approaches to writing materials'. In Tomlinson, B. (ed). 2003a: 183–98.
— 2011. 'Squaring the circle – reconciling materials as constraint with materials as empowerment'. In B. Tomlinson (ed.) 2011a: 379–402 [revised version of paper with same title in Tomlinson, B. (ed.) 1998a: 279–94].
Mares, C. 2003. 'Writing a coursebook'. In B. Tomlinson (ed.) 2003a: 130–40.
Masuhara, H. 2011. 'What do teachers really want from coursebooks?' In B. Tomlinson (ed.) 2011a: 236–66 [revised version of paper with same title in Tomlinson, B. (ed.) 1998a: 239–60].
Masuhara, H., Haan, M., Yi, Y. and Tomlinson, B. 2008. 'Adult EFL courses'. *ELT Journal* 62.3: 294–312.
Masuhara, H. and Tomlinson, B. 2008. 'Materials for General English'. In B. Tomlinson (ed.) 2008a. *English Language Learning Materials: A Critical Review* (17–37). London: Continuum.
Matsumara, T. 2010. Coursework as part of MA TESOL module in Materials Evaluation and Design, University of Nottingham.
Matthews, A. 1985. 'Choosing the best available textbook'. In A. Matthews, M. Spratt and L. Dangerfield (eds) *At the Chalkface* (pp.202–6). London: Nelson.
McCarten, J. and McCarthy, M. 2010. 'Bridging the gap between corpus and course book: The case of conversation strategies'. In F. Mishan and A. Chambers (eds): 11–32.
McDonough, J. and Shaw, C. 1993. *Materials and Methods in ELT*. Oxford: Blackwell.
—. 2003 (2nd edn). *Materials and Methods in ELT*. Oxford: Blackwell.
McDonough, J., Shaw, C. and Masuhara, H. (3rd edn, in press). *Materials and Methods in ELT*. Oxford: Blackwell.
McElroy, H. 1934. 'Selecting a basic textbook'. *The Modern Language Journal* 19.1: 5–8. Retrieved 18 May 2010 from www.jstor.org/stable/pdfplus/315419.pdf/
McGrath, I. 1994. 'The open slot'. *Practical English Teaching* 14.4: 19–21.
— (ed.) 1997. *Learning to Train*. Hemel Hempstead, Herts: Prentice Hall.
— 2000. 'Teacher autonomy'. In B. Sinclair, I. McGrath and T. Lamb (eds) *Learner Autonomy, Teacher Autonomy: Future Directions* (pp.100–10). Harlow, Essex: Longman/British Council.
— 2002. *Materials Evaluation and Design for Language Teaching*. Edinburgh: Edinburgh University Press.
— 2004. 'The representation of people in educational materials'. *RELC Journal* 35.3: 351–8.
— 2006. 'Teachers' and learners' images for coursebooks: Implications for teacher development'. *ELT Journal* 60.2: 171–80.
— 2007. 'Textbooks, technology and teachers'. In O. Alexander (ed.) *New Approaches to Materials Development for Language Learning. Proceedings of the Joint 2005 BALEAP/SATEFL Conference* (pp.343–58). Bern: Peter Lang.
— 2009. Aligning English Language Teacher Education in Materials Evaluation and Design with Teacher Needs. Paper presented at 18th MELTA International Conference, 11–13 June, 2009, Johor Bahru, Malaysia.
— 2013. 'Can primary-age pupils produce teaching materials?', In Zhang, J. and Ben Said, S. (eds) *Language Teachers and Teaching: Global Perspectives, Local Initiatives*. London: Routledge.
Meddings, L. and Thornbury, S. 2009. *Teaching Unplugged: Dogme in English Language Teaching*. London: Delta Publishing.
Mishan, F. 2005. *Designing Authenticity into Language Learning Materials*. Bristol: Intellect.
Mishan, F. and Chambers, A. (eds) 2010. *Perspectives on Language Learning Materials Development*. Bern: Peter Lang.

Morley, J. 1993. 'Textbook evaluation: The anatomy of a textbook'. In D. Freeman and S. Cornwell (eds) 1991: 101–4.
Mosback, G. 1984. 'Making a structure-based course more communicative'. *ELT Journal* 38.3: 178–86.
Mukundan, J. and Ahour, T. 2010. 'A review of textbook evaluation checklists across four decades (1970–2008)'. In B. Tomlinson and H. Masuhara (eds) 2010: 336–52.
Mukundan, J. and Nimehchisalem, V. 2008. 'Gender representation in Malaysian secondary school English language textbooks'. *Indonesian Journal of Language Teaching* 4.2: 155–73.
Nguyen Thi Cam Le 2005. 'From passive participant to active thinker: A learner-centred approach to materials development'. *English Teaching Forum* 43.3. Retrieved 24 February 2011 from http://eca.state.gov/forum/vols/vol43/no3/p2.htm
Ning Liu. 2009. 'When communicative approaches don't work'. *Modern English Teacher* 18.2: 64–9.
Nishigaki, C. nd. A study of learner's attitudes towards listening materials. Retrieved 15 November 2010 from http://mitizane.ll.chiba-u.jp/metadb/up/AN10494742/KJ00004297069.pdf
Nunan, D. 1988a. *The Learner-Centred Curriculum*. Cambridge: Cambridge University Press.
— 1988b. 'Principles for designing language teaching materials'. *Guidelines* 10.2: 1–24.
— 1989. *Designing Tasks for the Communicative Classroom*. Cambridge: Cambridge University Press.
— 1991. *Language Teaching Methodology*. Hemel Hempstead, Herts: Prentice Hall.
— 1992. 'The teacher as decision-maker'. In J. Flowerdew, M. Brock and S. Hsia (eds) *Perspectives English Language Learning Materials: A Critical Review on Second Language Teacher Education* (pp.135–65). Hong Kong: City University of Hong Kong.
O'Neill, R. 1982. 'Why use textbooks?' *ELT Journal* 36.2: 133–8.
Paltridge, B. 2002. 'Thesis and dissertation writing: An examination of published advice and actual practice'. *English for Specific Purposes* 21.2: 125–43.
Paran, A. 1996. 'Reading in EFL: Facts and fictions'. *ELT Journal* 50.1: 25–34.
— 2003. 'Helping learners to become critical: how coursebooks can help'. In Renandya, W. (ed.) 2003: 109–23.
Peacock, M. 1997a. 'Choosing the right book for your class'. *Essex Graduate Papers in Language and Linguistics*. Retrieved 10 September 2010 from www.essex.ac.uk/linguistics/publications/egspll/volume_1/pdf/PEACOCK1.pdf
— 1997b. 'The effect of authentic materials on the motivation of EFL learners'. *ELT Journal* 51.2: 144–54.
Pennycook, A. 1994. *The Cultural Politics of English as an International Language*. London: Longman.
Perren, G. (ed.) 1969. *Languages for Special Purposes*. CILT Reports and Papers No.1. London: Centre for Information on Language Teaching.
— (ed.) 1971. *Science and Technology in a Second Language*. CILT Reports and Papers No.7. London: Centre for Information on Language Teaching.
— (ed.) 1974. *Teaching Languages to Adults for Special Purposes*. CILT Reports and Papers No.11. London: Centre for Information on Language Teaching.
Phillipson, R. 1992. *Linguistic Imperialism*. Oxford: Oxford University Press.
Pogelschek, B. 2007. 'How textbooks are made: Insights from an Austrian publisher'. In M. Horsley and J. McCall (eds): 100–7.
Popovici, R. and Bolitho, R. 2003. 'Personal and professional development through writing: The Romanian Textbook Project'. In B. Tomlinson (ed.) 2003a: 505–17.
Prodromou, L. 1990. 'A mixed ability class'. *Practical English Teaching* 10.3: 28–9.
— 1992a. 'What culture? Which culture? Cross-cultural factors in language learning'. *ELT Journal* 46.1: 39–50.
— 1992b. *Mixed Ability Classes*. London: Macmillan.
— 2002. 'The great ELT textbook debate'. *Modern English Teacher* 11.4: 25–33.

Prowse, P. 2011. 'How writers write: testimony from authors'. In Tomlinson (ed.) 2011: 151–173 [revised version of paper with same title in Tomlinson, B. (ed.): 1998a: 130–145].

Ramírez Salas, M. 2004. 'English teachers as materials developers'. *Revista Electrónica Actualidades Investigativas en Educación* 4.002: 1–18. Retrieved 27 June 2010 from redalyc.uaemex.mx/pdf/447/44740214.pdf

Ramasamy, A. 2011. B.Ed coursework. National Institute of Education, Singapore.

Rashad, R. 2011. B.Ed coursework. National Institute of Education, Singapore.

Ravelonanahary, M. 2007. 'The use of textbooks and educational media: The Malagasy experience'. In M. Horsley and J. McCall (eds): 166–75.

Reinders, H. and Lewis, M. 2006. 'An evaluation checklist for self-access materials'. *ELT Journal* 60.3: 272–8.

Renandya, W. (ed.) 2003. *Methodology and Materials Design in Language Teaching: Current Perceptions and Practices and their Implications*. Anthology Series 44. Singapore: SEAMEO Regional Language Centre.

Riazi, A. (2003) 'What do textbook evaluation schemes tell us? A study of the textbook evaluation schemes of three decades'. In W. Renandya (ed.): 52–68.

Richards, J. (ed.) 1976. *Teaching English for Science and Technology*. Selected papers from the RELC seminar, Singapore April 21–25. Singapore: Singapore University Press.

— 1985. 'The secret life of methods'. In *The Context of Language Teaching* (pp.32–45). Cambridge: Cambridge University Press.

— 1995. 'Easier said than done: An insider's account of a textbook project'. In Hidalgo et al. (eds) 1995: 95–135.

— 1998a. 'Textbooks: Help or hindrance?' In *Beyond Training* (pp.125–40). Cambridge: Cambridge University Press.

— 1998b. 'What's the use of lesson plans?' In *Beyond Training* (pp.103–21). Cambridge: Cambridge University Press.

— 2001a. 'The role of instructional materials'. In *Curriculum Development in Language Teaching* (pp.251–85). Oxford: Oxford University Press.

— 2001b. 'The role of textbooks in a language program'. *RELC Guidelines* 23.2: 12–16.

— 2006. 'Materials development and research – making the connection'. *RELC Journal* 37.5: 5–26.

Richards, J. and Ho, B. 1998. 'Reflective thinking through journal writing'. In *Beyond Training* (pp.153–70). Cambridge: Cambridge University Press.

Richards, J. and Lockhart, C. 1994. *Reflective Teaching in Second Language Classrooms*. Cambridge: Cambridge University Press.

Richards, J. and Mahoney, D. 1996. 'Teachers and textbooks: A survey of beliefs and practices'. *Perspectives* (Working Papers of the Department of English, City University of Hong Kong) 8.1: 40–63.

Richards, J. and Nunan, D. (eds) 1990. *Second Language Teacher Education*. Cambridge: Cambridge University Press.

Richards, J. and Rodgers, T. 1986. *Approaches and Methods in Language Teaching*. Cambridge: Cambridge University Press.

— 2001. *Approaches and Methods in Language Teaching* (2nd edn). Cambridge: Cambridge University Press.

Riley, L. 2001. 'Pedagogical implications of an EFL materials evaluation'. *Proceedings of PAC 3 at JALT 2001* (pp.813–24). November 22–25, Kitakyushu, Japan. Retrieved 03 June 2011 from http://jalt-publications.org/archive/proceedings/2001/812.pdf

Rinvolucri, M. 2002. *Humanising Your Coursebook*. Peaslake, Surrey: Delta.

Rix, J. 2009. 'A model of simplification: The ways in which teachers simplify texts'. *Educational Studies* 35.2: 95–106.

Roberts, J. 1996. 'Demystifying materials evaluation'. *System* 24.3: 375–89.

Robinett, B. 1978. *Teaching English to Speakers of Other Languages*. University of Minnesota Press.

Robinson, P. 1980. *ESP: English for Specific Purposes*. Oxford: Pergamon.

Rossner, R. 1988. 'Materials for communicative language teaching and learning'. In Brumfit, C. (ed.) *Annual Review of Applied Linguistics* 8 (pp.140–63). Cambridge: Cambridge University Press.
Rubdy, R. 2003. 'Selection of materials'. In Tomlinson, 2003a: 37–57.
Salusbury, M. 2010. 'Global EFL industry gets tech appeal'. *EL Gazette*, April 2010: 29.
Sampson, N. 2009. Teaching materials and the autonomous language teacher: A study of tertiary English teachers in Hong Kong. Unpublished Ed.D thesis, University of Hong Kong. Retrieved 06 February 2011 from http://handle.net/10722/56640
Samuda, V. 2005. 'Expertise in pedagogic task design'. In K. Johnson (ed.) *Expertise in Second Language Learning and Teaching* (pp.230–54). Houndmills, Basingstoke: Palgrave Macmillan.
Saraceni, C. 2003. 'Adapting courses: A critical view'. In B. Tomlinson (ed.) 2003a: 72–85.
Schön, D. 1984. *The Reflective Practitioner: How Professionals Think in Action*. New York: Basic Books.
Scrivener, J. 2005. *Learning Teaching* (2nd edn). Oxford: Macmillan.
Sengupta, S. 1998. 'Peer evaluation: "I am not the teacher"'. *ELT Journal* 52.1: 19–28.
Senior, R. 2006. *The Experience of Language Teaching*. Cambridge: Cambridge University Press.
Sercu, L., Mendez Garcia, M. and Castro Prieto, P. 2004. 'Culture teaching in foreign language education: EFL teachers in Spain as cultural mediators'. *Porta Linguarum* 1: 85–102. Retrieved 20 January 2011 from www.ugr.es/~portalin/articulos/PL-numero1/sercu.pdf
Shaffie, A. 2011. M.Ed. coursework, National Institute of Education, Singapore.
Shawer, S., Gilmore, D. and Banks-Joseph, S. 2008. 'Student cognitive and affective development in the context of classroom-level curriculum development'. *Journal of the Scholarship of Teaching and Learning* 8.1: 1–28.
Sheerin, S. 1989. *Self-access*. Oxford: Oxford University Press.
Sheldon, L. (ed.) 1987a. *ELT Textbooks and Materials: Problems in Evaluation and Development*. ELT Documents 126. Oxford: The British Council/Modern English Publications.
— 1987b. 'Introduction'. In L. Sheldon (ed.) 1987a: 1–10.
— 1988. 'Evaluating ELT textbooks and materials'. *ELT Journal* 42.4: 237–46.
Skierso, A. 1991. 'Textbook selection and evaluation'. In M. Celce-Murcia (ed.) (2nd edn) *Teaching English as a Second or Foreign Language* (pp.432–53). Boston: Heinle & Heinle.
Smotrova, T. 2009. 'Globalization and English language teaching in Ukraine'. *TESOL Quarterly* 43.4: 727–32.
Spratt, M. 1999. 'How good are we at knowing what learners like?'. *System* 27.2: 141–55.
—. 2001. 'The value of finding out what classroom activities students like'. *RELC Journal* 32.2: 80–103.
St George, E. 2001. 'Textbooks as a vehicle for curriculum reform'. Unpublished doctoral dissertation, University of Florida.
St Louis, R., Trias, M. and Pereira, S. 2010. 'Designing materials for a twelve-week course for pre-university students'. In F. Mishan and A. Chambers (eds): 249–70.
Stevick, E. 1980. *Teaching Languages: A Way and Ways*. Rowley, MA: Newbury House.
Stillwell, C., Curabba, B., Alexander, K., Kidd, A., Kim, E., Stone, P. and Wyle, C. 2010. 'Students transcribing tasks: Noticing fluency, accuracy, and complexity'. *ELT Journal* 64.4: 445–55.
Stranks, J. 2003. 'Materials for the teaching of grammar'. In B. Tomlinson (ed.) 2003a: 329–39.
Swales, J. 1980. 'ESP: The textbook problem'. *English for Specific Purposes* 1.1: 11–23.
Swales, J. and Feak, C. 2004. *Academic Writing for Graduate Students*. Ann Arbor: University of Michigan Press.
Swan, M. 1992. 'The textbook: Bridge or wall?' *Applied Linguistics and Language Teaching* 2.1: 32–5.

Tanner, R. and Green, C. 1998. 16. 'You can't always get what you want: Materials evaluation and adaptation'. In *Tasks for Language Teacher Education* (pp.120–9). Harlow, Essex: Longman.

Tarnopolsky, O. 1996. 'EFL teaching in the Ukraine: State regulated or commercial'. *TESOL Quarterly* 30: 616–22.

Thornbury, S. 1999. 'Window-dressing vs cross-dressing in the EFL sub-culture'. *Folio* 5.2: 15–17. Retrieved 28 August 2011 from www.thornburyscott.com/assets/windowdressing.pdf

— 2000. 'A dogma for ELT'. *IATEFL Issues* 153 (Feb./Mar. 2000). Retrieved 16 April 2010 from www.thornburyscott.com/tu/sources.htm

— 2010. T is for Taboo. Retrieved 15 September 2011 from http://scottthornbury.wordpress.com/2010/06/27/t-is-for-taboo

Thornbury, S. and Meddings, L. 2001. 'Coursebooks: The roaring in the chimney'. *Modern English Teacher* 10.3: 11–13.

— 2002. 'Using a coursebook the Dogme way'. *Modern English Teacher* 11.1: 36–40.

Tice, J. 1991. 'The textbook straitjacket'. *Practical English Teaching* 11.3: 23.

— 1997. *The Mixed Ability Class*. London: Richmond Publishing.

Todd Trimble, M., Trimble, L. and Drobnic, K. (eds) 1978. *English for Specific Purposes: Science and Technology*. English Language Institute, Oregon State University.

Tomlinson, B. (ed.) 1998a. *Materials Development in Language Teaching*. Cambridge: Cambridge University Press.

— 1998b. 'Glossary of basic terms for materials development in language teaching'. In B. Tomlinson (ed.) 1998a: viii–xiv.

— 1998c. 'Conclusions'. In B. Tomlinson (ed.) 1998a: 340–4.

— 1999. 'Developing criteria for evaluating L2 materials'. *IATEFL Issues* Feb–Mar. 1999: 10–13.

— 2001. 'Materials development'. In R. Carter and D. Nunan (eds) *Teaching English to Speakers of Other Languages* (pp.66–71). Cambridge: Cambridge University Press.

— (ed.) 2003a. *Developing Materials for Language Teaching*. London: Continuum.

— 2003b. 'Humanizing the coursebook'. In B. Tomlinson (ed.) 2003a: 162–73.

— 2003c. 'Materials development courses'. In B. Tomlinson (ed.) 2003a: 445–61.

— (ed.) 2008a. *English Language Teaching Materials: A Critical Review*. London: Continuum.

— 2008b. 'Conclusions about ELT materials in use around the world'. In B. Tomlinson (ed.) 2008a: 319–22.

— 2010a. 'Principles of effective materials development'. In N. Harwood 2010a: 81–108.

— 2010b. 'What do teachers think about EFL coursebooks?' *Modern English Teacher* 19.4: 5–9.

— (ed.) 2011a (2nd edn) *Materials Development in Language Teaching*. Cambridge: Cambridge University Press.

— 2011b. 'Introduction: Principles and procedures of materials development'. In B. Tomlinson (ed.) 2011a: 1–31.

— 2011c. 'Comments on Part B'. In B. Tomlinson (ed.) 2011a: 174–6.

— 2011d. 'Conclusions'. In B. Tomlinson (ed.) 2011a: 437–42.

— 2011e. 'Comments on Part C'. In B. Tomlinson (ed.) 2011a: 296–300.

Tomlinson, B., Dat, B., Masuhara, H. and Rubdy, R. 2001. 'EFL courses for adults'. *ELT Journal* 55.1: 80–101.

Tomlinson, B. and Masuhara, H. 2003. 'Simulations in materials development'. In B. Tomlinson (ed.) 2003a: 462–78.

— 2004. *Developing Language Course Materials*. Singapore: SEAMEO RELC.

— 2010a. *Research in Materials Development for Language Learning: Evidence for Best Practice*. London: Continuum.

— 2010b. 'Published research on materials development for language learning'. In B. Tomlinson and H. Masuhara 2010a: 1–18.

— 2010c. 'Applications of the research results for second language acquisition theory and research'. In B. Tomlinson and H. Masuhara 2010a: 399–409.

Tsobanoglou, S. 2008. 'What can we learn by researching the use of textbooks and other support materials by teachers and learners'. Unpublished MA dissertation, University of Nottingham.

Tsui, A. 2003. *Understanding Expertise in Teaching: Case Studies of ESL Teachers.* Cambridge: Cambridge University Press.

Tucker, C. 1975. 'Evaluating beginning textbooks'. *English Teaching Forum* 13.3/4 (Special Issue Part 2): 355–61 [originally printed in 1968 in *English Teaching Forum* 6.5: 8–15, and subsequently reprinted as Appendix 3 in
H. Madsen & J. Bowen (1978) *Adaptation in Language Teaching* (pp.219–37). Rowley, MA: Newbury House.

Tudor, I. 1993. 'Teacher roles in the learner-centred classroom'. *ELT Journal* 47.1: 22–31.

— 1996. *Learner-Centredness as Language Education.* Cambridge: Cambridge University Press.

Twine, G. 2010. 'Freedom, what freedom?' *English Teaching Professional* 68: 48–51.

Underhill, A. nd. Teaching without a coursebook. Retrieved 16 April 2010 from www.thornburyscott.com/tu/sources.htm

University of Cambridge ESOL Examinations. 2011. CELTA (Certificate in Teaching English to Speakers of Other Languages). Retrieved 27 May 2011 from http//www.cambridgeesol.org/exams/celta/index.htm

Ur, P. 1996. *A Course in Language Teaching: Practice and Theory.* Cambridge: Cambridge University Press.

— 2009. English as a lingua franca and some implications for English teachers. Plenary address at TESOL France, 2009. Retrieved 08 September 2011 from www.tesol-france.org/Colloquium09/Ur_Plenary_Handouts.pdf

Wala, D. 2003a. 'A coursebook is what it is because of what it has to do: An editor's perspective'. In B. Tomlinson (ed.) 2003a: 58–71.

— 2003b 'Publishing a coursebook: Completing the materials development circle'. In B. Tomlinson (ed.) 2003a: 141–61.

Wallace, M. 1991. *Training Foreign Language Teachers: A Reflective Approach.* Cambridge: Cambridge University Press.

Wang, L.-Y. 2005. 'A study of junior high school English teachers' perceptions of the liberalization of the authorized English textbooks and their experience of textbook evaluation and selection'. Unpublished MA dissertation, National Yunlin University of Science and Technology, Taiwan.

Watkins, P. 2010. 'Giving learners a voice in correction and feedback'. *ELT WorldOnline* Vol 2. Retrieved 26 April 2011 from http://blog.nus.edu.sg/eltwo/2010/01/29/giving-learners-a-voice-in-correction-and-feedback

Williams, D. 1983. 'Developing criteria for textbook evaluation'. *ELT Journal* 37.3: 251–5.

Williams, M. 1988. 'Language taught for meetings and language used in meetings. Is there anything in common?' *Applied Linguistics* 9.1: 45–58.

Williams, R. 1981. 'A procedure for ESP textbook analysis and evaluation on teacher education courses'. *ESP Journal* 1.2: 155–62.

Wong, J. 2001. 'Applying conversation analysis in applied linguistics: Evaluating dialogue in English as a second language textbooks'. *International Review of Applied Linguistics* 40.1: 37–60.

Woodward, T. 1991. *Models and Metaphors in Language Teacher Training.* Cambridge: Cambridge University Press.

— 1992. *Ways of Training.* Harlow, Essex: Longman.

— 2001. *Planning Lessons and Courses.* Cambridge: Cambridge University Press.

Wraight, A. and Suzuki, I. nd. Effective use of the textbook – using supplementary materials. Retrieved 22 October 2011 from www.c-english.com/files/effectiveuseofthetext_awraight

Wright, A. 1976. *Visual Materials for the Language Teacher.* London: Longman.

Wright, T. 1987. *Roles of Teachers and Learners*. Oxford: Oxford University Press.
Wright, T. and Bolitho, R. 2007. *Trainer Development*. www.lulu.com.
Xu, I. 2004. 'Investigating criteria for assessing ESL textbooks'. Unpublished PhD thesis, University of Alberta, Canada.
Yakhontova, T. 2001. 'Textbooks, contexts, and learners'. *English for Specific Purposes* Vol. 20, Supplement 1: 397–415. Retrieved 23 February 2011 from www.sciencedirect.com. . . . . . ./
Yalden, J. 1987. *Principles of Course Design for Language Teaching*. Cambridge: Cambridge University Press.
Yan, C. 2007. 'Investigating English teachers' materials adaptation'. *Humanising Language Teaching* 9.4. Retrieved 14 July 2008 from www.hltmag.co.uk/Jul07/mart01.htm/
Young, R. 1980. *Modular course design. ELT Documents special – Projects in Materials Design*. London: The British Council: 222–31.
Yuen, K. 1997. Review of Allwright's (1981) paper 'Why use textbooks?' BEd assignment, University of Nottingham.
Zacharias, N. 2005. 'Teachers' beliefs about internationally-published materials: A survey of tertiary English teachers in Indonesia'. *RELC Journal* 36.1: 23–38.
Zheng, X.-m. and Davison, C. 2008. *Changing Pedagogy: Analysing ELT Teachers in China*. London: Continuum.

# AUTHOR INDEX

This index lists authors who are quoted in the text and/or whose ideas are referred to.

Acklam, R. 23, 143–4, 212, 214
Akbulut, Y. 180–1
Alamri, A. 106–7
Alexander, K. 164–5
Allwright, D. 13, 79, 92
Al-Senaidi, F. 94, 218–19
Al-Sinani, S. 94, 218–19
Altan, M. 10, 68
Al-Yousef, H. 108–9, 112, 151, 171, 180
Amrani, F. 32, 34, 35, 36
Angouri, J. 11
Appel, J. 66, 74
Arakaki, L. 167, 178, 181, 202
Arikan, A. 172
Arva, V. 142

Bahumaid, S. 26, 56
Balajee, D. 163
Banks-Joseph, S. 128, 147, 156
Bathmaker, A.-M. 143, 169, 187, 193
Bell, J. 38, 39, 42, 43, 44, 45, 46, 47, 168, 197
Block, D. 26, 75, 150
Bolitho, R. 17–21, 44, 78, 93–4, 95, 96, 151
Botelho, M. 9, 116, 119, 120, 132
Bowen, J. 24, 61, 62, 71
Boys, O. 11
Breen, M. 90, 95, 205, 209
Brown, H. 212
Brumfit, C. 13, 22, 89, 90, 93, 95
Burns, A. 127, 144
Byrd, P. 5, 51–2, 54, 55–6, 82, 96

Çakır, I. 110, 151
Canagarajah, A. 10
Candlin, C. 90, 95, 205, 209
Canniveng, C. 26, 100
Castro Prieto, P. 116–18, 119

Caterina 151–2
Celce-Murcia, M. 58
Chandran, S. 113, 121, 143
Chavez, E. 170, 178, 181–2
Chowdhury, R. 173–4
Cohen, D. 87–8
Copland, F. 127, 144
Crawford, J. 9, 85
Crookes, G. 167, 176, 178, 181, 202
Cunningsworth, A. x, 25, 54, 55, 63, 64, 78, 207, 208
Curabba, B. 164–5

Dam, L. 95, 205, 209
Daoud, A.-M. 58
Darian, S. 69
Dat, B. 37–8, 40, 42–3, 160, 196, 197
Davis, P. 189
Davison, C. 168, 184
Donovan, P. 34, 35
Duarte, S. 152
Dudley-Evans, T. x, 23–4, 25, 26
Dunford, N. 127, 129–30

Edwards, T. 1, 14
Ellis, R. 12, 52, 78, 183, 210
Erdoğan, S. 179
Escobar, L. 152
Etherton, S. 94, 218–19
Ewer, J. 11

Farooqui, S. 171, 172, 177
Flack, R. 160
Fortune, A. 160
Fredriksson, C. 26, 105, 114, 120, 125, 147

Gabrielsen, G. 95, 205, 209
Garinger, D. 55, 56, 71

Garside, B. 189
Garton, S. 127, 144
Gebhard, 16, 17, 219
Gilmore, A. 9, 11, 158
Gilmore, D. 128, 147, 156
Gomes de Matos, F. 55
González Moncada, A. 26, 99, 171
Gower, R. 38, 39, 42, 43, 44, 45, 46, 47, 168, 197
Grant, N. 22, 55
Graves, K. xi, 10, 11, 50, 52, 53–4, 60, 64, 65, 68, 70, 76, 77, 144–5, 160, 179–80, 210, 212, 213, 214, 215
Gray, J. 12, 132, 138, 139–40
Green, C. 207, 211, 217
Greenall, S. 32, 41–2
Guefrachi, H. 205, 209

Hadfield, C. 17
Hadfield, J. 17
Hann, M. 12, 37, 40, 42, 196, 197
Harmer, J. 6, 8, 15, 38, 59, 64, 70, 76, 82, 84, 89, 208, 211
Harwood, N. 10, 11
Hassan, F. 171–2, 175–6
Hayashi, C. 143, 175, 177
Hayes, D. 113, 167, 169, 174–5
Helgesen, M. 70
Henrichsen, L. 25
Holliday, A. 9
Horsley, M. 85–7
Howard, J. 75–6
Howatt, A. 4
Hsiao, J. 128, 177
Hu, Z. 149, 154–6
Huang, S.-E. 122–3
Hughes, J. 74, 212–13
Hutchinson, T. xii, 5, 11, 12, 14, 15, 25, 61, 133, 150, 179
Hutchinson, 76, 90

Inal, B. 105, 113
Islam, C. 45–6, 61, 70, 71

Jazadi, I. 4, 11, 113, 121, 128, 142–3
Johansson, T. 146–7, 156–7, 175, 190
Johnson, K. 88, 123
Jolly, D. 44, 78, 93–4, 95, 96, 151

Kanchana, P. 163
Katz, A. 148
Kayapinar, U. 109–10

Kennedy, J. 215
Kesen, A. 154–5
Kidd, A. 164–5
Kim, E. 123, 164–5
Kiss, T. 220
Krajka, J. 159–60

Lackman, K. 78
Lamie, J. 74
Law, W.-H. 105, 115–16, 124, 125, 175, 178, 181
Lee, R. 143, 169, 187, 193
Li, D. 179
Liu, N. 123, 173
Littlejohn, A. xii, 12, 53, 210
Litz, D. 110–12, 150
Lockhart, C. 220
Loewenberg-Ball, D. 87–8
Lund, R. 10, 45

McDonough, J. 11, 54, 62, 64, 65, 66, 67, 68, 69
McElroy, H. 1, 22, 25, 55
McGrath, I. xii, 3, 6, 7, 8, 15, 47, 49, 52, 53, 54, 55, 57, 58, 62, 64, 65, 66, 69, 71, 72, 73, 75, 76, 78, 80, 149, 152–4, 164, 183, 190, 208, 209, 210, 211, 212, 218, 221–2
Madsen, H. 24, 61, 62, 71
Mahoney, D. 128, 138, 140, 141–2, 147
Major, J. 75–6
Maley, A. xii, xiii, xiv, 64, 65, 68, 76, 169, 222
Mares, C. 29, 38, 39, 45–6, 61, 70, 71
Martinez, M. 26, 100
Masuhara, H. xi, xii, 9, 11, 12, 37–8, 40, 42–3, 44, 50–1, 56, 64, 65, 74, 78, 100, 196, 197, 209
Matsumara, T. 176, 183
Matthews, A. 54
Meddings, L. 11, 14
Medgyes, P. 142
Mendez Garcia, M. 116–18, 119
Morley, J. 214
Mukundan, J. 12

Nava, A. 123
Nguyen, T. 157–8
Nimehchisalem, V. 12
Nishigaki, C. 158
Nunan, D. ix, 76

Olsson, R. 26, 105, 114, 120, 125, 147
O'Neill, R. 88

Peacock, M. 158–9
Pennycook, A. 10
Pereira, S. 160
Perkins, D. 123
Pinter, A. 215
Pogelschek, B. 31, 34, 37, 40, 41
Prodromou, L. 49, 60, 62, 68–9
Prowse, P. 33, 36, 38, 40

Ramasamy, A. 163
Ramírez Salas, M. 150, 182
Rashad, R. 163
Ravelonanahary, M. 128, 138, 142, 152, 170, 172, 180
Richards, J. ix, x, 5, 6, 13, 16, 19–20, 25, 29, 31, 32, 33, 34, 37, 38, 46, 56, 60, 61–2, 64, 91, 128, 133–5, 138, 140–2, 147, 198, 208, 210, 215, 220
Rinvolucri, M. 8, 9, 189
Roberts, J. 56, 58
Rodgers, T. x
Rossner, R. 12, 89, 90, 93, 95
Rubdy, R. 37–8, 40, 42–3, 196, 197

St John, M. x, 23–4, 25, 26
St Louis, R. 160
Salusbury, M. 8
Sampson, N. 125, 129, 135–8, 139, 140, 168, 174, 183
Samuda, V. xi, 24, 72, 94, 215
Saraceni, C. 70, 71, 162
Schön, D. 77
Scrivener, J. 210–11
Selamat, N. 171–2, 175–6
Sengupta, S. 165–6
Senior, R. 59, 89
Sercu, L. 116–18, 119
Shaffie, A. 91
Shaw, C. 11, 54, 62, 64, 65, 66, 67, 68, 69
Shawer, S. 128, 147, 156
Sheldon, L. 8, 12, 22, 187, 195, 203
Skierso, A. 55
Smith, A.-M. 123
Smotrova, T. 173

Soler-Canela, O. 123
Spratt, M. 160
Stillwell, C. 164–5
Stone, P. 164–5
Swan, M. 13

Tanner, R. 207, 211, 217
Thornbury, S. 11, 14, 84–5
Tice, J. 62, 70
Tomlinson, B. xi, xii, 3, 4, 5, 9, 11, 12, 26, 37–8, 40, 42–3, 44, 56, 64, 65, 69, 73, 74, 78, 100, 121, 125, 149, 188, 196, 197, 213, 214, 216, 217, 219–20, 221
Torres, E. xii, 5, 11, 12, 14, 15, 25, 61, 133, 150, 179
Trias, M. 160
Troudi, S. 205, 209
Tsobanoglou, S. 131–2, 133, 138, 145–6, 176
Tsui, A. 94, 169, 192
Twine, G. 192

Underhill, A. 14
Ur, P. 6, 198–9

Wala, D. S. 30, 32, 37, 40–1, 44, 45
Wallace, M. 77
Wang, L.-Y. 114–15, 121–2, 123, 125, 172–3
Waters, A. 76, 90
Woodward, T. 69, 76, 202, 206, 217, 219
Wraight, A. 74
Wright, T. 79, 211, 217, 218, 220
Wyle, C. 164–5

Xu, I. 120–1

Yakhontova, T. 152
Yalden, J. 51
Yan, C. 130–1, 133, 138, 139, 142, 144, 148, 149–50, 171, 189
Yi, Y. 12, 37, 40, 42, 196, 197
Yuen, K. 87

Zacharias, N. 138, 140, 141
Zheng, X.-M. 168, 184
Zoughby, K. 10, 45

# SUBJECT INDEX

The Index lists key terms and concepts referred to in the text.

analysis,
   content 10–12
   context 53–4
   of coursebook packages 6–8
   vs evaluation 53, 89–90
   market 31–2, 43
   materials 53
   needs 50–1, 79, 89–90, 110–11, 160–2
authenticity,
   of language 10–11, 63, 112
   of tasks 118
autonomy *see* learner; teacher

checklists 55–8, 114–15, 122–3
   best known 55
   design 55–8
   and teacher attitudes 114–15, 120, 122–3, 125 *see also* teacher education
   value of 55, 120, 123, 182
coursebook,
   advantages of 5–8, 14
   alternatives to 13
   analysis *see* analysis
   criticisms of 8–14
   global 9–10
   learner attitudes to *see* learner responses to materials
   metaphors for 153–5
   national 10
   retrospective evaluation studies *see* evaluation
   reviews of 37–8, 197
   selection 54–8
   (theory), 113–25
   (practice) *see also* materials, evaluation
   and teacher education *see* teacher education
   teaching without a coursebook 15–17
   and technological development 6–8
   writers *see* materials, writers
     *see also* culture
cultural context 41–2, 44, 67, 156
culture,
   and coursebooks 6, 9–10, 109–10, 116–19, 122–3, 132, 138–41, 152, 173, 197–8
   and materials 157–8, 162

Dogme 14

English for Specific Purposes (ESP) x, 11, 23–4
evaluation *see* coursebook, selection; materials, evaluation

*Humanising English Teaching* 161–2

learner,
   activity preferences, topic preferences, interests 160–2
   autonomy 17–20, 21, 147, 166, 179
   -centred teaching 79, 162–4, 184, 189
   factors and materials evaluation *see* analysis, needs
   -generated materials 3, 21, 79–80, 92, 163–6
   involvement in materials evaluation 79
   metaphors for coursebooks 153–5
   and new roles 20–1
   responses to materials 147, 149–66

managers, institutional xii
   implications for 190–3, 199–200, 222

# SUBJECT INDEX

materials,
  adaptation,
    as addition 63–6, 133–8, 140
    as change 63–6, 73, 133–43
    definitions of 2–3, 59
    foci of 60, 62–3, 138
    forms of 24, 59–60, 63, 70, 72, 139–42 (teachers' practice)
    importance of 60–1
    principles 66–71, 131, 213
    proactive and reactive 60–2, 133
    purposes of 59–60, 62
    see also supplementation; teacher; teacher education
  analysis see coursebook
  authentic 2–3, 43, 73–4
  as-content 4–5
  and culture see culture
  design 50 see also teacher, roles (writing original materials)
  of checklists see checklists
  evaluation 50, 52
    checklists see checklists
    and design 50
    and lesson-planning 58–9
    phases/stages/steps in 52, 54–5, 78–9, 125, 183, 194
    studies, retrospective 106–13
    systematic, importance of 105, 126, 191
  as-language 4–5
  learner-generated see learner
  as object of study and research x–xi
  piloting 34–6, 77–8
  selection processes 54–8 (theory)
    see also coursebook, selection (practice)
  value of ix–x
  verbal and non-verbal 4
  writers,
    implications for 195–9
    perspectives 38–47
  Ministry of Education 40–2
    implications for 193–4

publisher,
  implications for 195–9
  perspectives of 30–2, 33–8, 39–47

research,
  applied linguistics 10–11, 12
  and coursebooks 198
  and curriculum adaptation 128
  foci of 199–202
  lack of x, 70, 126
  into learners' attitudes to materials
    see learner responses to materials
  by materials writers 32–3
  need for x, xii, xiv, 199–203
  by publishers 31–2, 33–6, 44
  and syllabuses 193
  into teachers' evaluation criteria 116–23
  into teachers' use of materials 129–48
  into teachers' views on coursebooks
    see materials, evaluation, studies

supplementation,
  vs adaptation 72
  definitions 71
  forms of 24, 72–4, 142–8
  reasons for 71–2, 129–32

teacher,
  autonomy 15, 17–20, 23, 87, 95, 127–8, 147, 184, 190, 192–3, 207
    lack of 12, 13, 81–2, 174–7, 191
  creativity 23–4, 45–6
  criticality see teacher education
  experience 90, 124, 134–9, 183
  implications for 188–90
  individual factors 167–84
    see also teacher, experience; teacher, NESTs and NNESTs
  NESTs and NNESTs 118–19, 135–7, 139–41, 173
  practices see coursebook selection (practice); research into teachers' use of materials
  as reflective practitioner 77–8
  relationship with materials and learners 17–20
  roles of 21–4, 81–2, 97–8
    course planning 50–2
    evaluation see materials
    lesson planning 52, 58–9, 143–4
    materials adaptation 45–6
    materials selection 21–3, 24, 52, 54–8
    supplementation 24, 71, 73, 90
    writing original materials 75–6, 92–6
  status of xiii
  and teaching context Chapter 8
  and technology 2–3, 14, 74, 123, 146, 196 see also teacher education

teacher education,
    implications for 194–5, 202–3
    and materials 26, 82, 100, 202
    in materials evaluation and
        design 81–101, 194–5, 203–19
    aims and objectives of 83
    content of 83–101
    and coursebook analysis 210
    and coursebook selection 207–9
    and coursebooks 83–7, 89–92,
        207–9
    and criticality 221–2
    in-service 90–2, 100–1, 203–19
    and materials adaptation 211–14
    and materials evaluation 183,
        207–9
    and materials writing 87–8, 92–6,
        214–15, 216
    method 203–19
    need for 24, 26, 91–2, 100, 124,
        183, 194, 222
    pre-service 89–90, 96–100, 203–19
    provision 26
    and supplementation 92, 214
    and teaching context 99–100
    and technology 17, 82, 85, 96–9
teacher educator,
    implications for 203–19
    perspectives of 81–101
technology *see* coursebook; teacher;
    teacher education
textbook *see* coursebook